Managerial Decision Analysis Series

Decision Making Under Uncertainty

David E. Bell • Arthur Schleifer, Jr.
Harvard Business School, Boston, MA

Course
TECHNOLOGY

Course Technology, Inc. *One Main Street, Cambridge, MA 02142*
An International Thomson Publishing Company

IP

Albany • Bonn • Boston • Cincinnati • London • Madrid • Melbourne • Mexico City
New York • Paris • San Francisco • Singapore • Tokyo • Toronto • Washington

Decision Making Under Uncertainty is published by Course Technology, Inc.

Managing Editor	Mac Mendelsohn
Production Editor	Christine Spillett
Text Designer	Susannah K. Lean
Cover Designer	John Gamache

Copyright © 1995 Course Technology, Inc.
A Division of International Thomson Publishing, Inc.

For more information contact:

Course Technology, Inc.
One Main Street
Cambridge, MA 02142

International Thomson Publishing Europe
Berkshire House 168-173
High Holborn
London WCIV 7AA
England

International Thomson Publishing GmbH
Königswinterer Strasse 418
53227 Bonn
Germany

Thomas Nelson Australia
102 Dodds Street
South Melbourne, 3205
Victoria, Australia

International Thomson Publishing Asia
211 Henderson Road
#05-10 Henderson Building
Singapore

Nelson Canada
1120 Birchmount Road
Scarborough, Ontario
Canada M1K 5G4

International Thomson Publishing Japan
Hirakawacho Kyowa Building, 3F
2-2-1 Hirakawacho
Chiyoda-ku, Tokyo 102
Japan

International Thomson Editores
Campos Eliseos 385, Piso 7
Col. Polanco
11560 Mexico D.F. Mexico

Case material of the Harvard Graduate School of Business Administration is made possible by the cooperation of business firms and other organizations which may wish to remain anonymous by having names, quantities, and other identifying details disguised while maintaining basic relationships. Cases are prepared as the basis for class discussion rather than to illustrate either effective or ineffective handling of an administrative situation.

Library of Congress Catalog Card no.: 95-67518

Trade Marks
Course Technology and the open book logo are registered trademarks of Course Technology, Inc. ITP The ITP logo is a trademark under license. Microsoft Excel and Windows are trademarks of Microsoft Corporation. Some product names used in this book have been used for identification purposes only and may be trademarks or registered trademarks of their respective manufacturers and sellers.

Disclaimer
Course Technology, Inc. reserves the right to revise this publication and make changes in content from time to time without notice.

1-56527-275-7

Printed in the United States of America

10 9 8 7 6 5 4 3 2 1

To Howard Raiffa and Robert O. Schlaifer

FROM THE PUBLISHER

At Course Technology, Inc., we believe that technology will transform the way that people teach and learn. We are very excited about bringing you, professors and students, the most practical and affordable technology-related products available.

The Course Technology Development Process

Our development process is unparalleled in the higher education publishing industry. Every product we create goes through an exacting process of design, development, review, and testing. Reviewers give us direction and insight that shape our manuscripts and bring them up to the latest standards. Every manuscript is quality tested.

The Course Technology Team

This book will suit your needs because it was delivered quickly, efficiently, and affordably. In every aspect of our business, we rely on a commitment to quality and the use of technology. Every employee contributes to this process. The names of all of our employees are listed below:

Diana Armington, Tim Ashe, Debora Barrow, Stephen M. Bayle, Ann Marie Buconjic, Jody Buttafoco, Kerry Cannell, Jei Lee Chong, Jim Chrysikos, Barbara Clemens, Susan Collins, John M. Connolly, Stephanie Crayton, Myrna D'Addario, Lisa D'Alessandro, Jodi Davis, Howard S. Diamond, Kathryn Dinovo, Jennifer Dolan, Joseph B. Dougherty, Patti Dowley, Laurie Duncan, Karen Dwyer, MaryJane Dwyer, Kristin Dyer, Chris Elkhill, Don Fabricant, Jane Fraser, Viktor Frengut, Jeff Goding, Laurie Gomes, Eileen Gorham, Catherine Griffin, Jamie Harper, Roslyn Hooley, Marjorie Hunt, Nicole Jones Pinard, Matt Kenslea, Marybeth LaFauci, Susannah Lean, Brian Leussler, Kim Mai, Margaret Makowski, Tammy Marciano, Elizabeth Martinez, Debbie Masi, Don Maynard, Kathleen McCann, Sarah McLean, Jay McNamara, Mac Mendelsohn, Karla Mitchell, Kim Munsell, Michael Ormsby, Debbie Parlee, Kristin Patrick, Charlie Patsios, Darren Perl, Kevin Phaneuf, George J. Pilla, Nancy Ray, Brian Romer, Laura Sacks, Carla Sharpe, Deborah Shute, Roger Skilling, Jennifer Slivinski, Christine Spillett, Audrey Tortolani, Michelle Tucker, David Upton, Jim Valente, Mark Valentine, Karen Wadsworth, Renee Walkup, Tracy Wells, Donna Whiting, Rob Williams, Janet Wilson, Lisa Yameen.

CONTENTS

OVERVIEW

This book is one of a series entitled *Managerial Decision Analysis*. This series of four books represents the output of three long-term course-development projects with which we have been associated at Harvard Business School. Both of us spent several years, at various times, heading the semester-long Managerial Economics course, required of all 800 first-year MBA students. We have separated this material into two parts, according to whether it concerns a decision made under conditions of complete knowledge (Decision Making Under Certainty) or a decision made under some degree of uncertainty (Decision Making Under Uncertainty). The first of these two books covers topics such as relevant costs, net present value, and linear programming. The second covers material on decision trees, simulation, inventory control and cases involving negotiation and auction bidding.

Both of us have also taught elective courses to second-year MBA students. Schleifer developed a course on Business Forecasting that is the foundation of our third book, *Data Analysis, Regression, and Forecasting*. Bell developed a course that integrates approaches to decision making under risk, whether business, personal, or societal. This material is presented in our fourth book, Risk Management.

Together, these four books provide unprecedented case coverage of issues, concepts, and techniques for analyzing managerial problems. Each book is self-contained and can serve as a stand-alone text in a one-semester course (which is how the material was used in our classrooms) or as a supplemental volume for those seeking a set of demanding real-world applications for students in a more traditional text and lecture course.

Learning concepts and techniques through the case method may be a new experience for some. It takes time to adjust to the notion that problems do not always have neat, clear solutions, and, more profoundly, that learning is often greater when they don't. We believe that this set of material covers not only what a future manager should know as an intelligent user of quantitative methods but also as an intelligent consumer of analyses others have done.

As the reader will see, some of the cases and notes were prepared by our colleagues; we are grateful for the opportunity to use them. What will not be apparent is the debt we owe to those of our colleagues that have gone before us in heading the Managerial Economics course: Robert Schlaifer, John Pratt, John Bishop, Paul Vatter, Stephen Bradley, and Richard Meyer. We also thank the Division of Research at the Harvard Business School for their financial support of all the course development reflected in these volumes. Finally, we wish to express our appreciation to Rowena Foss and Laurie Fitzgerald of the Harvard Business School, and to Mac Mendelsohn of Course Technology, for their substantial efforts both keeping this project on track and contributing to its quality. Rowena Foss has been our secretary, at times individually, but for the most part jointly, since 1978. To her we owe a special debt of gratitude.

PREFACE

Decision Making Under Uncertainty

People have a natural tendency to believe that the world is more certain than it is. Tests show that people are unrealistically confident about predicting the future; particularly people think they are right more often than proves to be the case. This trait appears not only in social gambling situations, but also among managers who believe that they "know" what the competition (or the customer, or the supplier) will do. Pretending that uncertainty can be ignored is foolhardy; many of our most difficult decisions stem from our lack of certainty about the future. Yet having acknowledged the importance of uncertainty, we need some means for thinking about it.

Decision Making Under Uncertainty presents a systematic approach that will help the student correct the worst excesses of his/her current thinking. It considers ways to structure problems so as to capture the explicit effects of uncertainty and to make allowances that correct for the presence of uncertainty in decision making.

The book may be thought of as having two parts. In the first part we establish tools and terminology for use in contexts where the uncertainty is exogenous to the decision making process. Examples of such uncertainties include the weather, or the actions of larger competitors whose decisions are made independently of our own. In the second part of the book we consider problems where the resolution of an uncertainty may depend on our own actions. For example the price set by a competitor may well depend on the price we set.

Chapter 1   Decison Trees

The first chapter, "Decision Trees", introduces probability as the language of uncertainty and decision trees as a structure for analyzing problems in a systematic way.

The first case, *The Sant-Iago,* describes a situation that is characteristic of an unstructured decision problem under uncertainty. A galleon that sank 250 years ago is somewhere at the bottom of the Indian Ocean; it may or may not contain a fortune in gold and precious jewels. Should you put together a consortium of investors to try and salvage the vessel? This case is designed to permit a discussion of how to structure a decision that involves uncertainty and to identify the data one might need to reach an analytic conclusion. This case is followed by a note that describes the technique of **decision trees**.

Freemark Abbey Winery describes a case problem in which the owner of a vineyard is looking at a weather report suggesting that a storm is headed up the Napa Valley. Such a storm could severely damage his grapes. But the grapes aren't quite ripe. Should he cut his losses or gamble that the storm will not appear?

While the Freemark Abbey case pretty much lays out the permissable alternatives, the *Ventron* case requires some creativity to identify suitable alternatives. Ventron is making rotor blades for a government helicopter contract. Though the job is routine, engineers have suggested that this might give the company a chance to develop a new manufacturing technology. Management worries that the job may not be finished on time if this development is permitted. Options considered include varying the sequence in which parts are manufactured or even undertaking parallel development.

Ligature is a small company considering a change in the way it collects fees for writing school textbooks. Hired by publishing houses to supplement their in-house staff, Ligature had traditionally been paid a flat fee. They were now considering a royalty arrangement. However, the problem of establishing a fair royalty rate was complicated by the fact that the royalties would be paid over several years and would be subject to the uncertainty of the books' market success. What royalty rate should make the old and new payment schemes equally attractive?

The last case in this chapter looks at a complex issue in which outcomes cannot be summarized in terms of dollars and cents. Although, the *EPA* is charged with regulating pesticides, they sometimes permit previously banned pesticides to be used in situations where the benefits greatly outweigh the environmental costs. The case describes one such example.

Chapter 2   Inventory Decisions

Chapter 2 looks at a particular class of decisions under uncertainty, those associated with inventory decisions. In the first case, *Union Carbide* is concerned that the butane gas supply at one of its factories will be interrupted by a storm at sea. How much of a butane reserve should they truck in to prevent having to shut down the factory in case of a storm? Of course the trucked butane costs more than normal. This case is characteristic of many problems facing managers: how big a reserve is enough?

This case is followed by two notes. The first outlines a clever procedure for solving these inventory problems: we call it the **critical fractile method**. The second note describes how graphs of **probability distributions** can be used in these kinds of problems. (This note will also be very useful in tackling the cases in the next chapter.) Cases in which these two techniques may be applied include the *Confederated Pulp and Paper Company*, which is building a reserve of logs to see itself through the upcoming winter, and *Auto Mag*, which is a want ad newspaper. Each week *Auto Mag* has nearly 30% of their print run returned from newsagents: are they printing too many? Finally the *L.L. Bean* case looks at the item forecasting and inventory stocking problems of the well-known mail order company.

Chapter 3   Simulation

The third chapter considers an additional tool for analyzing decisions under uncertainty: simulation. Each of the cases in this chapter may be analyzed by sketching a suitable decision tree and then constructing a matching spreadsheet to simulate the situation. An appropriate spreadsheet will contain certain parameters that are uncertain. By repeatedly recalculating the spreadsheet, or by using a commercial simulation package, one can see how results vary with the parameters. This is the essence of the simulation technique.

The first case in this chapter, *Hannaford Brothers*, concerns a supermarket reordering items for its warehouse inventory. There are two uncertainties to consider: how long the supplier's truck will take to arrive and the consumption rate of inventory items will be during that time.

Marsh & McLennan describes a problem faced by Eastern Airlines: how to insure their fleet of planes. The company's insurance broker has identified two fairly distinct reimbursement plans. The economics of these two plans depends on the actual losses that Eastern suffers in the next three years. Simulation can be used to examine the cost of the two plans under various representative scenarios.

DMA is a start-up company facing a dilemma typical for a new venture. Should they market their new product themselves or sell through an agent? The problem becomes complex because of the variables involved. How hard will the agent push the product? When will the product become obsolete? And so forth.

Great Western Steel Corporation faces a typical queuing analysis problem: how much will they save in ship idle time if they build an extra unloading dock? As with all queuing problems, taking averages gets nowhere close to the correct solution.

The Zeckendorf Company is building a skyscraper in Manhattan. With a $50 million line of credit, the company is understandably nervous about potential fluctuations in prevailing interest rates. Their bank has offered a number of schemes for locking or capping rates at acceptable levels. But each plan comes at a cost. How should Zeckendorf figure out if these plans are worthwhile? Remember, intuition isn't a perfect guide. Simulation helps.

Chapter 4   The Value of Information

Chapter 4 covers a significant application of the decision tree methodology, namely in determining the value of information. An initial note sets the scene in some detail. Next a set of exercises is divided between cases in which the information to be obtained is accurate (perfect) and cases in which the information may not be entirely accurate (imperfect). Despite the lack of case material in this chapter, the application of decision trees to the valuing of information is a very important one. Too many companies waste time and money on market research that is never used, or delay a decision in the hope of receiving late-breaking news that never comes.

Chapter 5   Bidding

Chapter 5, "Bidding", looks at generic situations in which your decision is to select a price to bid at an auction. Of course in traditional auctions, where people bid higher and higher until an item is sold, there is little analysis to be done except for assigning a fair value to the item that is for sale. But many auctions require some consideration of the actions of competing bidders. *Portsmouth Paper Company* and *The S.S.Kuniang*, how how the methodology of decision trees is applied to bidding situations. In these cases the decision maker must estimate the probability that competitors will bid at various levels.

In the remaining cases the situation is not so straightforward because strategic gaming is involved. In *Maxco and the Gambit Company*, one bidder knows that a tract of land contains oil, whereas the other does not. This superior knowledge is of great value to the informed company. But how does the company take advantage of the information in preparing an optimal bid?

The final case, *The RCA Transponder Auction* describes a unique situation in which seven identical items were sequentially put up for auction. No one bidder would wish to purchase more than one of them. What is the appropriate bidding strategy to use?

Chapter 6   Contracts and Incentives

Chapter 6, "Contracts and Incentives", shows how to sort out the twisted incentives that occur when negotiating a deal. We can identify the difficulties by drawing a decision tree for all interested parties. *CK Coolidge* is a classic case in which a company is sued for patent infringement; the case analysis is useful in determining just exactly where Coolidge's interests lie. *Brockway and Coates* is a publisher negotiating a book contract with a flamboyant, elderly US Senator. The Senator has high royalty expectations but can he, and will he, deliver?

Chapter 7   Negotiation

Chapter 7, which concerns negotiation, is also very relevant to the topic of contracts and incentives. This material is presented separately because each of the cases is set up for two roles, permitting (indeed encouraging) explicit negotiating between students.

The first case, which describes the circumstances surrounding *The 1987 National Football League Strike*, can form the basis of a very rich discussion of the foundations of negotiation analysis. After a note on negotiation concepts, an exercise based on the *NFL Strike* shows how difficult it is to see one's way through the implications of moves and counter moves. The *Joan Mitchell/Brown & Kenney* cases describe a multiple-issue negotiation over a store lease. When students use these materials to negotiate before class, it is easy to see what tactical approaches worked best. The *RCI/Southeastern* cases describe two sides negotiating over the electricity generated by a waste disposal plant. In both of these cases, confidential information is not printed in this book; it can be obtained from the data diskette (using the password given in the Teacher's Manual).

Chapter 8   Strategic Decisions

Chapter 8, "Strategic Decisions", looks at arm's length gaming. After a set of exercises (one of which describes the famous Prisoner's Dilemma situation) there are three cases. The first, *CGE vs. Dowpont,* shows that price wars can easily result from non-strategic thinking; it also shows that the final result is very sensitive to initial conditions. *Judo and the Art of Entry* looks at the strategic options of a small player in a big market. The final case of this book, *Fouraker/Siegel,* looks at the dilemma of a customer whose supplier is manipulating prices to increase profits at the customer's expense.

Decision Making Under Uncertainty encourages you to use *both* your intuition and and the analytic techniques described in the book when uncertainty is part of the decsion making process. As you know, intuitive beliefs can be stronger than reason—and can lead to unrealistic conclusions—so you can't rely on intuition alone. By applying the techniques offered in this book, you can develop objective data to guide your decision making. However, your intuition can help you judge whether it is appropriate to use decision tree analysis, critical fractiles, probability distributions, simulation, or other techniques to obtain the information you need for effective decsion making.

Other Materials

A data diskette is available with the text. It contains spreadsheet data for some of the cases, exhibits, and exercises in the text. A Teacher's Manual is also available to instructors. It provides analyses and teaching strategies for each of the cases, solutions to exercises, a summary of the important points in the text, and some discussion of the pedagogy.

To the Student

The techniques and approaches described in this book are covered in many traditional text books. However, the cases assembled in this text are both relevant to the world in which you move (or hope to move) and carefully selected to provide focused discussion of the issues involved. They are designed so that learning will be a pleasure rather than just another assignment. To get the most out of the book you should read each case very carefully then spend time thinking about what you would do if faced with the same problem as the protagonist in the case.

READ THIS BEFORE YOU BEGIN

To the Student

A few of the cases have substantial amounts of accompanying data. The data is available on the *Data Diskette* in spreadsheet format. If your instructor does not provide you with the disk, it may be obtained from Course Technology, Inc., by calling 1-800-648-7450 or by sending a FAX to (617) 225-7976.

To the Instructor

Data Diskette: The instructor's copy of this book is bundled with the *Data Diskette* which contains data in a spreadsheet format for some of the cases in this book.

Instructions for installing the files contained on the Data Diskette are found in the README.TXT file on the disk. The README.TXT file may be opened by using the Windows Notepad.

DECISION TREES

Would you rather be: a) rich and happy, or b) poor and ill? It's an amusing question simply because such a clear-cut choice never seems to arise in life. All of us make decisions regularly where the wisdom of our choice depends on a whole host of factors beyond our control. Sometimes we learn whether we did the right thing and sometimes we don't. But the kind of feedback we get is very uneven. Imagine trying to learn algebra if the teacher only sometimes tells you the answers and even then often misleads you as to whether you had the problem solved correctly or not. But that's the haphazard way we all learn how to make decisions under uncertainty! No wonder we need help.

In this chapter, you will learn how to think about decision problems in a systematic way. It is important to learn how to construct decision trees, but more than that, it is essential that you be convinced that they are the right way to think about these kinds of problems. We certainly think they are.

CASE

THE SANT-IAGO

The Strait of Madagascar, October 1585

The *Sant-Iago*, as headship of a small merchant fleet, was leading the way up the channel between Madagascar and Mozambique. Around the Cape of Good Hope, at the end of the fleet's three-month voyage from Lisbon, lay Goa. In this port on the west coast of the Indies, the *Sant-Iago*'s owners would buy pepper and spices in exchange for gold and silver, then head home to Portugal with their precious cargo. Portugal controlled the lucrative Eastern spice trade by sea. Because pepper prices in Europe had hit an all-time high, Portuguese entrepreneurs and the Crown were getting rich, very rich. Venice might still be the dominant maritime power in the Mediterranean, but Portugal had locked up the trade routes to the Indies, around the southern tip of Africa.

On this October night, the *Sant-Iago*'s crew was sound asleep. The sea was calm. Gaspar Gozalves, the pilot, steered his ship up the strait. He knew these waters well; he had been here many times. He never could stand amateurs interfering with his duties: amateurs, all of them, the captain no better. De Mendoça should mind his own business...

Harvard Business School Case 9-189-183, revised August 10, 1994. This case was written by Professors Christian Schaack and Arthur Schleifer. Copyright © 1989 by the President and Fellows of Harvard College.

Bàssas da India lay squarely across the route of the *Sant-Iago*, just beneath the surface of the water. At low tide, the helmsman would have seen the surf break on the shallow reef, but on this fateful night the tide was high and the reef was covered. Without warning, the *Sant-Iago* burst upon the little island and sprang a large leak under the waterline. In the confusion, the captain, the priest, and the wealthy merchants took hold of the *Sant-Iago*'s lifeboats, leaving crew, passengers, and ship to be swallowed by the ocean. The Saint of Compostelle had forsaken his namesake and her men.

The *Sant-Iago*'s survivors made it to Madagascar, then returned to Lisbon, where they gave a detailed account of their ill-fated expedition to the corporation that had commissioned the voyage.

Boston, June 1987

Barry Clifford invited Bruce Heafitz to a room at the Park Plaza Hotel. Waiting for them were the Baron Erick Surcouf, the French archivist Michel Paret, and Clifford's lawyer. In his hands, Erick Surcouf held a permit from the French authorities to excavate shipwrecks on Bàssas da India, a semi-submerged atoll in the Indian Ocean, which, through a twist of fate, lies in French territorial waters.

Clifford explained that a Portuguese galleon worth $50 million to $100 million suffered shipwreck on this atoll in the late 1500s. With Surcouf's permit and Heafitz's financial support, he continued, they could excavate the *Sant-Iago*, the way they were currently excavating the *Whydah*. Would Heafitz be interested in funding the search for the *Sant-Iago* in exchange for a piece of the action?

The Treasure Hunting Business

Treasure hunting, though not a mainstream business activity, nevertheless has a long tradition. Grave robbers have been documented in Egypt since early antiquity. During the 1980s, treasure hunting came into the limelight when Mel Fisher found the wreck of two Spanish galleons off the Florida coast. Fisher's search for the *Atocha* is typical of how many treasure hunters operate.

The two galleons, *Nuestra Señora de Atocha* and *Santa Margarita*, had been en route from Havana to Spain in 1622 when they sank off Key West in a terrible storm. Fisher became obsessed by the gold on the *Atocha*. For 16 years he searched for the two wrecks. On July 20, 1985, he finally located them at a 50 foot depth, under four feet of sand, 40 miles off Key West. The treasure of the *Atocha* and the *Santa Margarita*, apart from cannons and other historical artifacts, consisted of gold bars, gold and silver coins, and silver bullion. It was worth $400 million, according to Fisher. Other sources quoted $40 million to $100 million as more realistic figures.

Fisher discovered some creative ways to market the treasure. The treasure recovered to date from the *Atocha* and her sister ship had largely been distributed in kind to Mr. Fisher's backers, making it difficult to assess the value of the salvaged artifacts.

In June 1988, Christie's, the renowned New York auction house, offered 400 lots from the two wrecks for sale. These lots, representing about 8% of what had been salvaged to date, fetched at the low end of the $3 million to $5 million range that the sellers had expected. Still, a third of the lots remained unsold. An elaborate marketing campaign had preceded the auction, including a well-distributed videotape showing the salvage operations, as well as a traveling exhibition of some of the artifacts.

Fisher discovered that seventeenth-century Spanish pieces of eight are worth more when they are recovered from a wreck than when they are of unknown provenance. His gift shop in Florida "was selling pieces of eight for as little as $180 to as much as $1,200, depending on the quality of their markings." Yet, professional numismatists were selling similar pieces of eight found during the early days of the search for the *Atocha* for $85.[1]

Bruce Heafitz

Since 1985 Bruce Heafitz had been giving serious thought to the treasure hunting business. Heafitz had grown up in Springfield, Massachusetts. "After receiving a B.A. from Harvard College and an L.L.B. and an M.B.A. from Columbia University," he recalled, "I was involved in making investments in primarily underdeveloped countries in South America, putting together venture capital projects. When I returned to the United States, I joined Merrill Lynch, participating in the start-up of their new mergers and acquisitions department. Like venture capital projects in South America, investment banking is generally a project- or transaction-oriented activity. I was engaged in merger and acquisition activity on Wall Street into the mid-1970s, when the first oil crisis occurred. I developed expertise in merging small independent oil exploration companies into larger oil development firms."

When he left Merrill Lynch, Heafitz went into the oil business on his own: "In return for learning the oil and gas business, I gave a number of independent oilmen a short financial education." In 1983 he founded a private investment banking firm, Heafitz Energy Management Inc., which managed his personal investments and those of a number of partnerships and corporate entities with interests in oil and gas fields. Heafitz owned varying shares of these oil and gas ventures.

In 1984, during a slump in oil prices, Bruce Heafitz's career shifted to a new activity: archaeology.

It all started, he liked to relate, with a trip to Egypt he took with his wife, at a time when his oil and gas investments were in the doldrums. In the Valley of the Kings, the Heafitzes were visiting the tomb of Tutankhamen when their local guide remarked that if the Americans were impressed by the tomb of King Tut, who after all was a minor figure in the pharaonic succession, how surprised they would be when the tomb of a great pharaoh was found and opened. Many such tombs were still undiscovered. Heafitz, turning to his wife, interjected, "I know this fellow in Boston who could find another tomb in no time flat."

A few days later, the Heafitzes were admiring the artifacts from Tutankhamen's tomb in the Cairo Museum, when another guide claimed there were undiscovered pharaonic tombs many times more splendid than this one. Heafitz again found himself boasting that he knew a gentleman in Boston who had the technology to explore and find these tombs. His wife, who had heard this once too often, said, "Stop talking about it, Bruce, and go do it!" And so he did.

Upon his return to New York, Heafitz contacted Vincent Murphy, a Massachusetts-based geophysicist. In Heafitz's words: "I came back and called Vinny, and he hastened off to Egypt and confirmed my belief." Indeed, within two weeks of their conversation, Murphy went to Egypt with his scientific gear.

---

[1] "The Curious Deals behind the Key West Treasure," *Money,* Sept. 1985.

Heafitz had met Murphy in 1980 "by coincidence." Murphy was the cofounder of Weston Geophysical, a small geophysics firm in the greater Boston area. The company's specialty was the exploration and analysis of the surface hundred feet of the earth. Heafitz explained, "Oil companies are largely active in using sound waves in the form of seismics to detect hydrocarbon-bearing sands, in some cases down to five miles deep. Mr. Murphy's company utilizes radio waves, sound waves, magnetic, and electrical waves to detect anomalies in the surface hundred feet. The practical applications on which Vinny has built an outstanding company consist in determining the integrity of roadbeds, sites for nuclear power plants, bridges, or dams, and in determining groundwater penetration in waste dumps or the location of hazardous chemicals on EPA sites. The tools of his trade are radar, seismographs, magnetometers, and side-scan sonar. Weston's expertise is equally useful on land and under water."

A few days after arriving in Egypt, Murphy had used seismic, radar, and magnetometric techniques to find two magnetic anomalies that were likely candidates for tomb sites. Excavation around these sites revealed that one was a cavity with a dead end. The other most likely was the tomb of the 12 sons of Ramses II who died before him. According to Professor Kent Weeks of the University of California at Berkeley, the archaeologist in charge of the dig, this tomb could represent the first major discovery in Egyptology since the opening of the tomb of Tutankhamen in 1922.[2]

The *Whydah*

In 1985, shortly after this success, Barry Clifford, a treasure hunter, approached Heafitz. Clifford needed cash to pursue his quest for the *Whydah*, an eighteenth-century slave ship that had sunk off the coast of Cape Cod.

Barry Clifford, not unlike Mel Fisher searching for the *Atocha*, had spent years dreaming about the *Whydah*. He had made it his business to find the wreck and raise its treasure. He collected newspaper accounts—the *Whydah* had made headlines in 1717—and court records. By piecing together these documents, he believed he had at last located the wreck. He estimated the cargo of the *Whydah* to be worth hundreds of millions of dollars.

In 1985, Clifford was exploring the possibility of raising $6 million from private sources, mostly through E.F. Hutton, a large investment banking firm. These funds were to salvage, under archaeological supervision, the wreck's contents. Clifford approached Bruce Heafitz as a second source of funds; Heafitz decided to take an 8% stake in this unorthodox business venture.

The History of the *Whydah*

The *Whydah* was a ship of the British North Africa Company. In 1717 it was returning, loaded with rum, from Barbados, where it had sold its slave cargo. When it spotted three run-down pirate ships giving chase, it turned and fled. A ship of the class of the *Whydah* should have had no difficulty outsailing the pirates; but every night, when she lay at anchor, the pirates somehow managed to keep within sight of her. On the third morning, the skipper of the *Whydah*, in a state of panic and despair, decided to surrender to the pirate Samuel (Black Sam) Bellamy. Black Sam, preferring the *Whydah* to his own scummy ship,

---

[2] "Technology Opens Ancient Doors," *New York Times*, 24 Feb. 1987.

transferred his crew to the *Whydah* as well as loot from the 50 ships he had pillaged. [Black Sam gave the unfortunate skipper of the *Whydah* his ship in exchange. The latter returned safely to England to be given another command.] Then Black Sam sailed north to Cape Cod, where he was rumored to have a lady friend. In violent seas, the *Whydah* hit a sandbar off Wellfleet, Massachusetts, and sank within sight of land. Some of the crew survived, to be tried and hanged. During the court proceedings they told the story of the *Whydah*. The chronicles record that for several weeks following the shipwreck, the locals scavenged objects that washed ashore. Most of the ship's load, however, sank deeply into the sand.

Convincing evidence for the discovery of the *Whydah*, in the form of a ship's bell engraved with the ship's name, was found, and the salvaging venture was incorporated under the name Maritime Explorations, Inc. The proceeds of the excavation would go to the shareholders of Maritime Explorations: the E.F. Hutton partnership, Clifford, and Heafitz. (The Commonwealth of Massachusetts originally claimed 25% of the proceeds from the *Whydah*, but a Superior Court judge ruled in 1987 that the State had no right to the wreck.)

A laboratory was set up on Cape Cod for the preservation and treatment of the archaeological artifacts retrieved from the *Whydah*. As the first pirate ship to be excavated in U.S. waters, the wreck was of primary archaeological importance.

In 1987 the excavation of the *Whydah* was progressing at a steady pace. The precise market value of the artifacts salvaged from the ship was not known. One major auction house quoted a figure of $2,500 apiece for the coins that had been retrieved; another quoted $800. As of late 1987, a few hundred coins had been recovered. Three to four more tons of similar coins were believed to remain on the wreck.

As a result of his investment in the *Whydah*, Bruce Heafitz had become intrigued by the treasure hunting business. The oil business and the treasure hunting business seemed to have similar economics. One spent a certain amount of money up front to drill an exploration well or to locate a wreck. More often than not, the well was dry. (Bruce Heafitz remembered that, 10 years earlier, it had taken him 26 dry holes before he finally struck oil.) Once oil was found, it took more money to extract it, but the risks were, of course, smaller at that stage of a venture. To use oil industry parlance, the *Whydah* was an exploitation well; the *Sant-Iago* was a wildcat exploration well.

The more Heafitz thought about it, the more he believed that treasure hunting and oil exploration were two sides of the same coin. If anything, the economics of the treasure business were more favorable, if one had the necessary scientific expertise. Indeed, the *Sant-Iago* could be the first in a long string of such investments. That way he could play the odds. You don't just drill one wildcat well. The analogies did not stop there. Heafitz could tell where the bottlenecks in the treasure business were going to be: obtaining permits and maintaining cash flow. The key to success, he felt sure, lay in managing these bottlenecks. To limit cash outflows, exploitation would have to be kept low for a number of years. These years would be used to obtain as many exploration permits and exploitation leases as possible before too many competitors entered the playing field. Heafitz was familiar with the strategy. This was the way the oil industry had developed through the 1950s.

The *Sant-Iago* Venture

As the meeting convened at the Park Plaza, there seemed to be little doubt among the group that the *Sant-Iago* had sunk on Bàssas da India. Michel Paret had documents describing the circumstances of the shipwreck. Paret had worked for Barry Clifford as a researcher at the Spanish Maritime Archives in Seville, tracing Renaissance galleons. He had introduced Clifford to Erick Surcouf, who shared a passion for sunken treasure.

Clifford, of course, had known Heafitz since 1985, when Maritime Explorations was formed to raise the *Whydah*. Clifford was a treasure hunter at heart. Heafitz had come to appreciate his sense of purpose, the strong loyalty he commanded from his development team, and his public relations skills.

At the Park Plaza Hotel, Clifford introduced Surcouf as an "expert on wrecks in the Indian Ocean." Heafitz recalled his surprise at this warm endorsement of a rival treasure hunter. In the past, Clifford had made it abundantly clear that he considered most of his fellow treasure hunters scoundrels and charlatans. He made an exception for Erick Surcouf.

Erick Surcouf was a great-grandnephew of Robert Surcouf, the famous French corsair[3] who roamed the Indian Ocean in the late 1700's.[4] The young Surcouf was in the advertising business in Paris. His interest in ancient wrecks started with his search for the *Oxford*, the flagship of the British pirate Henry Morgan, which had sunk off Haiti in 1699, "after a night of drunken merriment." After locating the *Oxford*, Surcouf had to abandon all hope of excavating the site. The wreck was buried so deeply in mud that, for Surcouf and his backers (among them the French jewelry firm Cartier) salvaging the booty would have been prohibitively expensive.

Now, in June 1987, Surcouf turned to Bruce Heafitz for a second chance. The *Sant-Iago*, at Bàssas da India, promised rich rewards to whomever could raise it. Surcouf did not have the funds, but he did have the next best thing: permission from the French Ministry of Culture to excavate all sixteenth-, seventeenth-, and eighteenth-century wrecks he could find on Bàssas da India. His lease on the site was good for seven years. According to the agreement, France would receive 60% of the booty. The remaining 40% was Surcouf's, to share as he pleased with his financial backers.

"Bàssas da India," explained Surcouf to Heafitz, "is a ring-shaped coral reef of volcanic origin, some 12 kilometers across, halfway between Madagascar and Mozambique. At low tide the atoll rises three feet above the surface of the ocean; at high tide it is buried three feet underneath the surface."

In 1960, related Surcouf, the main island of Madagascar was granted its independence by France. The smaller islands surrounding Madagascar, including Bàssas da India, were to remain under French sovereignty.[5] Surcouf did not have a topographical map of the atoll of Bàssas because apparently no such

---

[3] *Corsair*, a term used to describe a swift ship or the captain of such a ship, comes from the French *la course*, the race.

[4] Robert Surcouf was born in Saint-Malo, Brittany. He left for the Indies at age 16. At 22 he became a corsair captain and raided ships of the British East Indies Company. He maintained his headquarters on Mauritius and Reunion. During this time, Surcouf captured 47 British vessels. When the "Course" was forbidden in 1810, Robert Surcouf settled in Saint-Malo, where he led the life of a businessman-shipowner. He died in 1827.

[5] The Malagasy contested the legitimacy of French claims over these islands. They contended that the islands are in the zone of economic influence of their country.

maps existed: since it was submerged much of the time, Bàssas da India was considered a navigational hazard rather than an island. On most maps it showed up as a small speck halfway between Mozambique and Madagascar, at about 20 degrees latitude.

At this point, Heafitz recalled that as a result of a *New York Times* article on the Valley of the Kings expedition, he had been contacted by Environmental Research Institute of Michigan (ERIM), a company expert in satellite photography. At the time he had not been interested, but now he was wondering if ERIM could help him out on Bàssas. Maybe satellite imaging techniques could provide topographical detail of the reef.

"What do you know about the galleon?" Heafitz now asked. "Well," replied Surcouf, "when the *Sant-Iago* sank, it had been on its way to the Indies, loaded with gold and silver, to purchase pepper for the English market. The precise amount of precious metals and coins carried by the *Sant-Iago* is unknown, but estimates of the outbound cargo for a typical pepper ship lie in the range of $50 million to $100 million in gold and silver coins."

After a pause he added, "Actually, we know of a second ship, of lesser importance, that sank on Bàssas da India: the *Sussex*, operated by the British East Indies Company. The *Sussex* was on its return voyage to England; it carried wares for the British market, mostly china." Bruce Heafitz remembered reading about the *Nanking Cargo*, a South Sea wreck, whose china had recently been sold for $20 million by Christie's, a sum 10 times what similar merchandise, of untraced provenance, would have fetched. "More than a hundred ships are supposed to have sunk on or off the reef over the centuries," he heard Surcouf conclude.

Committing $400,000

Bruce Heafitz was considering whether he should commit $400,000 to the exploration of the atoll. That was how much he thought it would take to conduct a scientific search for the *Sant-Iago*. In exchange for fully funding the Bàssas expedition, Heafitz was offered a 10% stake in the venture, a quarter of Surcouf's original share. Surcouf had already struck a deal for another quarter with Clifford.

"So I am taking on essentially 100% of the financial risks in exchange for 10% of the action," Heafitz commented to his would-be partners.

Of course, he was thinking to himself, the payoff, while uncertain, might be great. Or it might be a disaster. He did have a technological edge over people like Clifford or Surcouf, he thought. He would not be looking for a needle in a haystack as Mel Fisher had. No, Bruce Heafitz was no Mel Fisher. His *modus operandi* was different. If he decided to fund the venture, he would not take 20 years. He had Vincent Murphy, who could find anything. Had he not shown ample proof in the Valley of the Kings? If the ship was there, Heafitz felt sure he could find it.

The *Whydah*, Heafitz's first investment into "archaeology-for-profit," as he liked to call it, had been a good one, despite the fact that the terms of the contract heavily favored the E.F. Hutton partnership. He reminded himself that the *Sant-Iago* and the *Whydah* salvages were ventures of different types. Whereas the *Whydah* had been located by the time he had been approached for funds, the *Sant-Iago* on Bàssas da India was a different proposition altogether. The funds he was asked to commit at Bàssas da India were for the purpose of locating the wreck. There were many more unknowns than there had been for the *Whydah*.

The main uncertainty about the *Whydah* had been the market value of the artifacts and the 25% claim of the Commonwealth of Massachusetts. But the *Santiago* first had to be located, its cargo inspected, and the recoverability of the artifacts studied.

As he thought about it rationally, Heafitz tried to decide if Surcouf was offering him an attractive investment opportunity.

"Well, Bruce?" he thought to himself.

Exhibit 1 _____

MAP OF MADAGASCAR AND BÀSSAS DA INDIA

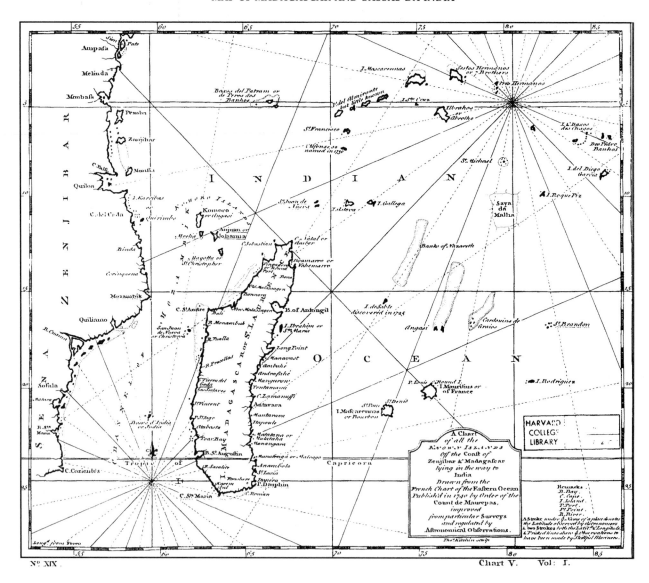

Exhibit 2 _____

EXCERPTS FROM BOOK VII OF DIOGO DE COUTO'S "DA ASIA,"

CHAPTERS 1 TO 3

As in this year 1585 the pepper contract came to an end that King Sebastian had established for three years [...], King Philip ordered a new contract for a duration of five years [...] with the following conditions:

That the contractors be obliged to send to India each year [buyers and] capital to purchase 30,000 quintals of pepper; [...]; that the contractors give the King the pepper [...] for 12 cruzados a quintal; that the King pay 4 cruzados a quintal for freight and 2.5% for losses.

[...] Since the shipping contract had been awarded to him, Manuel Caldeira quickly dispatched five vessels to India that same year [...], under fleet commander Fernão de Mendoça; and on April 10 they set sail, Commander [de Mendoça] on the ship *Santiago*, and the other captains, Diogo Tavira on the *San Francisco*, Miguel de Abreu on the ship *Salvador*, André Moreira on the *Santo Alberto*, and Fernão Cotta Falcão on the *San Loureaço*. [...] The ships sailed past the Cape of Good Hope; the flagship rounded the Cape last, on July 11. [The other ships went on their ways...]

The flagship, having passed the Cape of Good Hope took the inside route [through the Channel of Madagascar] and stayed in the land of Natal until August 13 because of many storms and tempests, while the other ships left Mozambique for India [...]. August 15 brought [the flagship] a good tailwind, and she made sail at great speed; and on the eighteenth, they shot the sun and found themselves at twenty-one and a third degrees, the latitude of Bassas da India [...]; since the middle of [the reef] lay at 21.5 degrees, it seemed that the rest of the day would be enough (given the strong tailwind) to clear the reef; but, since only God knows everything, not only had the pilot [Gaspar Gonzalves] made a mistake in his shooting of the sun, but also in his reckoning; and furthermore refused to listen to the admonitions of a sailor, a man expert at shooting the sun, who repeated numerous times that the reef was still ahead

[...] and that they should steer one quarter to the east to get away from the island [...]; but, as the pilots of this route consider themselves gods of the sea and think they know more than any noble man or passenger (who actually have better knowledge of the maps and study the height of the sun as well as they do and sometimes even better), since one cannot deny that in the course of time they become most expert in the art of navigation by virtue of the number of years they travel this route; for this reason, no matter how often the sailor was repeating and shouting [his warning], Captain Fernão de Mendoça refused to take action, so as not to upset the pilot, who unfortunately according to him had

DA ASIA
DE

DIOGO DE COUTO

Dos feitos, que os Portuguezes fizeram
na conquista, e descubrimento
das terras, e mares do Oriente.

DECADA DECIMA

PARTE SEGUNDA.

LISBOA

Na Regia Officina Typografica

ANNO M.DCC.LXXXVIII.

Com licença da Real Meza da Commissão Geral sobre o
Exame, e Censura dos Livros, e Privilegio Real.

bad habits and would tell him, as they all did, that [the captain] should mind his own business; and thus the ship continued on its course until evening when he thought he had left the reef to the west [...].

But the ship's master, being a sensible man, and very vigilant, ordered a few sailors whom he trusted to climb into the crow's nest and watch out for the reef, which they did; three quarters of an hour into the first watch they saw a shape ahead; as the night was dark they were not sure of what they were seeing, and while they were debating whether it was a cloud or the reef, the ship, with all sails set, hit the middle of [the reef]; for God, having decided that they should be lost on it, closed their mouths to all so that they would not shout their warning when they first saw the shape[...]

The lower part of the ship burst onto

IV   I N D I C E

pera o Mogor , e mettéram feus Capitães no Reyno de Verara.   109.
CAP. XVI. *Das novas que chegáram ao Viſo-Rey do Norte : e de como mandou lá Ruy Gomes da Gram com huma Armada : e de outras que mandou pera o Sul, e pera Malaca.*   115.

L I V R O VII.

CAP. I. *Da Armada que eſte anno de 1585. partio do Reyno, de que era Capitão Mór Fernão de Mendoça : e do novo contrato que ElRey fez eſte anno da pimenta : e do que aconteceo a todos na jornada: e de como Fernão de Mendoça ſe perdeo nos Baixos da India.*   121.
CAP. II. *Da deſcripção deſte baixo , em que a não deo : e das peſſoas que ſe ſalváram em o batel: e do que lhes aconteceo até chegar a terra.*   129.
CAP. III. *Do que aconteceo aos que ficáram nos baixos : e das jangadas que ordendráram : e de hum eſpantoſo milagre que féz o Lenho da Cruz de Chriſto : e do que aconteceo a Fernão de Mendoça, e aos do batel até chegarem a Moçambique.*   137.
CAP. IV. *De como o Viſo-Rey D. Duarte tratou de mandar huma Armada ao eſtreito*

the reef, which was made of rocks, and with the great force with which she was moving, she was cut as if with a saw, in such a way that the holds and the lower deck were submerged, while the upper decks sailed onto the reef more or less intact with the mast still [partially] standing.

[... The next morning] the stunned pilot [...] had tne skiff put in the sea, equipped with oars and sailors, and embarked on it with the captain: then arrived Father Fr. Thomaz Pinto of the Order of the Friars, Master in Holy Theology [...], whom the King had sent to be Inquisitor of India, who asked Fernão de Mendoça to take him on board which the latter refused to do, insisting he was going to check whether something he could see in the distance was an island [...] and giving his word he would return to the ship [no matter what...].

[The skiff] discovered only sea in all directions. [...] After that the captain hesitated to return to the ship since they could not save everyone in the skiff. Under the forceful suggestions of the [captain], who wanted to save his own person, [... the skiff] set sail for the coast of Cafraria. [...]

There were 400 people on the [*Santiago*].

Before the [second skiff] left, the ship's officers and the merchants took all the money they carried in "reales", a sum on the order of 400,000 cruzados, and buried it in deep wells in the rock of the reef, where the sea could not dislodge nor move it because of its weight, so they could return for it later; it probably still lies in this place, and it will remain there for many years, for water does not corrode silver [...].

The second boat departed the reef on August 22. [...] A sixteen year old boy by the name of Diogo de Couto was swimming after the boat, shouting and pleading that they take him on board in the name of the Virgin Our Lady who would make sure that they would all be saved. [...] He repeated this so often that the clergymen thought he was an angel [...] and asked the sailors to take him on board, which they did. [...]

▼   ▼   ▼

DECISION ANALYSIS

Managers often find making decisions difficult. One reason is that uncertainty is inherent in most important decisions. A product manager, for example, must decide whether to market a new product, even though she is uncertain of the eventual market size, competitive reaction, and production costs. A second reason is that decision makers may need to evaluate many alternatives or balance many conflicting objectives. It often becomes too difficult to make a decision based only on intuition: formal analysis may be necessary.

Harvard Business School Note 9-894-004, revised August 3, 1993. This case was written by Professor George Wu. Copyright © 1993 by the President and Fellows of Harvard College.

Decision analysis is a logical and systematic approach for analyzing decision problems. It takes a "divide and conquer" approach to decision making, breaking the process into a number of steps:

1. Identify the criteria for choosing among the competing alternatives.
2. Structure the decision problem, listing the alternatives and uncertain events in chronological order and representing them in a decision tree.
3. Assess the likelihood of the various uncertain events and assign values to the various outcomes of the decision problem.
4. Analyze the information provided in the first three steps to determine which alternative to undertake.
5. Determine if the decision is sensitive to changes in probabilities or other assumptions you have made.

A Simple Decision Problem

Consider the following simplified decision problem:

Sarah Chang is the owner of a small electronics company. In six months a proposal is due for an electronic timing system for the 1996 Olympic Games. For several years, Chang's company has been developing a new microprocessor, a critical component in a timing system that would be superior to any product currently on the market. However, progress in research and development has been slow, and Chang is unsure about whether her staff can produce the microprocessor in time. If they succeed in developing the microprocessor, there is an excellent chance that Chang's company will win the $1 million Olympic contract. If they do not, there is a small chance that she will still be able to win the same contract with an alternative, inferior timing system that has already been developed.

If she continues the project, Chang must invest $200,000 in research and development. In addition, making a proposal requires developing a prototype timing system at an additional cost of $50,000. Finally, if Chang wins the contract, the finished product will cost an additional $150,000 to produce. Chang must decide whether to abandon the project or whether to continue investing in the venture.

A Criterion for Decision Making

First, Chang needs to determine how she will choose among the competing alternatives. In this note, we assume that Sarah Chang wants to *maximize net cash flow;* that is, she wants to choose the alternative that yields the largest positive cash flow or smallest negative cash flow. Applying this criterion to a choice between $10 and $20 is straightforward. However, what if the choice is between $25 for sure and a .50 (or 50%) chance at $60? Because a .50 chance at $60 has two possible outcomes, $0 and $60, the criterion of maximizing net cash flow doesn't help.

How do we value a .50 chance at $60? Clearly, a .50 chance at $60 is worth less than $60, the best outcome. It is also worth more than $0, the worst outcome. Since the probability of receiving $60 is .50, the value of a .50 chance at $60 should be $30—halfway between $0 and $60. Similarly, the value of a .20 chance at $60 should be $12, or 20% of the way from $0 to $60.

In this example, $30 is the **expected monetary value (EMV)** of a .50 chance at $60. EMV is determined by multiplying each outcome by its probability and then summing these products. As another example, the EMV of a .30 chance at $50 and a .70 chance at $100 is:

$$.30(\$50) + .70(\$100) = \$85 \quad .$$

It is not always appropriate to use EMV. Some thoughtful individuals will value a .50 chance at $60 at less than its EMV of $30 because they dislike taking risks. A corporation with limited capital might reject a positive EMV alternative if the chance of a loss is too high. Even so, maximizing EMV is a reasonable criterion for a surprisingly large number of decision problems. It should be used when the stakes are small compared to the resources of the company or the individual decision maker. In addition, even when a decision maker wants her decision to reflect risk aversion, she might begin her analysis by evaluating the options in terms of EMV. In this example, we assume that Chang wants to maximize EMV.

Decision Trees, Alternatives, and Risks

In the next stage of analysis, Chang should identify the options available to her and the uncertainties she faces. We represent the chronological sequence of these options and uncertain events in a **decision tree**, which can be thought of as a roadmap of the decision problem.

It is six months prior to the proposal date. What can Chang do? First, Chang can abandon the project altogether, thereby avoiding the risks of failing to develop the microprocessor. On the other hand, Chang can continue to invest in the project. If these are the two possible options available to Chang, her decision tree begins with the two branches shown in Figure 1.1. Note that a decision is represented in a decision tree by a square, or **decision node**.

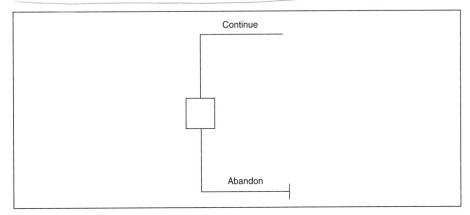

Figure 1.1

At this point, Chang should ask herself: "Then what?" If Chang abandons the investment, then she is done; she does not need to consider this path any further. On the other hand, what might happen if Chang decides to continue with the project? In the next six months, either Chang's engineers will succeed or fail in their effort to develop the microprocessor. Chang is unsure which of the two events will occur. In a decision tree, we represent an uncertain event with a circle, or **chance node**. Chang's decision tree so far is shown in Figure 1.2.

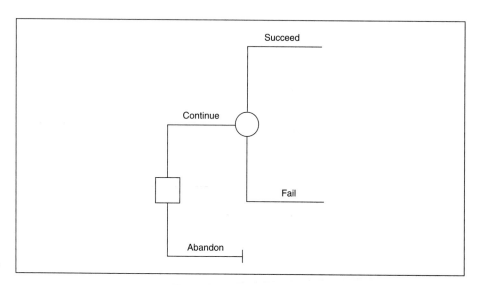

Figure 1.2

Chang should continue to ask herself, "Then what?" What could happen in the event of technological success or in the event of technological failure? First, suppose that Chang's engineers develop the microprocessor in time. Chang must then decide whether to make a proposal. Since it costs $50,000 to produce a prototype, it is not immediately obvious whether or not Chang should make a proposal. If Chang is unsure of whether an option is a good one, she should include it in the decision tree: if the alternative proves to be worse than another option, it will be eliminated naturally at a later stage in the analysis.

If she enters a proposal, she may either win or lose the contract (Figure 1.3). Of course, winning or losing the contract is an uncertain event.

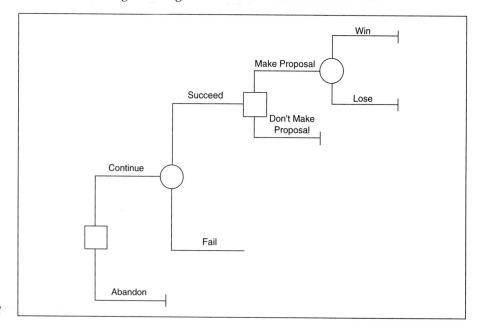

Figure 1.3

Finally, we can repeat this reasoning for the case of technological failure. Without the new microprocessor, Chang must decide whether to propose the alternative, inferior timing system. This situation is depicted in the decision tree shown in Figure 1.4.

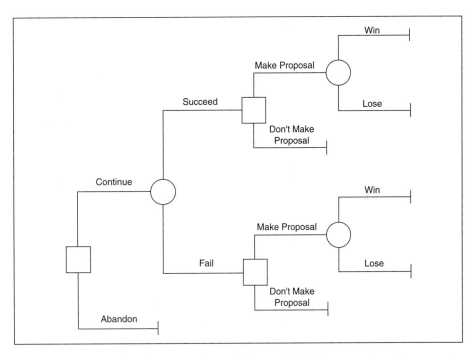

Figure 1.4

The process of Chang's asking "Then what?" has produced a concise description of her decision problem. The decision tree is a chronological depiction of the alternatives immediately available to Chang, as well as future alternatives and uncertainties. The decision tree can often clarify the problem immensely—perhaps providing enough insight that it becomes clear to the decision maker which alternative she should undertake. In this problem, if the chance of technological success is low, the costs of development high, and the rewards of winning the proposal low, then Chang might conclude that she should abandon the project. Problems that are not so clear-cut require a more complete analysis; the decision maker must assess the likelihood of the uncertain events and estimate the value of the possible outcomes.

In this example, the set of options and uncertainties is fairly small. In many real-world problems, however, the process of depicting a decision tree requires more creativity. Even in this simple problem, the analysis could easily be enhanced by considering additional alternatives: for example, investing $300,000 in development instead of $200,000; abandoning the effort after three months; etc. It is up to the manager to use her ingenuity and creativity to ensure that the decision tree captures all the reasonable options available to her. Creative decision makers can often conceive of alternatives others would overlook.

The Uncertain Future

In almost every important decision, the outcome of the decision depends not only on the alternatives the manager chooses but on external events that are not under the manager's control. For example, an investor's return depends on which stocks she owns (her decision) and whether these stocks appreciate or depreciate (an external event); a farmer's annual income depends on the crops planted (his decision) and the weather and market price for the crops (external events); and a publisher's profits depends on which books she publishes and promotes (her decision) and consumer demand for books and the state of the economy (external events).

Probabilities measure the likelihood of uncertain events. If the probability of an event is 0, then that event is impossible. If an event will happen for sure, then the probability of that event is 1. Probabilities provide us with a precise numerical language for communicating judgments about the uncertain future. Often you will hear statements like: "I think that there is a *pretty good* chance that our sales will be at an all-time high this year," or "It's *unlikely* that our competitor will change his price in the near future," or even "I'm *quite unsure* how the government will act on this issue." These phrases attempt to communicate a judgment about the uncertain future in a language that is imprecise at best. In contrast, probabilities require the decision maker to be explicit in her pronouncements: instead of merely saying that there is a "pretty good" chance, she must give a more precise estimate of what the chances will be.

In the current example, Chang must estimate the probability of developing the microprocessor. Naturally, Chang will want to obtain as much knowledge about the problem as possible, by talking to her engineers, reviewing past projects, and perhaps consulting outside experts. This research forms the input for her probability judgments.

Let's say that Chang believes that the probability of successfully developing the microprocessor in six months is .40, or 40%. (This means the chance of technological failure is .60, or 60%.) In addition, Chang indicates that there is .90 probability that she will win the proposal if she does develop the microprocessor. Without the microprocessor, she estimates that she has only a .05 chance of winning. These probabilities are reflected in the decision tree depicted in Figure 1.5.

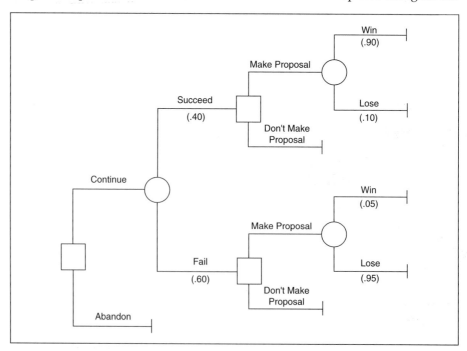

Figure 1.5

Although these judgments are necessarily subjective and hence not "right" or "wrong," they are not arbitrary. The probabilities reflect Sarah Chang's judgments about the likelihood of various events. But what does it really mean when Chang says that the probability of technological success is .40? If there is a bag containing 100 balls, 40 of which are red, then we all understand that the probability of choosing a red ball out of the bag is .40. Here the probability is "objective": If we drew a great many balls from the bag, replacing the drawn ball each time, about 40% of the balls drawn would be red. Although the probability of technological success does not have such a straightforward physical interpretation, it does have a meaning. Basically Chang is saying that she believes that developing the microprocessor is just as likely as drawing a red ball out of a bag in which 40% of the balls are red.

End Points and Monetary Consequences

Even if Sarah Chang had the decision tree in Figure 1.5, she could not make a decision unless she knew the value of the various outcomes. For example, how much better off is she winning the contract than failing to win it? In this stage of the process, Chang must evaluate each terminal point in the decision tree. For each path in the decision tree, or **scenario**, a unique set of choices and events has transpired. For example, in one scenario, Chang decides to continue with the project, her engineers are successful in developing the new microprocessor, and she is awarded the contract. Presumably this is the best scenario of all. But how good is it?

Recall that Chang wants to maximize the expected cash flow. Thus Chang must evaluate the net cash flow that results at each **end point**. In this step, she should identify all of the relevant costs incurred in the various activities, as well as the relevant revenues. If she wins the contract, then Chang will expend $200,000 in development costs, $50,000 in developing the prototype, and $150,000 in producing the final product. Thus the total costs to her will be $400,000. Since she wins a contract worth $1 million, the net cash flow is $600,000.[6] If she develops the technology, makes a proposal, but is not awarded the contract, then the net cash flow would be –$250,000 (the development costs plus the cost of developing the prototype). The other cash flows can be calculated by subtracting the relevant costs from the relevant revenues. They are shown for each scenario in Figure 1.6.

---

[6] A more detailed analysis would reflect the differential timing of the cash flows and the time value of money. Thus, the various cash flows would be expressed in terms of their **net present value**. We will not worry about these details in this note.

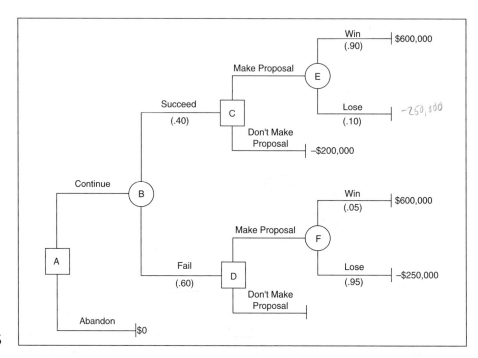

Figure 1.6

Consequences Not Contained in the Cash Flows

In most decisions, there are consequences other than purely monetary ones. In these situations the nonmonetary consequences should be evaluated and included in the analysis. In this example, we have simplified the situation by assuming that developing the microprocessor technology is valuable only because it increases the probability of winning the contract. However, having the technology in hand will often have considerable value outside this simple context: the microprocessor technology may open doors for other projects in the future, may enhance the reputation of Chang's company, etc. These benefits can be quite substantial and should be reflected in the analysis.

In general, if the manager believes that the various end points on her decision diagram leave her with different prospects for the future, she should assess the value for these future differences and add them to the cash flows. Thus, the analysis should reflect any differences in customer relations, employee morale, equipment, inventories, etc.

In our simple example, we assume that there are no differences in future prospects among the end points other than those contained in the evaluations of the monetary flows.

What's Best: Folding Back the Tree

At this point, Chang has structured the problem and used her judgment to assess the critical uncertainties and to evaluate the end points. Now she is ready to combine these judgments to determine the best course of action. We will start at the end points of the decision tree and work our way backwards to the present. Let's assume that Chang decided to continue the venture, that her engineers were successful in developing the microprocessor technology, and that she went ahead with the proposal. Thus she is at node (E) in the decision tree. At this juncture, she will either win or lose the contract. Recall that Chang wants to maximize EMV—expected monetary value. If we weight the "Win" and "Lose" outcomes by their respective probabilities, we find that the EMV for node (E) is .90($600,000) + .10(–$250,000), or $515,000. Thus we replace the uncertain event at node (E) with its EMV, $515,000 (Figure 1.7).

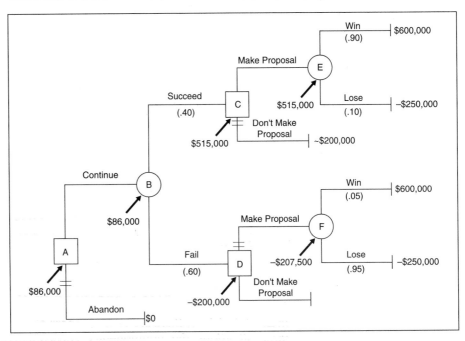

Figure 1.7

At node (C), Chang has a decision of whether or not to make a proposal. If she makes the proposal, then she can "expect" $515,000. However, if Chang does not make the proposal, then she will lose the $200,000 she expended in development costs. Clearly, she should make the proposal. Thus at node (C), we substitute the EMV of the better of the two decisions, "Make Proposal." We can "prune" the inferior option, "Don't Make Proposal," from the decision tree. *A pruned inferior option is denoted by two short parallel lines.*

We now have a procedure for analyzing the decision tree: we start at the end points of the decision tree, replace each chance node with its EMV and each decision node with the highest EMV of any of the alternatives, and work backwards toward the beginning of the tree. We call this process of simplifying the decision tree, **folding back the tree** or **backwards induction**. Chang can decide what to do initially at decision node (A), because she knows what she would choose if she were at decision node (C) or at decision node (D).

If we continue this process to the beginning of the tree, we find that Chang should continue investing in research and development and then make a proposal only if she does succeed in developing the microprocessor. The EMV of this strategy is $86,000. Figure 1.7 depicts the complete analysis.

Sensitivity Analysis

In a previous section, we discussed how Sarah Chang might think about the judgmental probabilities. She may indicate that the probability of winning the contract if she has the microprocessor technology is .90, but this judgment might be based on relatively little knowledge or experience. Chang might not feel particularly comfortable about investing such a large sum of money in this project without giving some more thought to the probability.

If Chang spent more time thinking about the chance of winning, perhaps reflecting on what her competitors might be up to, then the probability she assigns to winning might change. On the one hand, if, after further reflection, she decided that the probability of winning was actually higher than .90, then the decision to continue the project would be unaffected. On the other hand, how low could the probability of winning drop before "Continue" became worse than "Abandon"? First, Chang might choose some lower probability of winning, say .40, and fold back the tree with this new probability. In this case, she would find that the EMV of "Continue" has become negative, –$84,000. After some trial and error (or some simple algebra), Chang would determine that the EMV of "Continue" is positive when the probability of winning is greater than .647; it is negative when the probability is less than .647. Even though Chang might not be able to state precisely the probability of winning, she might feel confident that the probability is higher than .647. In this case, it is not worth investing her time refining her original probability assessment, because further reflection on the probability of winning would not change her decision to continue with the project.

Chang determined whether her decision to continue the project was sensitive to different probabilities of winning. The reasoning used in **sensitivity analysis** can also be applied to other judgments a manager might make. Decision analysis is an iterative process. In the first stage, a decision maker may make a tentative assessment or valuation in order to reach a preliminary conclusion about which alternatives to undertake. For example, Chang chose to ignore the nonmonetary benefits of having the microprocessor technology. After folding back the tree, she should determine whether her decision to continue investing is sensitive to any of the tentative judgments she made earlier. In Chang's case, any benefits of developing the microprocessor technology only reinforce her decision to continue the project. On the other hand, if Chang finds that her decision is very sensitive to some other judgment, then she may want to invest some resources refining this judgment. Thus a smart decision maker can use sensitivity analysis to identify which judgments need to be considered more carefully and which do not.

Epilogue

Sarah Chang's decision problem was relatively simple. Most managerial decision problems are more complicated. The sheer size of these problems can often paralyze a decision maker. However, decision analysis offers a systematic approach to decision making, breaking the problem into smaller, more easily digestible pieces. At each step in the process—structuring, assessment and evaluation, analysis, and sensitivity analysis—the manager can gain insight into her decision problem. The end result will be better decisions.

Strategies and Risk Profiles

Backward induction is not the only method of analyzing a decision tree. In this section, we discuss a second method to determine the best course of action. This approach permits a decision maker who is not completely satisfied with using EMV as a criterion for choice to consider all possible outcomes in her decision making.

First, we define a **decision strategy**. A strategy is a course of action or a set of decisions conditional on *all* possible events. Thus the decision maker must specify which alternative she would choose at every decision node. The first obvious strategy is "Abandon"—the strategy of abandoning the project. A more complicated strategy is to *continue* with the investment; *make* a proposal if the development succeeds; *don't make* a proposal if the development fails. We will denote this strategy as "continue; make; don't make." You should check that the other possible strategies are "continue; make; make," "continue; don't make; make," and "continue; don't make; don't make."

Next we can look at the risk profiles for each strategy. A **risk profile** for a decision strategy describes all the outcomes that might result, as well as the probability associated with each outcome.

The first strategy, abandoning the project, has the simple risk profile shown in Table 1.1.

Table 1.1

STRATEGY 1—"ABANDON"	
Possible Consequences	Probability
$0	1.00

If Chang chooses the strategy "Abandon," the net cash flow will be $0 for sure.

Consider the strategy "continue; make; make" shown in Table 1.2. Chang will make a proposal, whether the microprocessor development succeeds or fails. The probability that the development succeeds is .40. If the development succeeds, then the chance of being awarded the contract is .90. Thus the chance that the development succeeds *and* Chang wins the proposal is the product of these two probabilities, .40 × .90, or .36. Chang is also awarded the contract if the development fails, provided that she win the proposal with the alternative, inferior system. The chance that the development fails but Chang still wins the contract is .60 × .05 = .03. Therefore, the total probability of winning the proposal is the sum of the probability of winning the proposal in these two different ways, .36 + .03 = .39. Recall that the cash flow associated with winning the proposal is $600,000. We can use the same reasoning to determine that the probability of losing the proposal is .61. The cash flow associated with losing the proposal is –$250,000.

Table 1.2

STRATEGY 2—"CONTINUE; MAKE; MAKE"	
Possible Consequences	Probability
$600,000	.39
–$250,000	.61

Let us look specifically at one more strategy, "continue; make; don't make" shown in Table 1.3—the strategy we determined had the highest EMV. The chance of winning the contract is now the chance of the joint event of the development succeeding and Chang winning the proposal, .40 × .90 = .36. By similar reasoning, the chance of losing the contract is .40 × .10 = .04. Finally, the last possible outcome, incurring only the research and development expense, occurs if the technology fails. Now we have the risk profile for this strategy:

Table 1.3

STRATEGY 3—"CONTINUE; MAKE; DON'T MAKE"	
Possible Consequences	Probability
$600,000	.36
–$200,000	.60
–$250,000	.04

We can also determine the risk profiles for the two other strategies, as shown in Tables 1.4 and 1.5.

Table 1.4

STRATEGY 4—"CONTINUE; DON'T MAKE; MAKE"	
Possible Consequences	**Probability**
$600,000	.03
–$200,000	.40
–$250,000	.57

Table 1.5

STRATEGY 5—"CONTINUE; DON'T MAKE; DON'T MAKE"	
Possible Consequences	**Probability**
–$200,000	1.00

What should Chang do? Although there is no "right answer" to this choice, it is easy to see that she should not choose Strategies 4 or 5. Strategy 1 *dominates* Strategy 5: It is clear that $0 for sure is better than –$200,000 for sure. We can also see that Strategy 4 is dominated by Strategy 3: Strategy 4 has a lower chance at the best outcome, $600,000, and a higher chance at the worst outcome, –$250,000.

Choosing between Strategies 1, 2, and 3 is not so simple. First, Chang can select the strategy with the highest EMV (Table 1.6).

Table 1.6

Strategy	EMV
1	$0
2	$81,500
3	$86,000

Strategy 3 has a slightly higher EMV than Strategy 2 and a much higher EMV than Strategy 1. Recall that we came to the same conclusion by folding back the tree. However, EMV is only one way of summarizing a risk profile; not all decision makers want to maximize EMV. If Chang has limited financial assets, she might prefer Strategy 1 because Strategies 2 and 3 are too risky: they each have a potential "down side" of –$250,000. On the other hand, Chang might look at the risk profiles and decide to be more aggressive and select Strategy 3. She might reason that it is worth risking a possible loss of $250,000 for the "up side" of $600,000. Finally, Strategy 2 is similar to Strategy 3, and has a slightly lower EMV; on the other hand, it has a higher probability of $600,000 and a lower probability of a negative outcome.

FREEMARK ABBEY WINERY

In September 1976 William Jaeger, a member of the partnership that owned Freemark Abbey Winery, had to make a decision: should he harvest the Riesling grapes immediately, or leave them on the vines despite the approaching storm? A storm just before the harvest is usually detrimental, often ruining the crop. A warm, light rain, however, will sometimes cause a beneficial mold, *Botrytis cinerea*, to form on the grape skins. The result is a luscious, complex sweet wine, highly valued by connoisseurs.

The Winery

Freemark Abbey was located in St. Helena, California, in the northern Napa Valley. The winery produced only premium wines from the best grape varieties. Of the 25,000 cases of wine bottled each year (about the same as Chateau Lafite-Rothschild), most were Cabernet Sauvignon and Chardonnay. About 1,000 cases of Riesling and 500 cases of Petite Syrah were also bottled. (A case contains 12 bottles of wine.)

The Napa Valley extends for 30 miles, from Calistoga in the north to Napa in the south. The average temperature decreases as one moves south, closer to San Francisco Bay and the cold ocean waters. Freemark Abbey's grapes came from an ideal climate in the central and southern parts of the valley.

Winemaking

Wine is produced when the fruit sugar, which is naturally present in the juice of grapes, is converted by yeast, through fermentation, into approximately equal molecular quantities of alcohol and carbon dioxide. Sparkling wines excepted, the carbon dioxide is allowed to bubble up and dissipate. The wine then ages in barrels for one or more years until it is ready for bottling.

By various decisions during vinification—for example, the type of wooden barrel used for aging—the winemaker influences the style of wine produced. The style adopted by a particular winery depends mainly on the owners' preferences, though it is influenced by marketing considerations. Usually, as the grapes ripen, the sugar levels increase and the acidity levels decrease. The winemaker tries to harvest the grapes when they have achieved the proper balance of sugar and acidity for the style of wine sought. The ripening process is variable, however, and if the weather is not favorable, the proper balance might never occur.

Several different styles of Riesling (more accurately, Johannisberg Riesling) are on the market. If the grapes are harvested at 20% sugar, the wine is fermented "dry" (all the sugar is converted to alcohol and carbon dioxide) or "near dry." The resulting wine, at about 10% alcohol, is light bodied. If the grapes are harvested at 25% sugar, the winemaker can produce a wine with the same 10% alcohol but with 5% residual sugar; this wine is sweet and relatively full bodied.

A third and rare style results when almost-ripe Riesling grapes are attacked by the botrytis mold. The skins of the grapes become porous, allowing water to evaporate while the sugar remains. Thus, the sugar concentration increases greatly, sometimes to 35% or more. The resulting wine, with about

Harvard Business School Case 9-181-027, revised March 24, 1994. This case was written by Professor William Krasker. Copyright © 1980 by the President and Fellows of Harvard College.

11% alcohol and 13% residual sugar, has extraordinary concentration, and the botrytis itself adds to the wine's complexity. Freemark Abbey had already produced a botrytis-affected Riesling (called Edelwein) from its 1973 vintage. Exhibit 1 shows the winery label for this Edelwein Riesling.

Jaeger's Decision Problem

From the weather reports, Jaeger concluded that there was a fifty-fifty chance that the rainstorm would hit the Napa Valley. Since the storm had originated over the warm waters off Mexico, he thought there was a 40% chance that, if the storm did strike, it would lead to the development of the botrytis mold. However, if the mold did not form, the rainwater, which would be absorbed into the grapes through the roots of the vines, would merely swell the berries by 5–10%, decreasing their concentration. This would yield a thin wine that would sell wholesale for only about $2.00 per bottle, about $0.85 less than Jaeger could obtain by harvesting the not-quite-ripe grapes immediately and eliminating the risk. Freemark Abbey always had the option of not bottling a wine that was not up to standards. It could sell the wine in bulk, or it could sell the grapes directly. These options would bring only half as much revenue, but would at least avoid damaging the winery's reputation, which would be risked by bottling an inferior product.

If Jaeger decided not to harvest the grapes immediately in anticipation of the storm, and the storm did not strike, Jaeger would probably leave the grapes to ripen more fully. With luck, the grapes would reach 25% sugar, resulting in a wine selling for around $3.50 wholesale. Even with less favorable weather, the sugar levels would probably top 20%, yielding a lighter wine selling at around $3.00. Jaeger thought these possibilities were equally likely. In the past, sugar levels occasionally failed to rise above 19%. Moreover, while the grower waits for sugar levels to rise, the acidity levels must also be monitored. When the acidity drops below about 0.7%, the grapes must be harvested whatever the sugar level. If this happened, the wine would be priced at only about $2.50. Jaeger felt that this event had only about .2 probability.

The wholesale price for an Edelwein Riesling would be about $8.00 per bottle. Unfortunately, the same process that resulted in increased sugar concentration also caused a 30% reduction in the total juice. The higher price was therefore partly offset by a reduction in quantity. Although fewer bottles would be produced, there would be essentially no savings in vinification costs. The costs to the winery were about the same for each of the possible styles of wine and were small relative to the wholesale price.

Exhibit 1

Winery Label

CASE

VENTRON ENGINEERING (A)

The Ventron Engineering Company has just been awarded a development contract by the U.S. Army Aviation Systems Command to design, develop, and demonstrate critical components of a new rotor system. The system will be part of the Heavy Lift Helicopter program, which is currently receiving much attention in the industry.

An integral part of the rotor system is the blade spar. The blade spar is a metal tube that runs the length of and provides strength to the helicopter blade. Due to the unusual length and size of the Heavy Lift Helicopter blade, Ventron is unable to produce a single-piece blade spar of the required dimensions, using existing extrusion equipment and material.

The engineering department has prepared two alternatives for developing the blade spar: sectioning or an improved extrusion process. Ventron must decide which process to use. The risk report prepared by the engineering department is shown in Exhibit 1.

Sectioning

This process involves joining several shorter lengths of extruded metal into a blade spar of sufficient length. This work will require extensive testing and rework over a 12-month period at a cost of $150,000 per month. While this process will definitely produce an adequate blade spar, it merely represents an extension of existing technology.

Extrusion

In order to extrude the blade spar as a single piece, it will be necessary to modify the extrusion press at a monthly cost of $160,000 and to improve the material used at a monthly cost of $50,000. Each of these steps would require six months of steady work.

If successful, this process would produce a blade spar of superior quality at a lower overall cost. Unfortunately, there is some risk that Ventron will be unable to perfect the extrusion process.

After studying the technical problems, the engineering department feels there is a nine-in-ten chance of perfecting the material. However, the other possibility (a one-in-ten chance) is that at the end of the six-month development effort it will know that a satisfactory material cannot be developed within any reasonable time and cost framework, and it will have to rely on sectioning.

The engineers believe there is a three-in-four chance of successfully modifying the extrusion press, but a one-in-four chance that the extrusion process will have to be abandoned at the end of a six-month press development project, because a press with the necessary capabilities will be shown to be infeasible.

Development of the blade spar must be completed within 18 months in order to avoid holding up the rest of the contract. It has also been determined that, if necessary, the sectioning work could be done on an accelerated basis in a six-month period at a monthly cost of $400,000.

The Director of Engineering, Dr. Smith, is most interested in the opportunity provided by this contract to explore new technology in the extrusion process. He feels that if Ventron is successful in producing the single-piece blade spar, the company's reputation in the field will be greatly enhanced. In addition, an improved extrusion process would allow the company to complete development of the blade spar well under budget.

After a preliminary review of the problem, Ventron's President, Bill Walters, has not yet reached a final decision. Like Dr. Smith, he is intrigued by the possibility of successfully developing the extrusion process. He feels that this would give Ventron an excellent chance at some additional contracts. However, he is concerned about the possibility of wasting money on unsuccessful development or of being forced to do sectioning on an accelerated basis.

Ventron's contract with the Army is for a fixed total amount spread over several years. Walters wants to minimize the expenditures on the blade spar portion to free up money for technical developments on other components of the rotor system, which would improve Ventron's position for future business, both defense and commercial.

Exhibit 1 _____

RISK REPORT: BLADE SPAR DEVELOPMENT

	Cost/month ($000)	Probability of success	Time required for effort (months)	Total cost ($000)
Extrusion development				
Material development	50	0.90	6	300
Press modification	160	0.75	6	960
Sectioning				
Normal basis	150	1.0	12	1,800
Accelerated	400	1.0	6	2,400

▼   ▼   ▼

CASE

LIGATURE, INC.

On January 6, 1988, Richard Anderson and Stuart Murphy sat in the conference room of their new office suite at 90 Canal Street, Boston. They were working on the final details of a royalty agreement that they had negotiated with a publisher, Brockway and Coates.[7] All that remained was to select a royalty rate acceptable to both sides.

Company History

The $1.5 billion a year market for elementary and high school textbooks was geared to adoption cycles created by the populous states. Many state education committees periodically (e.g., every six years) announced new standards for textbooks in a given subject: science, mathematics, reading and so on. Publishers responded by submitting a series of textbooks suitable for all elementary or high school grades, together with supporting materials such as teaching guides. The state committee then reviewed these textbooks and selected a short list of four to eight publishers: these would be the sanctioned series from which individual schools or school districts in that state could choose.

Harvard Business School Case 9-188-141. This case was written by Professor David E. Bell. Copyright © 1988 by the President and Fellows of Harvard College.

---

[7] The company name has been disguised.

Because large states such as California and Texas were the most lucrative markets, most publishers geared their book development procedure to the timetables of these states. The cyclical demands of this arrangement forced publishers to contract out much of the writing and development of some of their series. In 1980, Anderson and Murphy set up Ligature in order to take on some of this contract work. By early 1988 the company had offices in Chicago and St. Louis as well as Boston, with a total staff of 87 full-time professionals.

The Royalty Agreement

Ligature had always operated on a fixed fee basis. For each development project they would negotiate with the publisher for a given budget (labor plus allocated overhead plus margin). Though budgeted profit margins of around 25% were normal, Ligature had found that, in their desire to produce a high quality product, costs tended to overshoot the budgets and eat away at the margins.

In mid-1987, the partners decided to propose to their customers that they be paid on a cost-plus-royalty basis. Under this system they would receive a flat fee for estimated costs (labor and overhead) but would earn their profit margin in the form of a royalty. By this means Ligature hoped to recoup the "added value" they felt they were contributing to texts developed with the publisher. If a book sold really well, the royalty would be equivalent to a higher than normal margin; if not, the royalty could be quite low.

An opportunity to try this proposal came when Brockway and Coates, for whom Ligature was to develop a Social Studies program (grades 9–12), agreed in principle to the new arrangement. The cost component of the deal had been fixed at $4,150,000. Under a normal deal Ligature would have added a 25% margin and would have received a total fee of $5,187,500. The fee would have been paid over the course of the project in 18 monthly progress payments.

A major consideration in setting an appropriate royalty rate would be the size and timing of book sales. Ligature estimated that sales would begin before the end of the first year after completion. Roughly 10% of sales would occur within that first year, 20% in each of the second and third years, 30% in the fourth year and 20% in year five. (Ligature would receive its royalties on each anniversary of the book's completion.) At that point the book would be revised, quite possibly with Ligature, but the proposal permitted royalties only until the fifth year.

As for total sales over the five-year period, Ligature assessed the probability estimates shown in Table 1.7, all in current dollars:

Table 1.7

Sales	Probability
$25,000,000	.10
$30,000,000	.45
$50,000,000	.30
$70,000,000	.15

While Ligature was happy, indeed eager, to undertake the risk associated with the uncertain sales, they were concerned with the cash crunch this would create. Anderson intended discounting future earnings at a rate of 10% per year before comparing them with the fixed-payment alternative.

For their part, Brockway and Coates seemed content with the arrangement. Part of the agreement placed a cap on the amount Ligature could earn through the royalty scheme: the royalties, discounted back at a compound annual rate of 10%, could exceed no more than 33% of the costs. The final step was to agree on the royalty rate.

▼   ▼   ▼

ENVIRONMENTAL PROTECTION AGENCY: EMERGENCY PESTICIDE EXEMPTIONS

The Environmental Protection Agency (EPA) was set up with the goal of preventing significant deterioration of the environment, particularly with reference to man's industrial interference with it. The agency had directed considerable attention toward pesticides—especially DDT—and the potential, often subtle, harm that they caused to flora and fauna. The indiscriminate use of pesticides may affect not only the natural environment, but also dairy cattle, human drinking water and food. The EPA is responsible for registering pesticides; only registered pesticides may be used. In some cases a pesticide may be registered for some types of applications but not for others. The EPA may also deregister pesticides that had previously been registered.

Section 18 of the Federal Insecticide, Fungicide and Rodenticide Act (as amended by the Federal Pesticide Control Act of 1972) had given the EPA the authority to permit federal and state agencies to use unregistered pesticides in emergency situations, subject to case-by-case approval.

Exemptions can be granted only if the following three criteria are all met:

1. A pest outbreak has occurred or is about to occur; no pesticide registered for the particular use, or no alternative control method, is available to eradicate or control the pest.

2. Significant economic or health problems will occur without the use of the pesticide.

3. The time available from discovery or prediction of the pest outbreak is insufficient for a pesticide to be registered for the particular use.

There are three categories of exemption requests. **Specific** exemption requests are those involving pests endemic to the United States. **Quarantine** exemption requests are those for pests foreign to the United States; a decision on these requests could take anywhere from a week to three months. A **crisis** exemption request involves a pest outbreak that was unpredictable and that has created an immediate health or economic hazard. In this case, there is no time to file for one of the other two exemptions. A crisis request is usually filed *after* application of the pesticide.

Graham Beilby[8] was in charge of all emergency exemption requests. The EPA rules and regulations largely dictated many mechanical aspects of handling requests. The requester was required to submit a large amount of data

Harvard Business School Case 9-180-018, revised March 1984. This case was written by Professor David E. Bell. Copyright © 1979 by the President and Fellows of Harvard College.

[8] This name and some dates have been altered. The subjective opinions and probabilities expressed in this case are for illustration only. They do not necessarily reflect the opinion of any EPA staff member.

supporting the claim, and to describe the expected detrimental effects of using the requested pesticide. While the EPA did not normally have enough time to collect its own data on a given situation, it was usually evident whether the claims of the requester were basically true. Inflated claims were sufficient grounds for dismissal of the request. In any case, requesters would not wish to damage their credibility with the EPA and thus jeopardize possible future requests.

Requests for a crisis exemption were often discussed on the telephone by Beilby and the head of the requesting agency before the official application was filed and before the pesticide was applied. This was because the requester faced stiff legal penalties if a crisis exemption was not ultimately approved. Therefore, the discussion revolved around reaching an understanding as to what would or would not likely receive approval.

Beilby was concerned that this informal case-by-case evaluation was inadequate in the face of a growing volume of emergency exemption requests. Seven requests had been received in the first two years after the Pesticide Control Act of 1972, but 36 had been received in 1974 and even more seemed likely in 1975. (Of the 36 requests in '74, 12 were granted, 14 were denied, 2 were crisis requests, 7 were later withdrawn and 1 was still pending.)

In the spring of 1975 Beilby received an application for a specific exemption request from the U.S. Forest Service to permit the use of DDT on its forests in the Pacific Northwest. The tussock moth, endemic to the region, was responsible for periodically defoliating Douglas fir trees. Until 1968, the U.S. Forest Service had used DDT to control the moth but then voluntarily discontinued its use. In 1974 when it again wished to use DDT (by then deregistered), its request was denied by the EPA. The 1974 request, which projected losses of $13 million, was denied based on the belief that the nuclear polyhedrosis virus would cause a natural collapse of the moth. However, the moth did not collapse: instead it was blamed for $77 million in losses.

Beilby was well aware of the difference between a bad decision and a bad outcome, but this event could not have helped EPA's credibility, which was already suffering from the outcome of an earlier exemption decision. In that case, a state had requested an exemption to use DDT and the EPA had granted the request; however, the pest had disappeared naturally before doing any serious damage. Fortunately the pesticide had not been applied, but Beilby felt that this incident had undermined not only his own credibility but the image of the EPA in general. Both the U.S. Congress and the general public kept a watchful eye on EPA decisions. Certain exemption requests were politically explosive.

With this background in mind, Beilby looked over the current request. The Forest Service wished to use 490,000 pounds of DDT on 650,000 acres that included part of Washington, Oregon, and Idaho. Two-thirds of the land was federally-owned, one-sixth was state land and one-sixth was the Colville Indian Reservation. Forestry on the Indian land accounted for 40 to 50% of the Indians' employment and 95% of the total income to the tribe. Their forests had been particularly hard-hit by the defoliation of 1974. Repeated defoliation leads to tree death, which is not only an economic loss but which also substantially increases the chance of forest fires. This would be a severe hazard to the Colville Reservation.

The request was made conditional upon tests of egg mass samples to be taken after the 1975 egg hatch. The tests would show whether the larval population was being controlled naturally by the nuclear polyhedrosis virus. If this natural control was not occurring and if the request for DDT were denied, the Forest Service projected economic losses of $67 million.

Even though the projected losses were high, Beilby was not comfortable with the thought of approving the request. But if he chose to deny the request, he'd have to have his reasoning pretty explicit and defendable. It occurred to him that a study completed only in February for the EPA by a well-known Cambridge consulting firm should be useful for his current decision. After rereading its report he drew the following decision tree (Figure 1.8). Since the request would be withdrawn by the Forest Service if the egg test proved favorable, the probabilities he estimated presupposed that the egg tests were unfavorable.

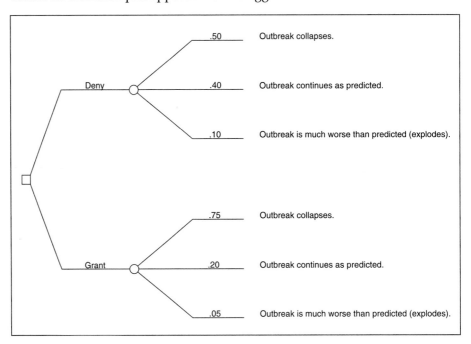

Figure 1.8

Beilby estimated economic losses in the best case (Outbreak collapses) at $3 million and in the worst case (Outbreak explodes) at $90 million. With these figures and the subjective probabilities that he had assessed he calculated expected losses of approximately $20 million for "Grant" versus $40 million for "Deny." It seemed to Beilby that both of these alternatives were bad. Although denying the request resulted in twice the losses as granting it, the use of DDT had to be weighed against the grant decision. Beyond this, he had a strong desire not to make the "wrong" decision again.

▼   ▼   ▼

INVENTORY DECISIONS

Remember the last time you organized a party and had to figure out how much food to buy? Unless you organize parties regularly, it's hard to know how much the typical person eats. You don't want to run out; on the other hand, even junk food gets pretty expensive when you're buying for lots of people. Businesses have this problem all the time, too. How many spare parts should you keep? How many books should you print? Fortunately, this is one problem we *really* know how to solve—and easily. You will, too, by the end of this chapter.

CASE UNION CARBIDE – BUTANE TRANSPORT

After completing the two-week butane use projection on the Monday morning after Thanksgiving, Ralph Hiecke, production coordinator, and Addie Locke, shipping supervisor at the Union Carbide Brownsville plant, were trying to decide whether to schedule extra butane by truck. A tow with two butane barges was due to leave Houston for Brownsville along the Intracoastal Waterway that noon. Locke was concerned, however, that bad weather might delay the barges. If the stored butane at Brownsville was consumed before the barges arrived, the plant would have to be shut down.

Background

In 1977, Union Carbide was among the 25 largest industrial companies in the United States, with sales of more than $7 billion. It employed more than 100,000 people and operated 500 plants, mines, and mills in 37 countries. Although Carbide was generally classified as a chemical company, chemicals and plastics accounted for only 40% of sales. The balance came from industrial gases, metals, and carbons (33%) and consumer and specialty products (27%).

Union Carbide was the nation's leading producer of many important products, including several large-volume chemicals for producing antifreeze, polyester fibers, auto and furniture cushioning, toiletries, and cosmetics. It also had fast-growing smaller businesses, which included agricultural products and

Harvard Business School case 9-180-017, revised March 29, 1994. This case was prepared by Frank Bondurant under the supervision of Professor Roy D. Shapiro.
Copyright © 1979 by the President and Fellows of Harvard College.

electronic components. Carbide marketed several well-known consumer products: Eveready batteries, Prestone antifreeze, Glad sandwich bags, and Simonize waxes and polishes.

At its Brownsville, Texas, plant, Union Carbide produced industrial chemicals, including acetic acid, methyl ethyl ketone, and ethyl acetate for use in the production of plastics and other chemicals. The plant used a process in which butane and oxygen were combined to form numerous products. The oxygen used in the process was removed from the atmosphere at an oxygen-refining unit located at the plant. The butane came to the plant via barges or trucks from Houston. The plant operated 24 hours per day, seven days per week and required 6,000 barrels (bbls) of butane per day.

Tows from Houston arrived every few days, bringing one to three barges of butane, as well as empty chemical barges to transport plant products to other locations. Each barge contained 13,000 barrels of butane. If the barges were delayed, trucks might be used to provide part of the butane requirements. Butane trucks carried 200 barrels each and could be unloaded at the rate of 143 bbls/hr. Costs associated with the two types of transportation are given in Exhibit 1.

The Intracoastal Waterway from Houston to Brownsville was 350 miles long, and barges took from three to seven days to deliver the butane, depending on weather conditions, the size of the tow, and tide conditions (see Exhibit 2). Without stopping, the tow could travel 85 to 125 miles per day, depending on conditions. Between November and April, however, frequent storms along the Texas coast caused barge delays (see Exhibit 3). Winds of 30 to 60 miles per hour could slow the tow's speed and create large waves in the Corpus Christi bay, which might break up the tow. If the waves were higher than normal, the captain of the tow might decide to stop on the north side of the bay and wait for the waves to subside. This waiting period had ranged from a few hours to three days.

Butane by Truck

The butane storage spheres at Brownsville were almost full, holding a total of 30,000 barrels at 8 A.M. that day. A tow with two butane barges was also due to leave Houston for Brownsville along the Intracoastal Waterway at noon. On the basis of weather forecasts for the coming week, Locke believed there was an 80% chance of stormy weather.

The decision on whether to truck butane had to be relayed to the Houston office by 4 P.M. Monday to assure delivery during that week. The number of truckloads to be delivered during the week would also have to be specified at that time.

Once the plant's stored butane was depleted, the operation would be shut down or cut back to a rate that could be sustained by trucked butane. Each day of lost production caused losses of approximately $30,000 in gross margin; in the event of a cutback, the cost would be proportional to the size of the cutback.

Exhibit 1

	TRANSPORTATION COSTS	
Item		**$/BBL**
Load barges or trucks at Houston		.525
Truck to Brownsville		1.482
Unload trucks		.189
Barge to Brownsville and unload		.336

Exhibit 2

TOW TRIP TIMES — HOUSTON TO BROWNSVILLE — JANUARY TO APRIL **1978**

Number	Trip Time (Hours)	Number	Trip Times (Hours)
1	96	17	165 *
2	90	18	114 *
3	74	19	83
4	84	20	120 *
5	135 *	21	82
6	68	22	144 *
7	94	23	93
8	95	24	92
9	76	25	141 *
10	140 *	26	85
11	79	27	80
12	78	28	83
13	142 *	29	111 *
14	144 *	30	92
15	112 *	31	88
16	140 *		

* Indicates a trip during which a storm occurred.

Exhibit 3

MAP OF TEXAS PORTS

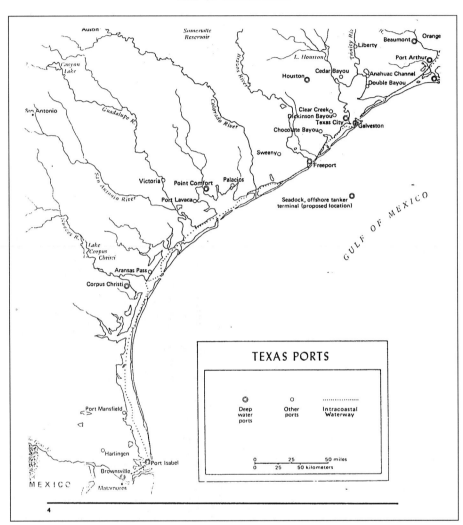

THE CRITICAL-FRACTILE METHOD FOR INVENTORY PLANNING

A popular author has written her latest book. How many copies should the publisher print? How many Nintendo sets should the local toy store buy for the Christmas season? These are examples of a common decision problem where, in the face of uncertain demand, a decision maker must balance the gain of having enough inventory on hand to satisfy demand against the loss incurred by ending up with too much: the toy store gains a per-unit gross margin on every

Harvard Business School case 9-191-132, revised November 7, 1994. Copyright © 1991 by the President and Fellows of Harvard College.

Nintendo set sold, but stands to lose the per-unit cost (less any salvage value obtained through liquidation) on every unit remaining unsold at the end of the season.

The Newsstand Problem

A teenager sells the local Sunday newspaper at a busy intersection in his home town. At 7 A.M. each Sunday, Terry meets the news truck and buys copies of the paper at a unit cost of $0.90. He resells them to passing motorists at the newsstand price of $1.50. At noon he goes home, discarding leftover newspapers in a nearby recycling bin.

Terry is frustrated by the wide swings in demand for papers. Some Sundays he sells hardly any; on others he sells all his copies by 9 A.M. Each Sunday at 7 A.M., when he has to make his purchasing decision, he is unable to forecast whether this particular Sunday will be a high-demand day or a low-demand day. All that he can do is assess the probability distribution for demand, shown in Table 2.1.

Table 2.1

Demand	Probability
0	0.04
1	0.07
2	0.09
3	0.12
4	0.13
5	0.17
6	0.13
7	0.10
8	0.07
9	0.05
10	0.03
	1.00

How many newspapers should Terry buy from the news truck?

One way to solve this problem is to draw the entire decision tree. Figure 2.1 shows the complete tree of the decisions to order three and to order four. To analyze the entire tree would be a huge task. A second approach is to use a spreadsheet to evaluate each possible order in turn and to see which one gives the highest expected contribution. Table 2.2 is a spreadsheet showing what Terry's sales and contribution would be for each possible demand scenario if he decided to buy three newspapers. The value of $1.275 at the bottom of the last column is his "expected contribution"—a probability-weighted average of the contribution he would have made for each possible value of demand. This is the same value that appeared as the expected value associated with the "Order 3" decision in Figure 2.1.

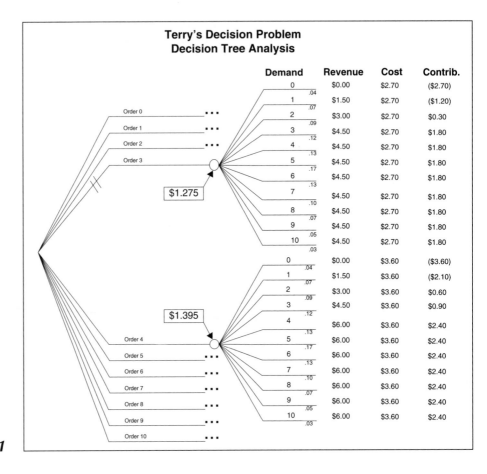

Figure 2.1

Table 2.2

TERRY'S DECISION PROBLEM

ANALYSIS OF THE DECISION TO ORDER THREE NEWSPAPERS

Decision: Buy   3
Per-Unit Revenue $1.50
Per-Unit Cost $0.90

Demand	Probability	Sales	Revenue	Cost	Contrib.	Prob.-weighted Contrib.
0	0.04	0	$0.00	$2.70	($2.70)	($0.108)
1	0.07	1	$1.50	$2.70	($1.20)	($0.084)
2	0.09	2	$3.00	$2.70	$0.30	$0.027
3	0.12	3	$4.50	$2.70	$1.80	$0.216
4	0.13	3	$4.50	$2.70	$1.80	$0.234
5	0.17	3	$4.50	$2.70	$1.80	$0.306
6	0.13	3	$4.50	$2.70	$1.80	$0.234
7	0.10	3	$4.50	$2.70	$1.80	$0.180
8	0.07	3	$4.50	$2.70	$1.80	$0.126
9	0.05	3	$4.50	$2.70	$1.80	$0.090
10	0.03	3	$4.50	$2.70	$1.80	$0.054
	1.00			Expected Contribution =		$1.275

Repeating these calculations for other purchase quantities would establish whether or not other quantities lead to higher expected contribution[1] and, in particular, what purchase quantity leads to the highest possible expected contribution. While this is a perfectly straightforward, though tedious, way of deciding how many newspapers to buy, we will gain more insight and reduce the amount of computation by thinking about this problem in an **incremental** or **marginal** fashion.

Suppose Terry has already decided to buy at least three copies of the newspaper and is considering whether to buy a fourth. As regards this incremental decision, there are just two possible outcomes: either the fourth copy will not be needed because there is no demand for it, or it will be needed to satisfy demand. If the fourth newspaper is not needed, he will suffer as a **loss** the purchase cost of the newspaper, or $0.90. If it is needed, he will achieve a **gain** equal to his gross margin, or $1.50 – $0.90 = $0.60. Given his uncertainty about demand, he cannot know for sure whether the fourth newspaper will or will not be needed, but he can compute probabilities of the two possible outcomes. The fourth newspaper will not be needed if three or fewer newspapers are demanded; it will be needed if more than three are demanded. The probability that demand will be for three or less is simply the probability that demand will be for exactly 0, 1, 2, or 3 newspapers, or 0.04 + 0.07 + 0.09 + 0.12 = 0.32, and the remaining 0.68 is the probability the demand will be for more than 3. Thus the expected incremental **net gain** or **contribution** of the decision to buy a fourth newspaper is:

$$\text{Exp. incr. net gain} = \$0.60 \times 0.68 - \$0.90 \times 0.32 = \$0.12 \quad .$$

Because this is positive, the decision to stock a fourth newspaper is better than the decision not to stock, for which the expected incremental contribution is obviously zero.

We could now go on to ask whether, having concluded that it is better to buy a fourth newspaper, we should also buy a fifth. Without doing any computations we can reason that the expected incremental contribution of a fifth newspaper must be less than $0.12. The gain if the fifth newspaper is needed will once again be $0.60, and the loss if it is not needed will be $0.90. But the probability that the fifth newspaper will not be needed must be greater than 0.32, and therefore the probability that it will be needed must be less than 0.68. Thus the expected incremental contribution of buying the fifth newspaper must be less than that of buying the fourth.

Having concluded this, it is still not clear whether to buy the fifth newspaper. Although its incremental contribution must be less than $0.12, the crucial question, which can be decided only by computing its value, is whether that quantity is positive or negative; if positive, we should buy the newspaper; otherwise, we should not. Table 2.3 is a spreadsheet in which we compute the expected incremental contribution of buying the first, second, ... newspapers. Notice that the increments decline steadily. The last incremental decision that has a positive expected contribution is the decision to stock the fourth newspaper. Thus we should stock four papers, but not five.

---

[1]For example, if you changed the buy decision from three to seven, you would find that expected contribution changed from $1.275 to $0.465. Try it! Buying seven newspapers clearly is not as good a decision as buying three.

In the last column of Table 2.3 we cumulate the incremental contribution. Notice that the cumulated expected incremental contribution of the first three newspapers is just the expected contribution of the decision to order three, as shown in Table 2.2 and Figure 2.1. Thus the incremental method permits you to compute total expected contribution, and leads to the same conclusion that you would reach by the more laborious total-expected-contribution method.

In Figure 2.2 we graph both the incremental and cumulative contribution associated with buying the first, second, ..., up to the tenth newspaper. Notice that the **total** contribution increases for each additional newspaper bought, up to the fourth; thereafter, it decreases. Correspondingly, the **incremental** contribution is positive for the first four newspapers bought, negative thereafter. The optimal number of newspapers to buy—the number that produced the highest **cumulative** expected contribution—is the highest number for which the **incremental** expected contribution is positive.

Table 2.3

INCREMENTAL ANALYSIS OF TERRY'S DECISION PROBLEM

Gain = $0.60
Loss = $0.90

Demand	Probability	Cumulative Prob.	Incremental Decision	Prob. that Incremental Unit Not Needed	Prob. that Incremental Unit Needed	Incremental Expected Contrib.	Cumulative Expected Contrib.
0	0.04	0.04					$0.000
1	0.07	0.11	First	0.04	0.96	$0.540	$0.540
2	0.09	0.20	Second	0.11	0.89	$0.435	$0.975
3	0.12	0.32	Third	0.20	0.80	$0.300	$1.275
4	0.13	0.45	Fourth	0.32	0.68	**$0.120**	**$1.395**
5	0.17	0.62	Fifth	0.45	0.55	($0.075)	$1.320
6	0.13	0.75	Sixth	0.62	0.38	($0.330)	$0.990
7	0.10	0.85	Seventh	0.75	0.25	($0.525)	$0.465
8	0.07	0.92	Eighth	0.85	0.15	($0.675)	($0.210)
9	0.05	0.97	Ninth	0.92	0.08	($0.780)	($0.990)
10	0.03	1.00	Tenth	0.97	0.03	($0.855)	($1.845)

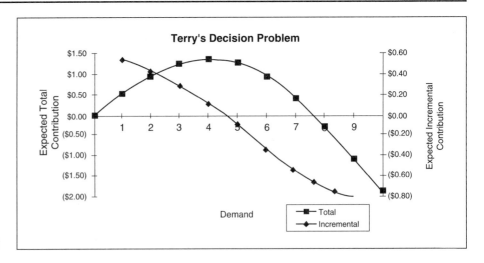

Figure 2.2

Generalization

Problems of this kind can be analyzed incrementally. Suppose you have already decided to stock $n-1$ units and are interested in whether you should stock the nth. Either the nth unit will be needed, in which case you will, in retrospect, be happy about your decision to stock it; or it will not be needed, in which case you will regret your decision in retrospect. Before knowing whether it will be needed or not, how can you balance the pluses and minuses? Let L be the amount you will *lose* if you stock the nth unit and it is *not* needed; similarly, let G be the amount you will *gain* if you stock the nth unit and it *is* needed. (Both L and G are increments in cash flow relative to the decision to stock $n-1$ units.) The probability that the nth unit is *not* needed (and therefore will not be sold) is the probability that demand will be for $n-1$ units or fewer; let's symbolize this by P_{n-1}. The probability that the nth unit *is* needed (and therefore will be sold) is then $1 - P_{n-1}$. Figure 2.3 shows the incremental decision diagram. Notice that both G and L are measured relative to the base-case scenario of stocking $n-1$ units. As you can see from Figure 2.3, the expected incremental contribution from stocking the nth unit is:

$$\text{Exp. incr. contribution} = G \times (1 - P_{n-1}) - L \times P_{n-1} \ . \tag{1}$$

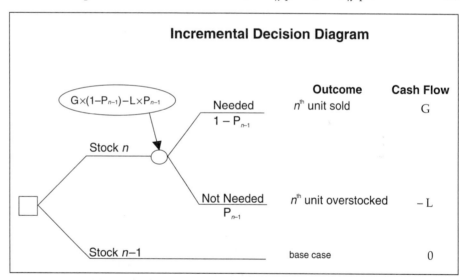

Figure 2.3

The nth unit should be stocked, if and only if, this expected incremental contribution is positive, i.e., if:

$$G - (G + L) \times P_{n-1} > 0 \ ;$$

which implies that:

$$P_{n-1} < G/(G + L) \ . \tag{2}$$

Suppose we determine that, according to this criterion, the nth unit should be stocked. Then how about the $(n+1)^{th}$? By identical reasoning, we *should* stock it if:

$$P_n < G/(G + L) \ ;$$

we should *not* stock it if:

$$P_n > G/(G + L) \ .$$

Thus, if $G/(G + L)$ is between P_{n-1} and P_n, i.e., if:

$$P_{n-1} \;<\; G/(G + L) \;<\; P_n \;\; , \tag{3}$$

we should stock *exactly n* units.

In the case of the newsstand problem, we have already seen that $G = \$0.60$, and $L = \$0.90$, and therefore the critical ratio is $\$0.60/(\$0.60 + \$0.90) = 0.40$. In Figure 2.4 we show a cumugram of the distribution of demand. The cumugram shows that $P_3 = 0.32 < 0.40$, that $P_4 = 0.45 > 0.40$, and that Terry should therefore stock four newspapers. In Figure 2.4, a horizontal line is drawn from the value of $G/(G + L) = 0.40$ on the vertical axis to the right until it hits the cumugram, and from there a vertical line is extended down until it reaches the horizontal axis at the value 4, Terry's optimal stocking level.

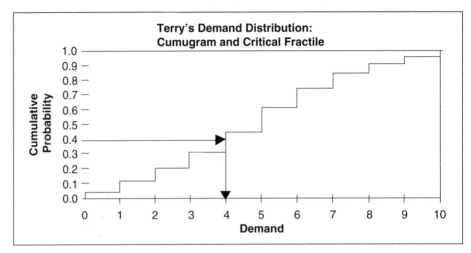

Figure 2.4

This method works in general. First, compute the **critical ratio** $G/(G + L)$. Then, the stock level that maximizes expected contribution is the value of n such that the critical ratio lies between P_{n-1} and P_n. This value of n can always be found by locating the value of the critical ratio on the vertical axis, moving horizontally to the right until you intersect the cumugram, and then down to the horizontal axis. For any value k between 0 and 1, the k fractile can be obtained in precisely the same way: locate k on the vertical axis, read over to the cumugram and down; the number you find on the horizontal axis is, by definition, the k fractile. Thus the optimal stocking level found by this incremental method of analysis is called the **critical fractile**, and the **critical-fractile method** refers to this way of finding the optimal stocking level.

In many real-world situations, there are so many possible values of demand that each value and its associated probability cannot be enumerated and represented by a stair-step cumugram like the one in Figure 2.4. Rather, the probability distribution of demand may be represented by a smooth, S-shaped curve. The critical-fractile method of finding the critical ratio, reading over to the curve and then down to the horizontal axis, will still permit you to find the optimal stocking level. The next section of this chapter gives more explanation about probability distributions.

Determining G and L

In an example like the newsstand problem, the values of G and L are respectively the margin (revenue minus cost) and the cost of stocking a unit, and the critical ratio is simply the margin expressed as a fraction of revenue. Other situations may be more complicated. Sometimes there is a salvage or liquidation value for excess stock; sometimes a sales commission is paid on items sold. Sometimes failure to satisfy demand can entail a goodwill loss as well as more tangible cash-flow losses; sometimes an unsatisfied demand can be backordered and subsequently sold.

Let r be the revenue gained if an item is sold; let c be the cost of acquiring the item, a cost that is incurred whether the item is sold or not. Let s be the salvage or liquidation value of unsold items. Let z be the sales commission that must be paid if an item is sold. Let g be the loss of goodwill that is incurred if an item that is demanded is out of stock, and let b be the backorder cost (including extra handling and loss of goodwill) if an out-of-stock item can be acquired and sold at a later date. A stockout will result either in lost demand and possible goodwill loss, or in a backorder that will be filled subsequently. We can represent the incremental decision problems for these two cases by the four-branched trees in Figure 2.5A and B, where the base case for each tree is the scenario in which we stock $n-1$ units and demand is for $n-1$ or fewer.

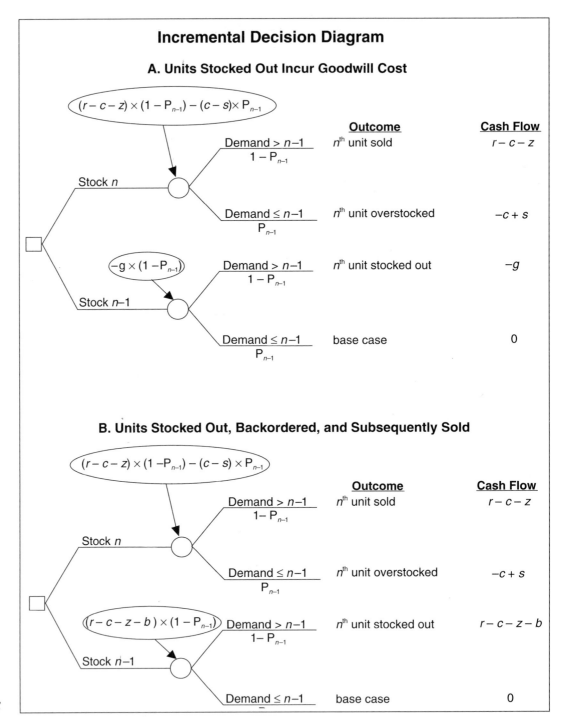

Incremental Decision Diagram

A. Units Stocked Out Incur Goodwill Cost

$(r - c - z) \times (1 - P_{n-1}) - (c - s) \times P_{n-1}$

| Outcome | Cash Flow |

Demand > $n-1$
$1 - P_{n-1}$ n^{th} unit sold $r - c - z$

Stock n

Demand ≤ $n-1$
P_{n-1} n^{th} unit overstocked $-c + s$

$-g \times (1 - P_{n-1})$

Demand > $n-1$
$1 - P_{n-1}$ n^{th} unit stocked out $-g$

Stock $n-1$

Demand ≤ $n-1$
P_{n-1} base case 0

B. Units Stocked Out, Backordered, and Subsequently Sold

$(r - c - z) \times (1 - P_{n-1}) - (c - s) \times P_{n-1}$

| Outcome | Cash Flow |

Demand > $n-1$
$1 - P_{n-1}$ n^{th} unit sold $r - c - z$

Stock n

Demand ≤ $n-1$
P_{n-1} n^{th} unit overstocked $-c + s$

$(r - c - z - b) \times (1 - P_{n-1})$

Demand > $n-1$
$1 - P_{n-1}$ n^{th} unit stocked out $r - c - z - b$

Stock $n-1$

Demand ≤ $n-1$ base case 0

Figure 2.5

If backordering is not possible (Figure 2.5A), the expected incremental contribution from stocking the nth unit is the difference between the expected values associated with the "Stock n" and "Stock $n-1$" decisions in Figure 2.5A, or

Exp. Incr. Contrib.

$$= (r - c - z) \times (1 - P_{n-1}) - (c - s) \times P_{n-1} + g \times (1 - P_{n-1})$$
$$= (r - c - z + g) \times (1 - P_{n-1}) - (c - s) \times P_{n-1} \; . \tag{4}$$

If we set $G = r - c - z + g$ and $L = c - s$, then equation (4) becomes equation (1), and the $G/(G + L)$ fractile provides the best stocking level.

If backordering is possible (Figure 2.5B), the expected incremental contribution from stocking the nth unit is

Exp. Incr. Contrib.

$$= (r - c - z) \times (1 - P_{n-1}) - (c - s) \times P_{n-1} - (r - c - z - b) \times (1 - P_{n-1})$$
$$= b \times (1 - P_{n-1}) - (c - s) \times P_{n-1} \; . \tag{5}$$

If we set $G = b$ and $L = c - s$, then equation (5) becomes equation (1), and the $G/(G + L)$ fractile once again provides the best stocking level. (Notice that the per-unit revenue r, the per-unit cost c, and the per-unit commission z all drop out of the expression for G, and indeed neither the revenue nor the sales commission is relevant to the stocking decision. In other words, if backordering is possible, all units demanded will ultimately be sold; revenue and commission are therefore not affected by the stocking decision. Notice also that if $b = 0$, then $G = 0$ and we should stock nothing. This corresponds to the situation where you can first observe demand and then fill it, i.e., make to order.)

Summary

The optimal stocking level in critical-fractile problems is the $G/(G + L)$ fractile of the distribution of demand. In the simplest situation, G is the margin per unit, L is the cost per unit, and the critical ratio is the margin expressed as a fraction of revenue. In more complicated situations, where there may be a salvage value s, a sales commission z, a loss of goodwill g if an item is out of stock and cannot be backordered, or a backorder cost if an item is out of stock but can eventually be sold, the values of G and L are as follows:

In the case of goodwill loss, $G = r - c - z + g$, $L = c - s$;

in the case of backordering, $G = b$, $L = c - s$.

Probabilistic Forecasts

Critical-fractile problems abound in the real world and are worth studying for that reason alone. In addition, they are one of the simplest illustrations of the need for explicitly quantifying your uncertainty. In practice, poor Terry would probably react to his uncertainty about newspaper demand by stating that the most likely demand was for five newspapers, and stocking that number. Or, if he were more sophisticated, he might calculate the mean of his distribution of demand as 4.77, and again conclude that he should stock the closest integral number of newspapers, or five. In both cases he would be wrong, and would make less money in the long run than he would if he chose to stock the quantity that maximized his expected contribution.

Although one might argue that the reduction in expected contribution resulting from stocking five rather than four newspapers is only $0.075, and that it hardly pays to go to all this trouble to avoid such a trivial loss, these results depend on the particular numerical values used in the example. In particular, because the values of G and L were fairly close, the critical ratio was 0.40, leading to an optimal stocking level near the center of the distribution of demand. Had G been very much larger than L , the critical ratio would have been close to 1, and the optimal stocking level would have been far out in the upper tail of the distribution, not anywhere near the mode or the mean. Conversely, if G had been very much smaller than L , the critical ratio would have been close to 0, and the optimal stocking level would have been far out in the lower tail of the distribution. In either of these cases, just stocking the mean or the mode of the distribution would have led to serious errors.

If we must make probabilistic forecasts of demand, how can we assess the probabilities? In the absence of relevant data, we would be relegated to probabilities assessed subjectively. If we had relevant data about variables that we believe affected demand, we might be able to make probabilistic forecasts based on some statistical model relating those variables to demand. In some instances we might believe that demand data on some set of past occasions were all equally representative of what demand will be on the future occasion for which we are forecasting, in which case a frequency distribution of past demand can serve as a probability distribution for future demand. One word of caution is needed, however. In many cases, past **sales** are recorded, but not past **demand**. Sales and demand may differ for several reasons, the most common being the result of stockouts. Basing a probability distribution of future demand on a frequency distribution of past sales can result in stocking decisions that are far from optimal if stockouts have occurred frequently.

Exercises

1.   A factory makes two products. It has capacity to produce a combined total of 100 units per week, in any combination. Product 1 costs $20 per unit to make and sells for $30. Demand for this product exceeds the factory's capacity. Product 2 costs $10 per unit to make, and sells for $100, but demand is uncertain. Product 2 is produced in batches once a week. Any units that are not sold by the end of the week must be thrown out: they have no salvage value. The probability distribution of demand for Product 2 is shown below. How many units, if any, should be produced?

Table 2.4

Demand	Probability
5	0.10
6	0.20
7	0.25
8	0.20
9	0.20
10	0.05

2.   Many companies make available to employees a tax-reducing flexible medical/dental spending account. The employee may designate an annual amount, up to $3,000, that will be deducted from his or her paycheck and

maintained by the employer in a special account that can be used to pay medical and dental expenses for the employee and his or her other tax dependents. The amount deducted is not subject to federal, state, or Social Security taxes. The catch is that under IRS regulations, any unused amount in an employee's account at the end of the calendar year cannot be refunded or used to make medical or dental payments in the following year, but must be retained by the employer.

Be prepared to discuss how you would decide how much money, if any, to designate in a flexible spending account of this sort.

3. Prior to 1978, civil aviation in the United States was regulated by the Civil Aeronautics Board (CAB), and route or fare changes took time. The 1978 Airline Deregulation Act gave airlines the freedom to enter or exit routes and alter fares at will. Perhaps the biggest change was the extent to which discount rates (usually including restrictions) became a phenomenon.

   Once prices and restrictions have been determined, it is yield management's responsibility to control the number of seats available in each fare category. An aircraft seat for a particular flight is a highly perishable commodity; once the plane takes off, the unsold product is lost forever. The challenge in yield management is to optimize the trade-off between the cost of an empty seat (the lost discount fare) and the cost of turning away a full-fare passenger (the difference between full and discount fare).[2]

   a. Consider a simple yield-management problem. An aircraft has 100 seats, and there are two types of fares: full ($500) and discount ($100). While there is unlimited demand for discount fares, demand for full fares is estimated to be equally likely anywhere between 10 and 30. How many seats should be protected for full-fare passengers?

   b. Be prepared to discuss in what ways this "simple" problem oversimplifies the real yield-management problem facing an airline.

CONFEDERATED PULP & PAPER

Desmond O'Hara wiped the perspiration from his forehead, looked out his window at the green countryside on this warm day of summer, and thought how the cold of the northern Quebec winters seemed always to affect his world. Today, with the temperature in the high eighties, he was worrying about the river freezing over and its effect on planning for his mill at Ste. Josette.

Supplying Wood to the Mill

The paper mill of Confederated Pulp & Paper, located in Ste. Josette, Quebec, was the largest of the company's seven mills. It produced newsprint continuously throughout a seven-day week. It had an annual capacity of 250,000 tons.

   Wood to supply the mill was cut 120 miles north of the mill in the company's timber holdings. After the trees were felled, they were cut into four-foot lengths and floated down the Moneskeg River to the mill. During the open

Harvard Business School case 9-191-065. This case is based on an earlier case by Professor Paul Vatter, Consolidated Pulp & Paper Limited, HBS #174-058. Copyright © 1990 by the President and Fellows of Harvard College.

[2]Problem abstracted from *American Airlines, Inc.: Revenue Management,* (Harvard Business School Case 190-029.) Included in *Decision Making Under Certainty.*

season on the river, logs were caught in a boom and moved directly into the mill as needed. The location of the timber lands and the mill made this an extremely efficient form of transportation.

The problems with this supply method began when the river froze over in the fall, and did not end until the spring thaw. To supply the mill during the freeze period, Confederated needed to build up an inventory of wood—The Block Pile—before the freeze; this inventory had to last until the regular flow resumed. Every year it seemed there were extended and sometimes heated discussions of how big The Block Pile should be. He knew this issue would be discussed at tomorrow's meeting, and he wondered what his position should be.

The Meeting—June 28, 1988

Desmond, as the mill manager at Ste. Josette, held this year's meeting in his office at the mill. The other participants in the meeting were Jacques Leveque of the Woodlands division and Harvey Wilson, an assistant treasurer from the home office in Montreal. Each participant had a copy of the information shown in Exhibit 1. This indicated the size of The Block Pile at the beginning of the freeze in each of the last six years and the size of the pile, if any, at the time the river opened again in the spring (this automatically became the start of the pile to be built for the following winter).

Desmond began the discussion, "You both remember, I am sure, the terrible problems we had in 1984 when we exhausted The Block Pile and had to buy wood locally to keep the mill operating. The same factors that caused us to run out—high paper demand and a long freeze—affected a number of other mills the same way. With that demand, our local farmers were able to charge us an effective price of about twice what it cost to buy and ship logs from the north country, and we had no alternative but to pay or shut down the mill. In fact, that's no alternative at all because the costs of stopping our operation and then restarting are prohibitive. But the point is this, the increased cost of wood wiped out all of the mill's profit contribution that year and in fact made the mill a drain on the company. I hope we can all agree at the outset that we will build The Block Pile big enough this year that we won't have a repetition of that fiasco."

Harvey Wilson frowned, tugged at his mustache, and said, "We all recognize the problem and in fact sympathize with you on it Desmond, but remember there is another side to the coin too. Eighty-four was really bad luck. Not only did we pick up much more newsprint business than we had forecast, but it was a devilishly long winter. It's not likely we'll run into that combination again. Certainly we can't do all of our planning protecting against every extreme contingency. Don't forget that The Block Pile really costs big money and we're not the old Cash Cow we used to be."

Desmond continued, "I'm not quite sure what you're driving at, Harvey, surely the costs of making the woodpile an adequate one are very small. After all, we will use any leftover wood the following winter."

Harvey broke in and said, "That's not really the point, Desmond. If we put too much wood on The Block Pile, it means that we have paid the loggers to *cut* that wood a year earlier than we needed to. It may not sound like a big deal to you, but our internal cost of funds is 20% per year, so tying up money in The Block Pile gets expensive. By the way, Jacques, what kind of logging costs are we looking at in Woodlands now?"

Jacques responded, "Well, we feel pretty comfortable with evaluating our full cost for cutting a cunit[3] at \$47.50, about \$23 of which is variable cost. In addition, the variable shipping cost when the log goes directly into the mill runs about \$8.00. Of course, when you have to put a log on the top of the pile and then later send it into the mill by conveyor from the bottom, it adds about \$2.00 per cunit to the cost. What kind of demand do you people at Ste. Josette plan to place on us this year?"

Desmond replied, "Demand and our backlog are such that we are almost certain we will operate through the entire winter at full capacity. That means each week we will use up 4,800 cunits of wood.

"The thing that bothers me is that how much wood I will need in The Block Pile depends not only on my rate of consumption of wood but on how long the river will stay frozen. Even the *Farmer's Almanac* doesn't give me the answer to that one, and it really makes a difference.

"When I looked back in our files I was able to piece together the length of the freeze in each of the past ten years. For each of the years I was able to get a good fix on the last day in the fall when we moved logs directly from the boom into the mill. From our operating records I could also learn the earliest date in each year on which logs from the river were again used in production."

As he passed a sheet to each of the others (see Exhibit 2), he added: "Here is the record I was able to come up with. As you can see there are tremendous differences from year to year. Harvey, it's all very well for you to come here from headquarters talking about internal cost of funds, but come the spring if the river is frozen and we're out of wood, we'll be at the mercy of the local farmers again, just like '84. We'll be paying \$65 a cunit [delivered to the mill] for sure. And that'll be in real dollars, not funny money."

Exhibit 1

| | SIZE OF BLOCK PILE AT BEGINNING AND END OF FREEZE, BY YEAR | |
Year	Size of Pile in Fall (000 of Cunits)	Size of Pile in Spring (000 of Cunits)
1982-83	100	12
1983-84	100	*
1984-85	125	40
1985-86	113	27
1986-87	110	5
1987-88	110	28

*The Pile was exhausted—12,000 cunits of wood were purchased locally.

---

[3]A cunit was a unit of measurement corresponding to 100 solid cubic feet of wood.

Exhibit 2 _____

LENGTH OF FREEZE OF MONESKEG RIVER, BY YEAR, **1978-1988**

Year	Freeze in Number of Days*
1978-79	142
1979-80	151
1980-81	120
1981-82	148
1982-83	144
1983-84	170
1984-85	138
1985-86	146
1986-87	159
1987-88	130

*Number of days between last day on which logs could arrive in the fall and the first day on which logs arrived in the spring.

▼   ▼   ▼

CUMULATIVE PROBABILITY DISTRIBUTIONS

When the outcome of an event is uncertain, each of its possible outcomes can be assigned a probability. For example, the outcome of a coin toss is uncertain: if you think the coin is fair, you will assign probability 0.5 to its coming up heads, and 0.5 to its coming up tails. Similarly, if the value of a variable is uncertain, its possible values can be assigned probabilities. The result of a roll of a six-sided die will be an integer between 1 and 6. If the die is fair, each outcome has probability 1/6. If the die appears to be asymmetric, or unevenly weighted, we may wish to assign judgmental probabilities different from 1/6 to the values, with our judgment based on whatever knowledge we possess about the die's asymmetry or unevenness.

In this note, we will first look at the problem of assessing probabilities for a variable that has many possible values—many more than the six possible values on the faces of a die. We shall see that the most straightforward way of carrying out such an assessment involves thinking in terms of cumulative probabilities—for example, the probability that the true value is less than 1 million, or greater than 5 million, or between 2 million and 4 million. Unfortunately, although assessing probabilities in this fashion makes sense, cumulative probabilities cannot be used directly in the evaluation or analysis of a decision tree. Thus, after discussing the problem of assessment, we shall turn to the problem of evaluation.

Assessing Probabilities for Many-Valued Variables

We will distinguish two cases. In the first case, you will have nothing but your expert judgment to go on. If any past data are relevant, they may be informally incorporated into your judgment, but will not be formally processed. In the sec-

This note was written by Professor Arthur Schleifer Jr..

ond case, you may have observations from the past that, in your judgment, bear equally on your assessment of the unknown value of the variable in which you are interested. We say, in these circumstances, that the observations come from indistinguishable situations, or the data are **indistinguishable**. Although indistinguishable situations are the exception, rather than the rule, it is often possible to take into account whatever factors cause individual data points to be distinguishable from one another and, having taken these factors into account, what is left may be indistinguishable. Therefore, assessing probabilities from indistinguishable data is useful in many contexts. We will start, however, with assessment based on pure judgment.

Judgmental Assessment

When there are many possible values of a variable, it is virtually impossible to think about assigning separate probabilities to each possible value. If your company's revenues next year could be between $100 million and $150 million, it is inconceivable that you could assign probabilities to every dollar value in the range. Even if you tried brackets $1 million wide, the task would be formidable, and if you used much wider brackets, say $10 million, it might be quite difficult to decide how much probability belonged in the $110–$120 million bracket and how much in the $120–$130 million bracket, for example. Most people find it considerably easier to think in terms of cumulative probabilities and fractiles. In fact, the three quartiles (the 0.25, 0.50, and 0.75 fractiles), are perhaps the easiest points on a cumulative probability distribution to assess. Why is this so?

It is usually difficult for people to have an intuitive feeling for an event with probability 0.32, or 0.85, or 0.41. It is much easier to ask oneself whether two possibilities, A and B, are equally likely, or whether A is more likely than B, or B more likely than A. Of course, if A and B are judged by you to be equally likely, then each has probability 0.5, in your judgment.

With this in mind, notice that the 0.50 fractile (the median of the distribution) is a value of a variable such that, in your judgment, it is just as likely that the true value will be below the median as above it. In the revenue example, your median will be $120 million if you are indifferent between the following two options illustrated in Figure 2.6: (A) receiving a valuable prize if revenues are less than $120 million and nothing if they exceed $120 million; and (B) receiving an identical prize if revenues exceed $120 million and nothing if they fall short of it. Observe that if you are indifferent between the two options, their expected values must be identical, and this can be the case only if $p = 1 - p$, which can be true only if $p = 0.5$; see Figure 2.6. It follows that if you are not indifferent, $120 cannot be your median. If you prefer Option A, by implication you think it is more likely that revenues will exceed $120 million than that they will fall short; your median should, therefore, be higher than $120 million. By similar logic, if you prefer Option B, your median should be lower than $120 million. How much higher or lower is a matter of judgment. Try a new value and ask yourself which option, if either, you would prefer, where the prize is now triggered on your new value; if you find options A and B equally attractive, the new value is your median.

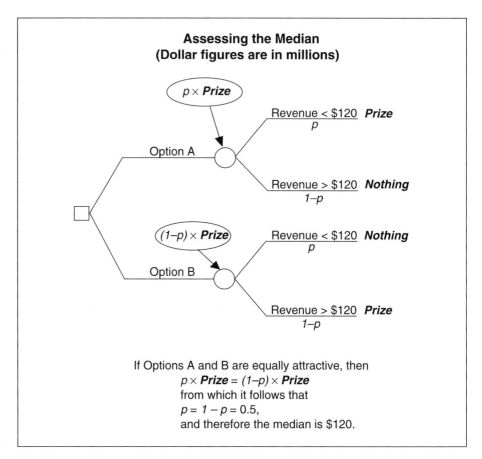

**Assessing the Median
(Dollar figures are in millions)**

$p \times$ **Prize**

Option A

Revenue $< \$120$ **Prize**
p

Revenue $> \$120$ **Nothing**
$1-p$

$(1-p) \times$ **Prize**

Option B

Revenue $< \$120$ **Nothing**
p

Revenue $> \$120$ **Prize**
$1-p$

If Options A and B are equally attractive, then
$p \times$ **Prize** $= (1-p) \times$ **Prize**
from which it follows that
$p = 1 - p = 0.5$,
and therefore the median is $120.

Figure 2.6

Just as the true value of a variable is likely to be above the median as below it, so the true value is likely to be between the first and third quartiles (the 0.25 and 0.75 fractiles), i.e., within the **interquartile range**, as it is to be outside the interquartile range. Furthermore, if you knew for sure that the true value was below the median, it would then be just as likely to be above the 0.25 fractile as below it, and similarly, if you knew for sure that the true value was above the median, it would be just as likely to be above the 0.75 fractile as below it. This provides a way of operationalizing the assessment of the first and third quartiles. We illustrate for the first quartile (the 0.25 fractile).

Suppose that you have assessed the median to be $120 million. Now suppose you are asked to choose between the following two options, illustrated in Figure 2.7. For both options, you receive nothing if revenue exceeds $120 million (the median), but if you choose Option C, you will receive a valuable prize if revenue falls short of $112 million and nothing if it exceeds $112 million, while if you choose Option D, you will receive an identical prize if revenue exceeds $112 million (but is less than the median of $120 million), and nothing if it is less than $112 million. If you find options C and D equally attractive, then $112 million is your 0.25 fractile, as shown in Figure 2.7. If you prefer Option C, then the first quartile must be less than $112 million; if you prefer Option D, it must be greater than $112 million. You should be able to adjust the amount that triggers the prize so that you will be indifferent between the two options; that amount is then your 0.25 fractile.

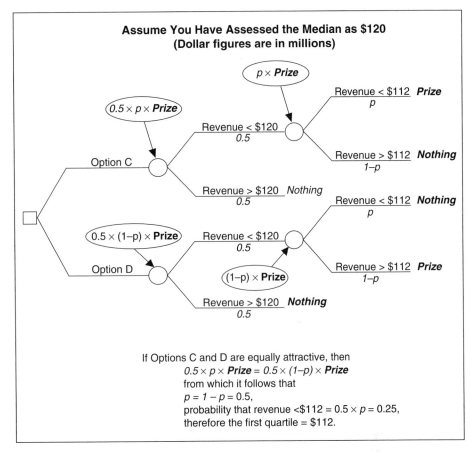

Figure 2.7

You should work through the very similar methodology for assessing the third quartile (the 0.75 fractile). Let's assume that after careful consideration, you decide that $134 million is your 0.75 fractile.

You will now have three points on your cumulative probability curve. You are not quite finished. You should assess two additional extreme values: a low number such that you believe there is only one chance in twenty that the true value of revenue will fall short of that number; and a high number such that you believe that there is only one chance in twenty that revenue will exceed it. These values are your 0.05 and 0.95 fractiles. Suppose you assess them to be $100 million and $150 million respectively. Figure 3 shows these five points. In principle, a probability distribution based on these five assessments should be a smooth S-shaped curve passing through all five assessed points. In practice, it is usually sufficient to approximate this smooth probability distribution by connecting the assessed points with straight lines. Figure 4 shows a smooth curve going through the five points and the straight-line approximation.

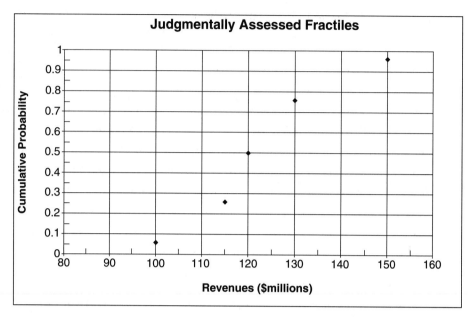

Figure 2.8

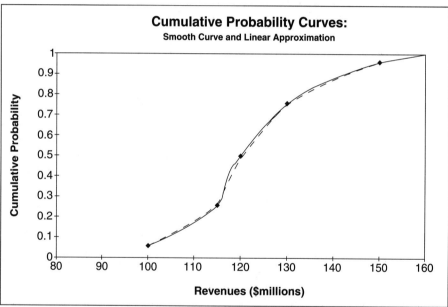

Figure 2.9

This method of subjectively assessing a probability distribution for a many-valued variable leaves one question unanswered: how do we use the assessed distribution in a decision-tree analysis? We will defer an answer to that question until we have discussed how probability distributions can be assessed from indistinguishable data.

Assessment Based on Indistinguishable Data

DMC, Inc., a direct-marketing company, is trying to decide how many dresses of Style X to order for its fall catalog. The decision will depend on a forecast of the demand that the dress in question will generate; at the beginning of the season, the buyer, who is responsible for the forecast is very uncertain about what the demand will be. She could, purely judgmentally, assess a median forecast, then the first and third quartiles, and finally two extreme fractiles, just as was done for the revenue forecast in the last section. Alternatively, she might have reason to think that this fall's demand will be like last fall's demand, and that the Style X dress whose demand she is forecasting might fare just about as well as any of ten dresses (Styles A, B, etc.) that were offered for sale in the prior year. Table 2.5 shows demand in the prior year for each of these ten dresses. If she believes that demand for Style X this year is as likely to be at the level of last year's demand for dress A as it is for dress B, dress C, etc., we can say that in her judgment demand for this year's Style X dress is indistinguishable from the actual demands for the ten styles from last year.

Table 2.5

Style	Demand
A	1,576
B	763
C	1,174
D	1,352
E	636
F	2,443
G	1,024
H	492
I	1,891
J	890

We have to be careful about asserting that data are indistinguishable. If the circulation of this fall's catalog is considerably different from that of last fall, this fall's demand will be distinguishable from last fall's. Similarly, if there is an upward (or downward) trend in response to the catalog, the past is distinguishable from the future. Furthermore, if one of last year's dresses was targeted towards a different set of buyers than this year's dress, the past and future demands will be distinguishable. Let's stipulate, however, that the buyer has in this case considered and rejected as inapplicable the various ways in which the past data might be distinguishable.

Given that the future demand for the Style X dress is viewed as indistinguishable from the past demands of Styles A, B, etc., there are two possible ways to proceed. The first is to treat the frequency distribution of past demands as a probability distribution for future demand. The other is first to smooth the frequency distribution and then to use the smoothed frequency distribution as a probability distribution of future demand.

Equating Past Frequencies to Future Probabilities

Because dress A experienced a demand of 1,576, and this was one of ten indistinguishable dresses, it would be reasonable to say that with probability 0.1, demand for this year's Style X dress will be 1,576. Figure 2.10A shows a cumugram of past demand, which can be used as a cumulative probability distribution of future demand for Style X; Figure 2.10B shows the same probability distribution in tree form. The possible values of demand and their probabilities could be used in any decision problem involving the uncertain demand for Style X dresses.

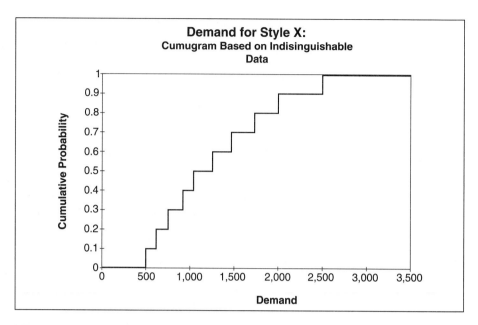

Figure 2.10A

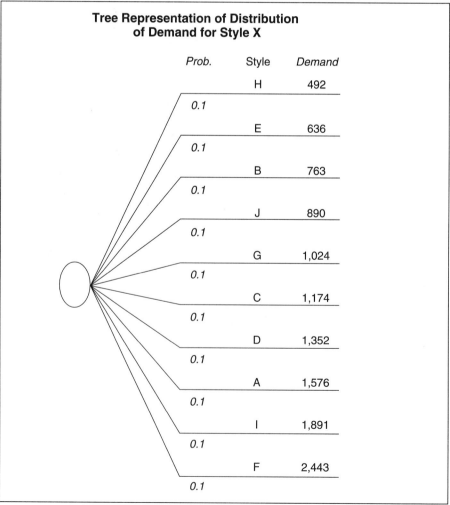

Figure 2.10B

Smoothing the Frequencies

Under some circumstances we might be dissatisfied representing the probability distribution of demand for Style X by a stair-step cumugram like Figure 10A. Taken literally, such a distribution asserts that a demand lower than the lowest observed demand (492) or higher than the highest observed demand (2,443) is impossible. Furthermore, it says that any level of demand in between two observed levels is impossible. For instance, 492 was the lowest demand and 636 the next lowest; treating the cumugram of Figure 2.10A as a probability distribution implies that a level of demand for Style X of 500, or 550, or 600 could not possibly occur.

Suppose we are trying to make a stocking decision for Style X based on the probability distribution of Figure 2.10A and the following costs and revenues: selling price = $60, cost = $25, salvage value = $15. Then G = $35, L = $10, and the critical ratio = $35/$45 = 0.778. Applying the critical fractile to Figure 2.10A, we would stock 1,576, the 0.778 fractile of demand. Notice that the decision to stock 1,576 would remain the same for any critical ratio between 0.70 and 0.80, even though common sense would suggest that a higher level of stocking should accompany a higher critical ratio. At the extremes—critical ratios in excess of 0.90 or less than 0.10—you would stock, respectively, the highest and lowest observed levels of demand, irrespective of whether the critical ratio was 0.90 or 0.99. This is a consequence of the stairstep cumugram, and suggests that a smooth approximation might be better. (Whether it will refine the decision sufficiently to be worth the trouble is not clear.)

Figure 2.11 shows a smooth curve drawn as an approximation to the stairstep cumugram. Notice that it extends below 492 and above 2,443, that it is smooth and S-shaped, rising at an increasing rate and then at a decreasing rate, and following reasonably closely the shape of the cumugram. If we were to use this curve instead of the cumugram as a probability distribution of demand, we would find that the critical 0.778 fractile was 1,606.

Normal Approximations

If the frequency distribution of past demands is reasonably symmetric, it may be reasonable to approximate this frequency distribution with a normal distribution. To do this, first calculate the mean m and standard deviation s of past demands. Using the Excel functions =AVERAGE() and =STDEV(), we find $m =$ 1,224, $s = 607$. You can then compute any fractile of a normal distribution having this mean and standard deviation using the Excel function =NORMINV(prob,m,s), where prob is a number between 0 and 1. For example, to compute the 0.1 fractile of the normal approximation to the probability distribution of demand, simply evaluate the function =NORMINV(0.1, 1224, 607) = 446. In Figure 2.12 we graph the cumugram of past demands and the fitted normal approximation. Because the cumugram arises from a distribution somewhat skewed to the right, the fit is not as good as that of the fitted curve in Figure 2.11.

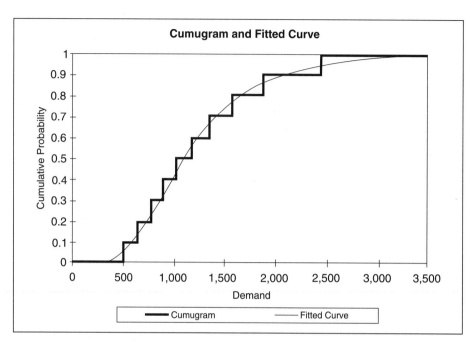

Figure 2.11

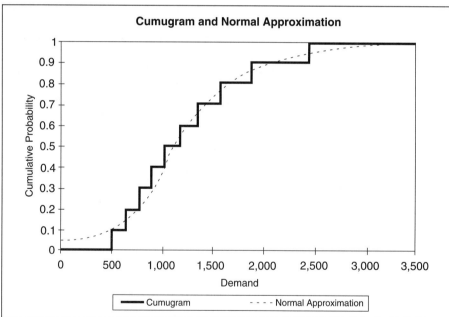

Figure 2.12

Pros and Cons

What is the best way to use indistinguishable past data to assess a probability distribution of some future value? Using the past frequency distribution results in an immediately applicable probability distribution, but the possible future values of demand are confined to the observed values of past demand.

A distribution that smoothes out the stairs in the cumugram avoids this problem, but creates two other problems: just how to smooth through a stairstep cumugram, and how to use the smoothed distribution to compute expected values.

The normal approximation has the virtue of smoothing the cumugram mechanically and, as we shall see, can be used mechanically to compute expected values, but it may be a totally inappropriate distribution if it does not provide a good fit to the cumugram. In particular, if the cumugram arose from a skewed distribution, or even from a symmetric distribution whose histogram was not appropriately "bell-shaped", the normal approximation will differ a great deal from a smoothed cumugram, and will be a poor approximation to a probability distribution.

Systematic Samples from a Smooth Cumulative Probability Distribution

A smooth cumulative probability distribution assigns probabilities to very many values of a variable. In using a smooth approximation to the probability distribution for number of Style X dresses demanded, we could, in principle, compute the probability that exactly 1,200 dresses would be demanded by subtracting the probability of 1,199 or less from the probability of 1,200 or less, and we could continue in this way to get the probability of every level of demand from 500, say, to 2,000. Obviously, such a procedure is not just tedious, but can add little value to one that uses not every possible level of demand, but rather a set of representative sample levels of demand. Let's see how we can use a representative sample of just five levels of demand.

For any distribution there is a 20% chance of falling below the 0.2 fractile, a 20% chance of falling between the 0.2 and 0.4 fractile, and 20% chances of falling between the 0.4 and 0.6, between the 0.6 and 0.8, and above the 0.8 fractiles. If we could find a representative value below the 0.2 fractile, between the 0.2 and 0.4 fractiles, between the 0.4 and 0.6 fractiles, etc., we could approximate the smooth probability distribution with a sample of five representative values, each of which stood for all the values in an interval that had probability 0.2. A convenient representative value is one that divides the probability interval in 2[1]. That is, the 0.1 fractile is reasonably representative of the set of values lying below the 0.2 fractile; the set of values lying below the 0.2 fractile have probability 0.2 of occurring. Similarly, the 0.3 fractile is reasonably representative of the values lying between the 0.2 and 0.4 fractiles, a set of values that also have probability 0.2 of occurring. We can continue in this way. In a nutshell, if we assign probability 0.2 each to the 0.1, 0.3, 0.5, 0.7, and 0.9 fractiles, we will have represented the continuous probability distribution by a systematic sample of five representative values. Of course, only five sample values may provide a poor approximation to a smooth curve; in principle, we could take a larger systematic sample (e.g., a sample of ten, using the 0.05, 0.15, ... , 0.95 fractiles, each representing probability of 0.1), but to demonstrate competency regarding decisions under uncertainty, it will be sufficient to use just five.

Figure 2.13A illustrates this discrete approximation method for the judgmentally assessed distribution of revenues shown in Figures 2.8 and 2.9, and Figure 2.13B shows this discrete approximation in decision-tree form.

---

[1]Remember that the median is the fractile corresponding to a probability that divides the vertical axis from 0 to 1 in two. Per analogy, if we use the vertical midpoints as representative values for brackets that go from 0 to 0.2, to 0.4, etc., these vertical midpoints are called **bracket medians**.

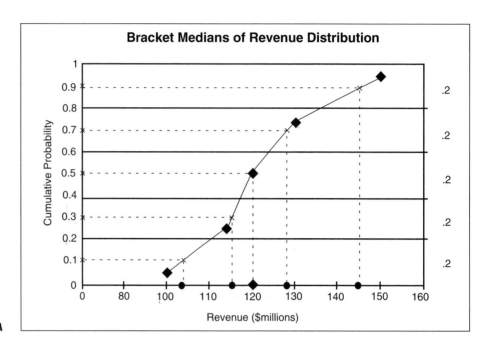

Figure 2.13A

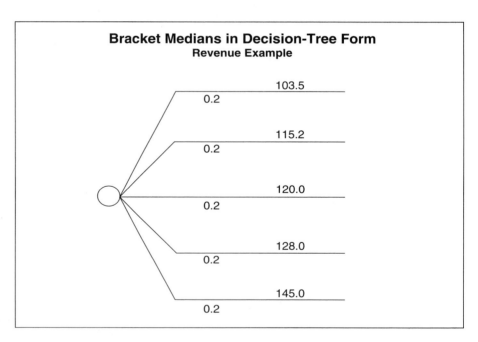

Figure 2.13B

In the case of the normal approximation, the five representative values can be derived by formula. If m and s are, respectively, the mean and standard deviation of the indistinguishable past observations, then the five representative values, each having probability 0.2, are:

$$m - 1.28s, \; m - 0.52s, \; m, \; m + 0.52s, \; m + 1.28s \, .$$

Indeed, we can use spreadsheets to obtain much finer discretizations of the normal approximation. For example, we can obtain 100 representative values, each with probability 0.01, using the Excel function =NORMINV(0.005,m,s),

=NORMINV(0.015,*m,s*), ... , =NORMINV(0.995,*m,s*). Figure 2.14 shows a five-point discrete approximation to the continuous normal approximation to the distribution of Style X dresses graphed in Figure 2.14.

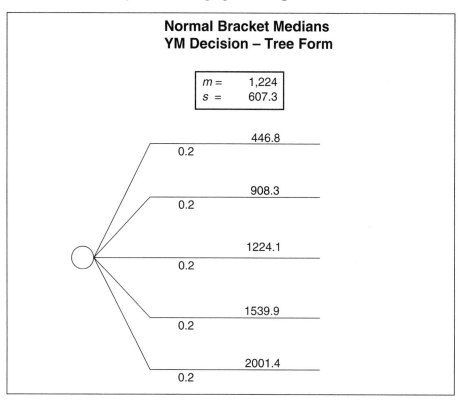

Figure 2.14

Using Discrete Approximations to Probability Distributions

Suppose DMC faces the following decision problem with respect to the Style X dress. It would like to order enough to meet demand for the season, but not so many that it must liquidate a large overstock position. The manufacturer of this dress proposes two options. Under the first option, she is willing to accept orders from DMC every week, supplying DMC out of finished-goods inventory, thus assuring that all demand will be met and there will be neither stockouts nor excess stock during or at the end of the season. Under the second option, the manufacturer has offered to produce a single order for as many dresses as DMC specifies, but because production facilities will then be devoted to other products, there will be no possibility of reordering as demand materializes. Under this option, DMC may run out of stock if demand exceeds expectations, or end the season with excess stock if demand falls short of expectations. DMC's cost under the first option is $30/dress; under the second, which permits the manufacturer to use her facilities much more efficiently, DMC's cost is $25/dress.

The dress sells through the catalog for $60. Any excess merchandise can be liquidated for $15 per dress. For the purpose of this example, assume that the only uncertainty facing DMC concerns total demand and not demand by size of dress: if they exercise the second option, for example, they will not end the season short of some sizes and overstocked with respect to others.

Figure 2.15 analyzes this decision problem using probability distributions of demand based on five bracket medians from the fitted curve in Figure 2.12. As exercises, you should do similar analyses using five normal bracket medians, the ten historical relative frequencies and, as an Excel exercise, 100 normal bracket medians. The results are as follows:

Method	Critical Fractile	Order in Advance	Make to Order
Fitted Curve, 5 bracket medians	1,606	$33,881	$36,126
Normal Approximation, 5 bracket medians	1,689	$35,335	$36,723
10 Historical Relative Frequencies	1,576	$34,005	$36,723
Normal Approx., 100 bracket medians	2,689	$34,773	$36,723

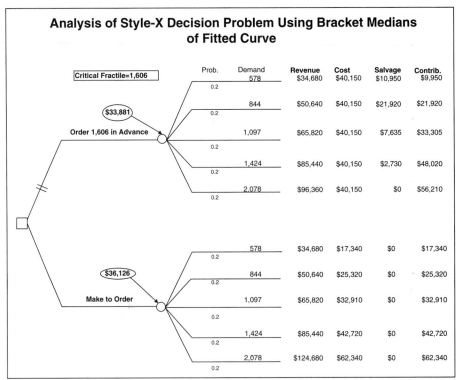

Figure 2.15

In all cases, make to order is the better decision. (If the cost per dress under the make-to-order option were $32 instead of $30, the order-in-advance option turns out to be slightly better under all approximations except the ten historical frequencies. If the cost per dress under the make-to-order option were $33, all approximation methods would favor the order-in-advance option.)

Summary

The following list shows the three ways we have discussed to derive a probability distribution from data arising from indistinguishable situations. It lists the properties of the cumulative probability distributions, and how to compute the expected value.

Method of Evaluation	Properties of Cumulative Probability Distribution	Expected Values
Stairstep Cumugram	Probabilities exist only for past observed values.	Direct computation; if there are n indistinguishable values, each has probability $1/n$.
Smooth Approximation to the Cumugram	Probabilities exist for all values.	Need to compute fit by drawing smooth discrete curve. approx- imation using bracket medians obtained from graph of smooth approximation.
Normal Approximation	Probabilities exist for all values. Fit mechanically, but approximation may be inappropriate.	Need to compute discrete approximation using bracket medians, but these are easy to obtain mechanically.

CASE

AUTO MAG

John MacBain waved a hand at the piles of magazines stacked in a corridor of the Auto Mag building. "Look at all these returns," he said. "I think we are spending too much on magazines we don't sell." The returns were copies of Auto Mag publications that had not sold on the newsstands the previous week and had been returned for destruction. At the time, returns were approximately 30% of circulation.

Since his graduation from Harvard Business School John MacBain (HBS '84) had been working for Power Financial Corporation, a major Canadian holding company. In June 1987 he heard that the owners of Auto Hebdo, a Montreal-based specialty magazine publishing company, were interested in selling their business. John knew he had to act quickly in order to snatch the deal away from three other interested parties. They included Auto Hebdo's printers, a Toronto-based publisher of magazines similar to those of Auto Hebdo, and one other publisher. With the help of his wife Louise, MacBain managed to secure the necessary several million dollars in financing and closed the deal within a period of only two weeks.

Auto Hebdo published seven magazines. Each of the magazines, except one, contained want advertisements for a specific category of product, as follows: (1) American cars; (2) imports; (3) antiques; (4) boats, motorcycles, and recreational vehicles; (5) trucks; and (6) heavy construction equipment. The seventh magazine contained want advertisements for miscellaneous products. The magazines were written in French and included photos of the products for sale. (See Exhibit 1 for a sample page from *Voitures Americaines*.) The publications were distributed across the province of Quebec through 5,000 newsstands.

Harvard Business School case 9-189-034, revised May 7, 1991. Najib Hashem prepared this case under the supervision of Professor David E. Bell. Some numbers in the case have been disguised to protect confidential information.

John Describes the Concept

"A customer phones us with an item to sell (for example, a car, boat, or motorcycle). We record the details and four lines of textual description. Then one of our free-lance photographers contacts the customer and arranges a time and location for the photo session. The process couldn't be simpler, and the cost of the ad is $20. There are no other commissions or sales charges. The photograph and four-line description appear in the next two editions. We contract a lot of advertising business with second-hand car and equipment dealers. Just think of it. We have 100% advertising, and on top of that, we sell, not give away, the magazines."

An average of 700 telephone orders per week were received to place ads in one of the four weekly magazines. Of these, 25% were advertisement renewals beyond the initial two weeks (see Exhibit 2 for a listing of all magazines). A staff of eight answered the phones. A separate telemarketing staff contacted people who had placed advertisements in the Montreal daily papers but had not placed ads in Auto Mag. That effort alone resulted in 200 new customers. About 300 people were walk-ins (individuals who were in the area and placed last-minute photos). The regular automobile garage advertisers accounted for approximately another 600 photos, depending upon the season. In addition, the company had commercial advertising contracts with its larger clients. Revenues from the larger clients are summarized in Exhibit 3.

The Printing and Distribution Process

The number of pages in each magazine, typically 100 to 120, depended on the amount of advertising and the packing density of the individual photographs. (The density range was 14 to 18 photos per page.) Every Tuesday the final pages of the new magazine editions were collated and delivered to the printers for overnight reproduction. At that time the decision was made regarding how many copies to print. (See Exhibit 4 for typical printing costs.)

Magazine distribution occurred each Wednesday. Each of the 70 distributors was responsible for a specific geographic territory. The distributors, referred to by Auto Hebdo as "Entrepreneurs in Marketing," were independent part-time workers. Many of these entrepreneurs were retired, or they were between jobs and needed to supplement their income. On the average, one day's pay was C$120. Turnover among distributors was a problem. (See Figure 2.16 for selected costs.)

Selected Costs

Photographers received C$4.50 per photo to cover all expenses. Film was supplied at no charge.

Entrepreneurs received C$0.18 per copy sold, with a minimum of C$1.50 per store for the stores selling fewer than eight copies per week.

Magazines were tied in bundles of 25. Entrepreneurs stocked just enough copies (rounded up to the nearest whole bundle) to cover their routes.

Figure 2.16

Entrepreneurs were assigned predefined routes. They contracted to collect the magazines from the printers, deliver them, return unsold copies of previous editions, adjust in-store display racks to enhance their appearance, and issue bills to each of their stores. Entrepreneurs received the magazines on a prepaid basis but received credit for copies not sold. The entrepreneurs delivered to Auto Hebdo all returns, as well as copies of the current edition that had not been displayed on racks within the stores. A computer compiled the sales data and completed the billing. The process was similar for the bimonthly and monthly publications (see Exhibit 2), except the cycle lasted either two weeks or one month.

The Sales Forecasting System

Auto Mag used a TRS-80-based microcomputer system to handle all of its accounting needs and to determine, for each publication, the optimum number of copies to display in the different stores. Director of Information Systems Michel Moore and his assistant Vincent Guilbert had experimented with many forecasting methodologies. The latest one was deceptively simple. For each publication, the computer program reviewed the latest sales figures store by store and adjusted the forecast to aim for a return of one in stores where fewer than six copies were delivered and for a return of two in all other stores. For example, if a store sold all of its 10 copies, 12 copies would be sent on the next occasion. If a store sold seven out of 10 copies, nine copies would be forecasted for the next delivery. Robert Perreault, the director of marketing, believed that the program was very effective, but was it the best?

The bills contained a listing of the recommended numbers of magazines in each category to be placed in each store. Exhibit 5 presents a sample distribution/billing sales slip. The entrepreneurs were still learning to trust the forecasts. Some preferred to use intuition and adjust the quantities they gave to a store on the spot. An occasional odd occurrence, such as road repairs outside a store, would require a reduction in the quantity delivered. Such an event could not be "known" to the computer, and an adjustment by the entrepreneur would be entirely appropriate. The format of the bill allowed for the recording of information regarding adjustments in quantities delivered. Adjusted figures were entered into the computer for recalculation the following week.

John's Decision

In order to meet the interest payments on the loan for the leveraged buy-out, John had to maintain his cash flow and improve profitability. The new budgeting and reporting procedures he had implemented were a good beginning. John was grateful that the general manager, Gordon Crevier, had chosen to stay with the company. He was certainly going to need Gordon's advice and experience. With a view toward expanding the product line John had come up with several ideas, as follows: new magazines with more targeted audiences; special editions at the beginning of each season; a cable television show; and, in Montreal, a new interactive home shopping system entitled *Minitel*. Because the networks of free-lance photographers, salespeople, and distributors were already in place, very little effort would be involved in taking the extra photo or delivering a new magazine or product within the same geographic area. Operating leverage was the key.

John knew that to maximize this leverage he must ensure that his distribution network was efficient. Should Auto Mag eliminate the stores that sell only one or two magazines a week? Invariably the percentage of returns from these stores was the highest. John recognized that dropping certain stores would incur future difficulties if he ever wished to sell to them again. By eliminating certain stores, was he investing in the future or not? What about the other stores? How many magazines should Auto Mag be displaying? Displaying too many magazines resulted in high returns and wasted copies. Displaying too few magazines meant that Auto Mag lost sales.

John reviewed these issues and decided to reevaluate the effectiveness of computer forecasts. The more pressing problem remained to be solved—the impact of unsold copies on profit.

Exhibit 1

RETAIL SALES AND MARGINS PER AUTO MAG PUBLICATION

Magazine	Store Price (C$)†	Retail Margin (C$)†	Average Unit Sales High Season	Average Unit Sales Low Season	Frequency of Publication
Americaines	1.25	0.25	15,500	10,000	Weekly
Importees	1.25	0.25	13,000	8,500	Weekly
Camions	1.25	0.25	19,000	14,000	Weekly
Moto Bateau	0.95	0.19	15,000	10,000	Weekly
Achat Vente	1.25	0.25	5,300		Fortnightly
Old Car	3.50	0.70	6,000		Monthly
Equip Lourd	3.50	0.70	3,600		Monthly
Special	1.95	0.39	20,000		One Off

Source: Company data.

†In Canadian dollars.

Exhibit 2

TYPICAL QUOTED PRINTING RATES

			Flat Rate for First 8,000 Copies		Cost per additional 1,000 Copies
Edition	88 pages:		C$3,095.13†	+	C$172.79
Size	96 pages:		C$3,215.01	+	C$185.14
	104 pages:		C$3,466.98	+	C$198.06
	112 pages:		C$3,717.92	+	C$211.87
	120 pages:		C$3,979.49	+	C$225.67
	128 pages:		C$4,483.40	+	C$240.64
	136 pages:		C$4,471.03	+	C$254.44
	144 pages:		C$4,733.64	+	C$267.90

Source: Company data.

†In Canadian dollars.

Exhibit 3

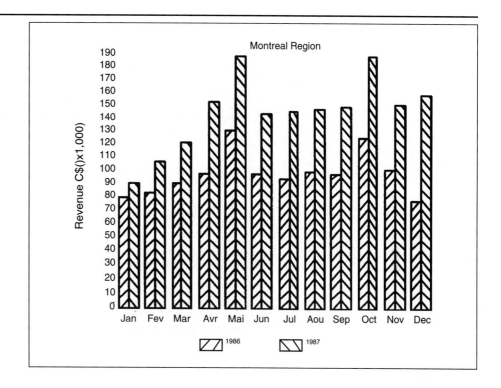

Exhibit 4

EXAMPLE OF A DISTRIBUTION/BILLING SALES SLIP

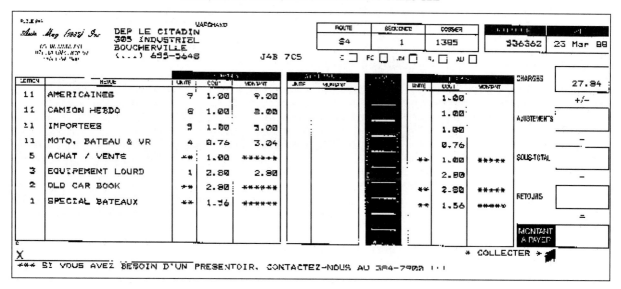

Exhibit 5

AUTO D'EXPOSITION CHEVROLET CORVETTE 1976, originale, 350 L 82, automatique, s.f., s.d., vitres électriques, am/fm stéréo, air climatisé, intérieur en cuir véritable, volant inclinable et télescopique, roues mags, plusieurs pièces chromées toutes les options disponibles en 1976 sont incluse, seulement 6,320 milles, millage original garantie, impeccable, voiture idéal pour collectionneur, il faut voir pour le croire, acheteur sérieux seulement S.V.P. au (514) 682-6500 jour ou le soir au 621-8719. RG6(3-4-5PDA)

MERCURY COUGAR 1979, bonne mécanique, vente cause décès, prix $1,000.00 ou meilleure offre au (514) 329-3076 après 18h00. LPG3(6A)

ACADIAN 1981, 4 vitesses, 93,000km, radio Blaupunkt, couleur noire, très propre, demande $1,500.00 au (514) 252-0843. UG4(15A)

TROIS-RIVIÈRES

FORD ESCORT GT 1986, 17,000km, noire, 5 vitesses, remisée l'hiver, garantie, prix $10,000.00 au (819) 375-0401. TRG2(25A)

GRAND PRIX 1979, baket seat, transmission au plancher, air climatisé, vitres électriques, door lock, tilt steering, freins neufs aux 4 roues, am/fm radio cassette et booster digital, prix $3,250.00 discutable au (514) 645-1122 après 15h30. BG7(3A)

FEMME PROPRIÉTAIRE

FIREBIRD 1980, 6 cylindres, automatique, p.s., p.b., spoiler, mags, pneus neufs, rouge vin, intérieur blanc peinture originale, très propre, prix $2,995.00, Hubert Fafard (514) 326-6637. UG1(10A)

FORD MUSTANG 1980, 6 cylindres, automatique, très bonne condition, garantie disponible, mécanique A1, prix $2,800.00, J.P. Auto au (514) 676-6484. GEG3(6A*)

CHEVROLET CAVALIER 1983, 76,000km, 4 portes, manuelle 5 vitesses, radio am/fm stéréo, bonne condition, prix $4,200.00 discutable au (514) 585-4333. EG3(12A)

THUNDERBIRD 1983, comme neuf, excellente condition, 1 seul propriétaire, vitres et miroirs électriques, bien chaussé, 62,000 km, prix $7,400.00 au (514) 445-6179 demandez Christian. GEG3(2A)

CHEVETTE 1981, 80,000km, 4 portes, automatique, moteur en bonne condition, conduit par une femme, prix $1,750.00 jour (514) 721-7560 ou 665-3257. UG1(7A)

PLYMOUTH RELIANT 1983, 72,000km, 4 cylindres, 2.2 litres, p.b., p.s., 4 portes, automatique, très propre, prix $2,900.00 ferme au (514) 668-7616. VG3(4A)

$5,650.00

MERCURY COUGAR LS 1983, vitres, portes électriques, bas millage, intérieur velours, broches, (195.00 par mois), Beaudry Autos Inc. au (514) 645-7042. EG8(9A*)

FORD MUSTANG 1981, 2 doors, 4 cylinders, 4 speed, 80,000km, price $1,800.00 at (514) 745-5821. DG6(4A)

ESCORT GT 1986, blanche, intérieur gris, 4 mags + 4 roues hiver, masque avant, radio MEI avec booster equalizer, toit ouvrant, vitres teintées, garantie transférable, prix $10,800.00 au (514) 655-3251 après 19h00, Dany. IG8(4-5-6PDA)

L.L. BEAN, INC.

Item Forecasting and Inventory Management

"When you order an item from an L.L. Bean catalog and we're out of stock, I'm the guy to blame. And if we end up liquidating a bunch of women's wool cashmere blazers, it's my fault. No one understands how tough it is." Mark Fasold, Vice President of Inventory Management, was describing the challenge of item forecasting at L.L. Bean. "Forecasting demand at the aggregate level is a piece of cake—if we're running short of expectations, we just dip deeper into our customer list and send out some more catalogs. But we have to decide how many chamois shirts and how many chino trousers to buy, and if we're too high on one and too low on the other, it's no solace to know that we were exactly right on the average. Top management understands this in principle, but they are understandably disturbed that errors at the item level are so large.

"In a catalog business like ours, you really capture demand. That's the good news. The bad news is, you learn what a lousy job you're doing trying to match demand with supply. It's not like that in a department store, say, where a customer may come in looking for a dress shirt and lets the display of available shirts generate the demand for a particular item. Or if a customer has some particular item in mind but it's not available, he or she may just walk out of the store. In a department store you never know the real demand or the consequences of understocking. But in our business every sale is generated by a customer demanding a particular item, either by mail or by phone. If we haven't got it, and the customer cancels the order, we know it."

Rol Fessenden, Manager of Inventory Systems, added, "We know that forecast errors are inevitable. Competition, the economy, and weather are all factors. But demand at the item level is also affected by customer behavior, which is very hard to predict, or even to explain in retrospect. Every so often some item takes off and becomes a runaway, far exceeding our demand forecasts. Once in a while we can detect the trend early on and, with a cooperative vendor, get more product manufactured in a hurry and chase demand; most of the time, however, the runaways leave us just turning customers away. And for every runaway, there's a dog item that sells way below expectations and that you couldn't even give away to customers."

Annual costs of lost sales and backorders were conservatively estimated to be $11 million; costs associated with having too much of the wrong inventory were an additional $10 million.

L.L. Bean Background

In 1912 Leon Leonwood Bean invented the Maine Hunting Shoe (a combination of lightweight leather uppers and rubber bottoms). He obtained a list of non-resident Maine hunting license holders, prepared a descriptive mail-order circular, set up shop in his brother's basement in Freeport, Maine, and started a nationwide mail-order business. The inauguration of the U.S. Post Office's domestic parcel post service in that year provided a means of delivering orders to customers. When L.L. Bean died in 1967, at the age of 94, sales had reached $4.75 million, his company employed 200 people, and an annual catalog was distributed to a mailing list of 600,000 people.

Harvard Business School case 9-893-003, revised September 7, 1993. This case was written by Professor Arthur Schleifer, Jr. Copyright © 1992 by the President and Fellows of Harvard College.

L.L.'s Golden Rule had been, "Sell good merchandise at a reasonable profit, treat your customers like human beings, and they'll always come back for more." When Leon Gorman, L.L.'s grandson, succeeded him as president in 1967, he sought to expand and modernize the business without deviating from his grandfather's Golden Rule. By 1991, L.L. Bean, Inc. was a major cataloger, manufacturer, and retailer in the outdoor sporting specialty field: catalog sales in 1990 were $528 million, with an additional $71 million in sales from the company's 50,000-square-foot retail store in Freeport. Twenty-two different catalogs (often referred to as "books" by company employees)—114 million pieces in all—were mailed that year. There were 6 million active customers.

The mail-order business had been giving way to telephone orders after the company installed nationwide "800" service in 1986. By 1991, 80% of all orders came in by telephone.

Major direct-mail competitors included Land's End, Eddie Bauer, Talbot's, and Orvis. A 1991 *Consumer Reports* survey on customer satisfaction with "mail-order" companies found L.L. Bean heading the list for overall satisfaction in every category for which they offered merchandise.

In explaining why L.L. Bean had not expanded its retail operations beyond the one store in Freeport, Leon Gorman contrasted the direct-marketing (catalog) and retail businesses. "The two approaches require very different kinds of management. Mail-order marketers are very analytic, quantitatively oriented. Retailers have to be creative, promotional, pizzazzy, merchandise-oriented. It's tough to assemble one management team that can handle both functions."[4]

Product Lines

L.L. Bean's product line was classified hierarchically (see Exhibit 1). At the highest level of aggregation were Merchandise Groups: men's and women's accessories, men's and women's apparel, men's and women's footwear, camping equipment, etc. Within each Group were Demand Centers; for instance, the Demand Centers for women's apparel were knit shirts, sweaters, pants, skirts, jackets and pullovers, etc. Each Demand Center was further broken down into Item Sequences; for example, women's sweaters consisted of Midnight Mesa handknit cardigans, Indian Point pullovers, lambswool turtlenecks, and about twenty other products. Item Sequences were further broken down into individual items, distinguished primarily by color; it was at this item level that forecasts had to be issued and, ultimately, purchase commitments had to be made.[5] About 6,000 items appeared in one or another of the catalogs issued in the course of a year.

Items were also classified into three seasonal categories (spring, fall, and all year) and into two additional categories ("new" or "never out") that described whether the item was a recent or more permanent member of the company's offerings, and consequently characterized the amount of historical demand data available for the item.

---

[4]*L.L. Bean, Inc.: Corporate Strategy*, Harvard Business School Case (581-159), 1981.

[5]Items were further broken down by size into stock-keeping units, or SKUs. This was done by applying standard size-distribution breakdowns. Although an inappropriate distribution could lead to excessive inventory of some sizes and stockouts of others, management concern was directed to the item level, since there was no evidence of a better system than assuming that the distribution of demand by size would behave in the future as it had in the past, and would be indistinguishable from one item to another.

The Bean Catalogs

The major catalogs—spring, summer, fall, and Christmas—each came out in several versions. A "full" catalog, running from 116 to 152 pages, went to Bean's regular customers. A smaller "prospect" catalog was circulated to potential customers; it contained primarily a subset of items from the full catalog. (Bean identified such prospect customers in a variety of ways—for example, through the purchase of mailing lists or by recording recipients of gifts from other Bean customers.) In addition, a number of specialty catalogs—Spring Weekend, Summer Camp, Fly Fishing, etc.—presented items that were unique to that catalog, as well as some items found in the major catalogs.

There was some overlap in circulation: the best customers received almost all the catalogs, and those customers known, through past purchasing behavior, to be interested in various specialties might receive an appropriate specialty catalog in addition to the seasonal full catalogs.

Item Forecasting

Each catalog had a gestation period of about nine months, and its creation involved merchandising, design, product, and inventory specialists. For example, the initial conceptualization for the Fall 1991 season began in October, 1990. Preliminary forecasts of total sales for each catalog were made in December. Product managers developed preliminary item forecasts by book in the December, 1990 to March, 1991 time frame. Layout and pagination of the books began in January, 1991. Initial commitments to vendors were made in January and February. In the subsequent months, as the catalogs took shape, item forecasts were repeatedly revised and finally "frozen" by May 1. By early July a black-and-white version of the layout was available internally. At this point, the product managers handed off their product line to the inventory managers.

The completed Fall 1991 catalogs were in the hands of customers around August 1. As the catalog generated demand, inventory managers decided on additional commitments to vendors, scheduled replenishments, handled back-orders, etc. This catalog remained active through January, 1992; inventory left over at that time might be liquidated, marked down and sold through special L.L. Bean promotions, or carried over to the next year.

Scott Sklar was a buyer for men's shirts. He described the forecasting process as follows: "Four or five of us—my inventory buyer, some product people, and I—meet to forecast shirt sales by book. We start by ranking various items in terms of expected dollar sales. Then we actually assign dollars in accordance with the ranking. There's discussion, arguments, complaints. People invent rules of thumb. I say 'invent,' because there aren't any good rules of thumb.

"We set this up on an Excel spreadsheet. We look at the book forecast and make adjustments accordingly. We look at the total of forecasted shirt sales and check it for reality. Does it feel good? Does it make sense? We do it book by book, item by item, and that's how we get an item level forecast.

"Of course, when we add a new item, we have to make a judgment: will this item generate incremental demand, and if not, from what items is it going to steal demand? And then those items need to be adjusted accordingly."

Barbara Hamaluk, a buyer for men's knit shirts, observed that the sum of the item forecasts for a catalog was often at variance with the dollar target for that book. "Usually this roll-up comes in on the high side, so you try to reduce forecasts on certain items. Or you can just say, if we're too high by 10%, we'll

just slash everything across the board by 10%. We really ought to have an inter-
mediate level of forecasts at the Demand Center level, reconcile item forecasts
with Demand Center forecasts, and the latter with the book forecast."

Production Commitments

The typical production lead time for most domestic orders was eight to twelve
weeks. (Of course, deliveries against a commitment could be scheduled to conform to the anticipated pattern of in-season demand.) With some vendors who
cooperated with L.L. Bean's "Quick Response" initiative, it was possible, after
observing some early-season demand, to place a *second* order, which would be
delivered in sufficient time to meet late-season demand. However, with many
domestic and most offshore vendors, lead times were sufficiently long so that
it was impractical to place a second commitment order in the course of the season. (In the remainder of this case, then, discussion will be limited to these
"one-shot" commitments.)

The commitments were generally *not* equal in size to the forecasts, but were
determined in two steps as follows: First, historical forecast errors (expressed as
"A/F ratios"—the ratio of actual demand to forecast demand) were computed
for each item in the previous year, and the frequency distribution of these errors
was compiled across items.[6] The frequency distribution of *past* forecast errors
was then used as a probability distribution for the as yet unrealized *future* forecast errors. For example, if 50% of the forecast errors for "new" items in the past
year had been between 0.7 and 1.6, then it would be assumed that with probability 0.5, the forecast error for any "new" item in the current year also would
fall between 0.7 and 1.6. So in such a case, if the frozen forecast for a particular
item were 1,000 units, it was then assumed that with probability 0.5, actual
demand for that item would end up being between 700 and 1,600 units.

Next, each item's commitment quantity was determined by balancing the
individual item's contribution margin if demanded against its liquidation cost
(or value) if not demanded. Suppose, for example, that an item cost Bean $15,
would regularly sell for $30, and could be sold at liquidation for $10. The gain
for selling a marginal unit would be $30–15 = $15; the loss for failing to sell the
marginal unit would be the cost less the liquidation value, i.e. $15–10 = $5.
Accordingly, the optimal order size should be the 0.75 fractile of the item's
probability distribution of *demand*. Suppose the 0.75 fractile of the distribution
of *forecast errors* was 1.3, and the frozen forecast for that item was for 1,000 units.
Then the 0.75 fractile of the demand distribution would be 1,000 × 1.3 = 1,300,
and Bean would make a commitment for 1,300 units.

Rol Fessenden expressed concern that the methodology treated the errors
associated with *all* "never out" items as equally representative of the forecast
errors that might be anticipated for the forecast demand of *any* "never out"
item (and similarly for "new" items). "You'd think that the error distribution
for some of our buyers might be tighter than for other buyers, or that the distribution for women's sweaters might have more dispersion than the distribution for men's footwear, but we can't find any real differences. Also, I'm not
entirely convinced that we go about estimating contribution margin and liquidation cost correctly."

---

[6]This was done separately for "new" items and for "never outs"; not surprisingly, the historical error distribution of "never outs" had less dispersion than that of "new" items. No other way of segmenting
items had revealed significantly different distributions of forecast errors.

Mark Fasold was worried about the wide dispersion in forecast errors, both for "never outs" and "new" items. He was also concerned about the implications of the methodology: "If the cost associated with understocking exceeds the cost of overstocking, which is the usual case here, we end up committing to *more* than the frozen forecast. And for 'new' items, about which we obviously know very little, the excess over the frozen forecast is even greater than for 'never outs.' The buyers are understandably upset when we commit to more than they forecast; they perceive us as going way out on a limb for 'new' items."

Exhibit 1

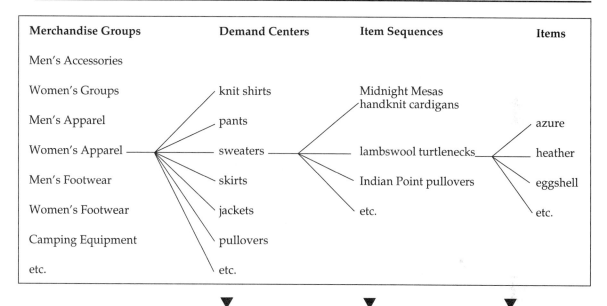

3 ▼ SIMULATION

Now you've learned about decision trees, and have also begun to think in terms of probabilities. The cases in Chapters 1 and 2 could each be analyzed on one or two pieces of paper, although there will be times when the problem is just too complex for that. If there are five uncertainties, each with four possible outcomes, and if you are considering three alternatives, that means a decision tree with $3 \times 4 \times 4 \times 4 \times 4 \times 4 = 3{,}072$ end points! Fortunately we can enlist the computer for this computation.

The technique we describe in this chapter can handle almost any number of end points—even millions. How? When the news media want to track the progress of a presidential candidate, they don't interview all 150 million registered voters; they interview a sample—maybe as few as 400 or so. That's the idea behind **simulation**.

USING SIMULATION

The methodology of decision trees provides an artful way to think through problems involving uncertainty. Without such a procedure, decision makers must approach situations involving uncertainty with a combination of intuition and experience. Consider Mr. Jaeger at Freemark Abbey Winery. How do you suppose he *really* would make the decision about harvesting grapes early in the face of an impending storm? This would not be the first time he had faced such a decision; it is reasonable to suppose he had developed a strategy, or decision rule, for handling such situations. The rule might have been simple ("always harvest") or complex ("never harvest unless the storm is expected to be very fierce or very likely"). The rule may have been refined over many years of experiences, both good and bad.

Learning by experience has two principal disadvantages as a route to effective decision making. First, it can be very slow. How many years must Mr. Jaeger wait until he has enough experience harvesting and not harvesting grapes before a storm? Second, people tend not to keep accurate records of their experiences, so that tapping history may be of little use.

Surprisingly, the experience needed for this approach to decision making doesn't have to evolve over the course of time; it can be artificially simulated, and such simulation can be used very effectively in many situations: it is the purpose of this chapter to show you how.

Harvard Business School Case N9-895-002, revised August 8, 1994. This note was written by Professor David E. Bell. Copyright © 1994 by the President and Fellows of Harvard College.

Freemark Abbey Revisited

Suppose your analysis of the Freemark Abbey case led you to believe that Mr. Jaeger should leave the Riesling grapes on the vine. Did you make the correct decision? Well, *on average* (given the numbers in the case), we can say that you did. But on this one occasion Mr. Jaeger might find that the storm ruined the crop. The case mentions two major uncertainties concerning the "don't harvest" strategy: whether the storm will arrive (yes, with probability 0.5), and whether it will produce botrytis (yes, with probability 0.4).

Let us pretend that this decision situation repeats exactly as described, year after year, but that the uncertainties resolve themselves according to their probabilities, i.e., half the time there is a storm, half the time there isn't, etc. How might Mr. Jaeger fare if he repeatedly selects the following strategy: don't harvest the grapes now but do harvest them if there is no storm?

In order to *simulate* a history, we must find a way to decide whether the storm hits the Napa Valley, and whether it brings botrytis if it does. The first event is easy to simulate. Simply toss a coin: heads the storm will come, tails it won't. But how do we simulate the 40% chance of the botrytis forming? One way would be to put ten playing cards (four red cards and six black cards) in a bag and pick one card at random (red meaning botrytis, black meaning no botrytis).

Our simulated history might look like the data shown in Table 3.1.

Table 3.1

	Result of Coin Toss	Color of Playing Card	Cash Flow from Riesling Grapes	Scenario
Year 1	Heads	Black	25,680	Storm, no botrytis
Year 2	Heads	Red	67,200	Storm, botrytis
Year 3	Tails	—	34,200	No storm
Year 4	Tails	—	34,200	No storm
Year 5	Heads	Red	67,200	Storm, botrytis
Year 6	Tails	—	34,200	No storm
		Total	262,680	
		Average	43,780	

The average cash flow resulting from a strategy of leaving the grapes was $43,780 over these six years. This does not match the expected monetary value calculated in the decision tree ($38,244 = 0.2 \times 67,200 + 0.3 \times 25,680 + 0.5 \times 34,200$) because the botrytis did not arrive exactly 40% of the time in the simulated history. However, had we performed a simulation of 1,000 "years," it is very likely that about 50% of the time the storm would arrive and on about 40% of those occasions, botrytis would form. If we simulated 100,000 years we could pretty much guarantee that the average cash flow from the simulation would match the expected value calculated from the decision tree. By repeating the simulation for each possible decision strategy, the decision with the best expected value can be identified.

Of course, there isn't much point going to all this trouble to analyze a problem as straightforward as that faced by Mr. Jaeger. The decision tree procedure is a much more effective solution than simulation in this case. We have merely used Mr. Jaeger's problem as an example. Simulation is an effective tool for more complex problems, where laying out a decision tree would be an overwhelming task.

Components of a Simulation

Although simulations can be very complicated, the ones we will consider will have four major components.

1. A list of strategies to be evaluated
2. A list of uncertainties and associated probabilities that impact the evaluation of the strategies
3. A system of generating scenarios
4. An evaluation system for each strategy/scenario pair

A **strategy** is a decision, or sequence of contingent decisions, that lays out in advance what the decision maker will do in all possible circumstances. In solving a problem by a decision tree, the best strategy emerges as a result of the backward induction process (folding back the tree). In simulation, however, all possible strategies must be specified in advance. For example, for an investor simulating the stockmarket, a strategy might be expressed quite simply as "keep 75% in stocks, 25% in bonds." Or the formula might be more complicated, where the percentage to be invested in stocks depends not only on recent stockmarket trends, but also on the investor's net wealth at the time.

A **list of uncertainties** should be sufficient to describe every possible outcome that might result from pursuing any one of the strategies. Associated with each such uncertainty there would be a probability, or a set of probabilities, that might well be contingent upon other uncertainties. If we wish to simulate an inventory planning problem, we might need to specify probabilities for each possible level of demand for each item under consideration, the probability that a customer who finds an item out of stock will return at a later time, and probabilities for the number of days it will take for a replenishment order to arrive.

A **scenario** is a single resolution of the list of uncertainties; it describes one possible version of the future. In a simulation we may want to generate 100 or perhaps 1,000, or 100,000 scenarios as a kind of pseudo-history. So long as the scenarios are generated randomly in accordance with the probabilities provided for the component uncertainties, we will be able to draw appropriate inferences about the likely quality of candidate strategies.

A **trial** is the simulation of one scenario to evaluate one strategy.

An **evaluation system** describes the statistics that are of interest from the simulation. Given a list of 1,000 scenarios, and given a particular strategy, what is it you would like to know about how well that strategy performed? In many business problems you may want to know the expected value, which is estimated by the average value generated by the strategy. But you may also like to see the lowest value achieved over the 1,000 trials.

You may also want to see a **risk profile** of all 1,000 scenarios. Typically this is represented as a graph with an appropriate measure of value on the horizontal axis (profit, for example) and percentages on the vertical axis. If the point ($500, 23%) were on the graph, it would mean that 23% of the simulated scenarios had a value less than or equal to $500.

We should point out that our terminology is not standardized. Some people use the term *strategy* to mean only the general aim of an approach ("my strategy is to steer clear of projects with high risk") rather than an implementable specification. Some use the term *scenario* to mean the consequence of a strategy and the resolution of all associated uncertainties. Some use *trial* in place of our term *scenario*. We will try to use our own terms precisely, however, because we feel this will provide for clearer explanations.

Let's illustrate the process of simulation with a worked example.

Example

Arthur has a small cake concession in a local supermarket. His cake supplier has agreed to deliver a fixed number of cakes every day for a week at $10 each. At the end of the week, Arthur may change his order for the following week. Arthur has kept close track of daily cake demand. It averages 3.3 cakes per day but varies from day to day as shown in Table 3.2.

Table 3.2

Probability that demand	=	1	0.10
	=	2	0.20
	=	3	0.25
	=	4	0.25
	=	5	0.15
	=	6	0.05

Arthur does not believe that being out of stock on a given day influences demand on future days; in particular, he believes that the demand distribution described above will hold on every day.

Arthur's initial inventory of cakes is zero. He always keeps any unsold cakes and tries selling them, at the full price of $18, on the second or subsequent days. Since Arthur is going on vacation in two weeks' time, any cakes left at that time will have to be donated to charity. How many cakes per day should Arthur order for this week?

Solution

Note that if Arthur orders five cakes per day this week, his order next week can be contingent on the number of cakes left over from this week. So, although the question doesn't make reference to what happens next week, we will need to consider that aspect as part of our analysis.

Our knowledge of critical-fractile analysis allows us to solve a closely related problem very easily. If the cakes needed to be sold fresh (that is, on the day Arthur received them), then each day would be an independent problem. The loss of having a cake when it is not demanded is $10; the gain of having one that is demanded is $8; and the critical ratio would be calculated as $8/(8+10) = 44\%$, from which we conclude that 3 cakes per day is the appropriate order.

However, since leftover cakes are not wasted, we can afford to be a little more aggressive. Would ordering 4 cakes per day make sense? 5? If we order 5 per day, we can expect lots of leftovers; but according to Arthur's policy, these may be sold the following week.

In the second week we should probably be a little more cautious, ordering either 3 or 4 cakes per day, assuming that any inventory at the end of day 7 is worthless. The best *strategy* for our order for the second week would be something like "order 4 per day if there are zero left over from the preceding week, 3 per day if there are between 1 and 7 leftovers, 2 per day if there are between 8 and 14 leftovers," and so on. Indeed a strategy in this problem must be of the form "order so many per day the first week and then a certain number per day in the second week, depending on the number left over from the first week."

The *list of uncertainties* is simply the probability distribution of demand for each of the 14 relevant days. Note how much more complex the structure of this problem would be if the demand varied from day to day—and particularly if it varied according to the sales of fresh and stale cakes!

A *scenario* would be a sequence of 14 daily demands.

The *evaluation* system is quite simple. Each cake ordered costs $10, each one sold generates $18. We shall ignore reputation effects, and the time value of money, although they could quite easily be incorporated in the analysis.

Performing the Simulation

Normally we will do the analysis on a spreadsheet, but first let us recognize how we might carry out the simulation more dramatically. Suppose we have 20 students available, six of whom have a strategy they would like to test out for Arthur (call these students A, B, C, D, E, F, and G). The remaining 14 students will each role-play one of the uncertainties in the problem (call these students 1, 2, ..., 14). Each of the 14 students needs a container with 20 pieces of paper, two of which are marked "Demand = 1," four marked "Demand = 2," etc..

Here's how the first trial will proceed. Student 1 draws out a piece of paper to reveal the demand for day 1. Students A to G note how many cakes they would sell and how much inventory is carried over to day 2. Student 1 replaces the piece of paper in the container. Now student 2 draws a piece of paper revealing the demand for day 2, and so it goes. After student 14 has played her role in the proceedings, each of students A to G can calculate how much money they would have made for Arthur using their strategy on the scenario played out by students 1 to 14.

It is easy to construct a spreadsheet to make life a little easier. See Exhibit 1. The *strategy* evaluated in the table is shown at the top left of the exhibit. In this trial, the week 1 daily order was set at 3. The week 2 daily order was chosen to be 4 if the ending inventory from week 1 equaled 0 or 1, 3 if inventory was 2 to 7, 2 if inventory equaled 8 or 9, and 1 if more than 9. The *scenario* is shown in the columns headed Day and Demand. The demand for day 1 was 5 cakes, for day 2 it was 2 cakes, and so on.

The *evaluation* is shown in the last two columns. In order to determine the revenue generated by Arthur during the two weeks we need to calculate how many cakes he would have sold under this scenario. On day 1 he would only have 3 cakes on hand, and since demand is 5, he would evidently sell 3 and leave 2 potential customers unsatisfied. The next day, day 2, he will again have 3 cakes but will only sell 2. On day 3 he will begin with 4 cakes: 3 fresh cakes plus 1 left over from the day before.

At the end of day 7 we see that in this scenario, Arthur would have zero cakes left. According to our *predetermined* strategy, this means he should submit an order of 4 cakes per day for the coming week.

We may now calculate his profit for the two weeks. First, let's calculate his costs. During the first week he bought 21 cakes at $10 each. In the second week he bought 28 cakes at $10 each. We can see that he sold 39 cakes (note that he has 10 left over) for a total revenue of 39 × $18 = $702. Less expenses of $490, this leaves a profit of $212—as shown in Exhibit 1.

This completes one trial of this strategy. Nine more trials were run with this strategy (the results are not shown here). The *average* profit over the ten trials was $287, with a range from $212 to $392.

Exhibit 2 shows a similar calculation with the week 1 order set at 4; the net profit for this trial was $248. The ten-trial average profit in this case was $352, substantially higher.

Can we conclude that it is better for Arthur to order 4 cakes per day than 3 cakes per day in the first week? The answer is no, for two reasons:

1. There is no reason to suppose that we have correctly chosen the week 2 strategy.

2. The average profit figures might change if we calculated more than ten trials, or selected (even randomly) a different set of ten trials.

In Exhibit 3 we show the results of 3,330 different trials of a simulation for this problem. We considered three strategies (order 3 per day in week 1, order 4 per day in week 1, and order 5 per day in week 1), each with the same week 2 strategy described above.

No one would ever report simulation results this way; we are doing it here only so that we may explain how results may vary depending on how many trials are conducted. In the first three columns of Exhibit 3 we see the results of performing ten trials for each of the three strategies. In the fourth through sixth columns we see the results we would have obtained had we performed ten sets of ten trials for each strategy. Thus in the fourth column $260 is the profit average of ten trials, $289 (at the foot of the column) is the average of 100 trials. Finally, the last three columns contain averages of 100 trials. The row at the foot of these columns shows the average of 1,000 trials.

Based on Exhibit 3 can we determine which of the three strategies under consideration is to be preferred? If we performed just *one* trial for each of the three strategies, say the first three numbers in row 1, we would have a profit of $212 for 3 cakes, $392 for 4 and $336 for 5, from which it would appear that 4 cakes is the preferred order. Even the average over the first ten trials still leaves ordering 4 cakes as the preferred alternative ($287 profit for 3, $352 for 4, $347 for 5). Yet, glancing over at the figures at the foot of the last three columns we see that, over 1,000 trials, the scores are $293 for 3, $320 for 4 and $334 for 5. Having been misled once, can we be satisfied with this result? Should we now do a set of 10,000 trials? 100,000 trials? When do we stop?

Determining the Correct Number of Trials

It is always more reliable to base a conclusion on more trials. This much we know. But when should we be satisfied that we have enough information?

The answer to this question is contained in the one set of figures in Exhibit 3 that we have yet to discuss. The final row in Exhibit 3 is the standard deviation of the ten sets of trials in the column above. So the ten single trials we conducted for the 3-cake strategy had a mean of $287 and a standard deviation of $48.

If the outcomes were normally distributed, this means that we might expect that about 2/3 of the time a trial will produce a result in the range ($287 − $48, $287 + $48), that is, $239 to $335. Indeed, if you look down the column, seven of the trials were in this range. (No, these numbers were not "chosen." They are the actual results from a spreadsheet [included in your Data Diskette].) We would also expect 95% of the trials to fall within two standard deviations of the mean, i.e., in the range $191 to $383. Indeed, nine of the results are in this range.

What this confirms is that taking one trial for each strategy is not sufficiently reliable for decision-making purposes. The result of any one trial could easily be as much as $100 away from the true long-run average (expected value) of that strategy.

But perhaps we can rely on the *average* of ten trials? To see if this is true, look at columns 4, 5, 6 of Exhibit 3. How wildly do *they* fluctuate? A quick glance down column 4 shows that the range of outcomes is $260 – $334, or $74. The standard deviation of these averages is $23, still not terribly reassuring.

Now let's go to the last three columns. Note that not only does "Order 5" have the highest mean profit ($334) but the results are all very much the same. The range is $325 – $339, or $14. The standard deviation is $4. I am very confident that even if I ran 100,000 trials, the average would come out somewhere close to $334. The "Order 4" strategy is similar. Although its grand average, $320, is quite close to $334, it would be quite surprising if, after running a million trials, we discovered that the true mean of "Order 4" was actually, say, $330 and the mean of "Order 5" was $326. To see this, look at the eighth column (the column showing 100 trials of "Order 4"). How surprised would you be if the next set of 100 trials turned out to have an average of $330? Well, it would be unlikely, given that the highest payoff to date was $328, but it wouldn't be astonishing. But how surprised would you be if the next 10,000 trials had an average of $330? The answer: very. On top of that, in order for the "Order 5" strategy to be worse than "Order 4," we would *also* have to be surprised by the next 10,000 trials of the "Order 5" strategy. It simply is too unlikely to worry about.

The Mathematics of Averages

Roughly speaking, the uncertainty surrounding the accuracy of an average taken over n trials falls in proportion to the square root of n.

So, if one trial has a standard deviation of 48, we would expect the standard deviation of an average of 10 trials to be $48/\sqrt{10}$, or about 15, and the standard deviation of 100 trials to be $48/\sqrt{100}$, or about 5. The actual standard deviations we obtained for the "Order 3" strategy were 48 for single trials, 23 for averages of 10 trials and 5 for averages of 100 trials. These results don't match the mathematical prediction accurately because (a) the 48 figure is itself only an *estimate* of the true standard deviation and (b) the 23 and 5 figures are *also* estimates. However, you can see that the general property holds quite well.

Another way to think about this property is that in order to *halve* the uncertainty, you have to perform four times as many trials.

It is not easy to determine *in advance* how many trials will be enough. Usually what happens is that one performs 100 trials (say) for each candidate strategy and then examines the results. If the results are convincing, you stop. If they're not, you continue. After 10 trials, however, we could make a very crude estimate of the number of trials that might be necessary. We see that the Order 4 and Order 5 results are very close after 10 trials (averages of $352 and $347 respectively). We ask ourselves: if these really are the true means, how many trials will we need to carry out in order to be convinced that Order 4 is really better than Order 5 and that these results aren't due to chance? We calculate that our uncertainty about $352 after 10 trials is $33/\sqrt{10} = 10.4$, and that of $347 is $23/\sqrt{10} = 7.3$.

Suppose we performed enough trials so that these results were $352 ± 1 and $347 ± 1. Would that be convincing evidence? (It certainly would convince me!) In order to achieve this level of accuracy, we would need to have $33/\sqrt{n} = 1$ which implies that $\sqrt{n} = 33$ or $n = 1,089$.

It may happen that the means have changed after 1,089 trials, and more trials may become necessary. To be realistic, of course, at some point the accuracy is not worth the effort. There is no point trying to distinguish further between a strategy with a payoff of $282.46 and one with a payoff of $282.62.

Blocking

It is almost always preferable to compare strategies against the same list of scenarios. Instead of generating 300 scenarios to perform 100 trials of three strategies, simply generate 100 scenarios and use each to evaluate all three strategies. We did this in Exhibits 1 and 2. We also did this in describing how 20 students might "act out" the simulation.

This procedure is called **blocking**. A very simple example shows how powerful blocking can be. Suppose that some strategy, "A," leads to a wide variety of potential payoffs, depending on the precise scenario generated. Suppose that strategy "B" leads to exactly the same payoff as "A" *plus one dollar*. That is, B always does better than A by exactly one dollar. Now if we think to take note of the *difference* in value of these two strategies, on a scenario-by-scenario basis, it will become apparent very quickly that B does better. This fact might take several thousand trials to make clear if the scenarios are generated independently.

Blocking should be used (if possible) whenever the performance of two strategies is likely to be positively correlated across scenarios.

Epilogue

The worked example about the cakes has served to illustrate both the good and bad aspects of simulation. Simulation is poor at handling situations where there are many, many strategies to be considered because each must be evaluated in turn. (Decision trees or dynamic programming are better tools in these cases.) But simulation is excellent for handling cases where there are many uncertainties. The power of statistical sampling is enormous; with some experience in interpreting results, it can be used with great effect.

Exhibit 1 _____

ARTHUR'S CAKES

STRATEGY		UNCERTAINTIES	
Week 1 Order =	3	Probability Distribution for Demand	
Week 2 Strategy =			
If Ending Inventory is	New Daily Order is		
0	4	1	0.1
1	4	2	0.2
2	3	3	0.25
3	3	4	0.25
4	3	5	0.15
5	3	6	0.05
6	3		
7	3		
8	2		
9	2		
10	1		

SCENARIO		EVALUATION	
Day	Demand	Supply	Sales
1	5	3	3
2	2	3	2
3	3	4	3
4	3	4	3
5	1	4	1
6	6	6	6
7	4	3	3
8	2	4	2
9	5	6	5
10	2	5	2
11	4	7	4
12	1	7	1
13	3	10	3
14	1	11	1

Net Profit = $212

Exhibit 2

ARTHUR'S CAKES

STRATEGY			UNCERTAINTIES	
Week 1 Order =		4	Probability Distribution for Demand	
Week 2 Strategy =				
If Ending Inventory is	New Daily Order is			
0	4		1	0.1
1	4		2	0.2
2	3		3	0.25
3	3		4	0.25
4	3		5	0.15
5	3		6	0.05
6	3			
7	3			
8	2			
9	2			
10	1			

SCENARIO		EVALUATION	
Day	Demand	Supply	Sales
1	5	4	4
2	2	4	2
3	3	6	3
4	3	7	3
5	1	8	1
6	6	11	6
7	4	9	4
8	2	8	2
9	5	9	5
10	2	7	2
11	4	8	4
12	1	7	1
13	3	9	3
14	1	9	1

Net Profit = $248

Exhibit 3

ARTHUR'S CAKES

Simulation Summary

	Each Number Represents the Result of 1 Trial			Each Number Represents the Average of 10 Trials			Each Number Represents the Average of 100 Trials		
Week 1 Daily Order =	**3**	**4**	**5**	**3**	**4**	**5**	**3**	**4**	**5**
1	212	392	336	260	323	339	292	321	339
2	302	302	392	271	328	335	284	315	333
3	284	338	336	307	331	357	291	328	333
4	266	338	336	285	351	342	296	319	325
5	248	374	336	281	328	353	293	321	334
6	338	338	336	317	293	314	299	318	337
7	248	392	336	267	311	355	301	321	336
8	284	392	336	334	322	340	295	315	336
9	392	300	394	276	316	347	297	321	333
10	300	356	336	295	354	309	285	319	332
Average	287	352	347	289	326	339	293	320	334
S.D	48	33	23	23	17	15	5	4	4

CASE

HANNAFORD BROTHERS WAREHOUSE INVENTORY

"It's nine a.m., cocktail hour!" It was June 30, 1986 and David Graham had already been at his desk for more than three hours when the computer went off-line for a regularly scheduled half hour of downtime in order that it might transmit items ordered so far to the warehouse and print out hard copies. David, along with his fellow buyers, used the time for coffee and breakfast.

The Hannaford Brothers warehouse, located in South Portland, Maine, acted as a wholesale distributor to more than 100 supermarkets in northern New England. About a third of these were independent stores and the remainder were wholly owned by Hannaford Brothers. As often as six days a week a supermarket would place an order for many hundreds of items needed to replenish its shelves. If the order was in by noon, a truck could be loaded that afternoon and the goods could be on the shelves by the next morning. Billing procedures were identical for each store.

Part of David's job was responsibility for keeping certain categories of products in the warehouse stocked at a sufficient level to ensure at least a 95% success rate in meeting supermarket orders. If a supermarket did not receive a certain item with an order, it was sure to reorder it the next day; thus a stockout that lasted seven days would count as seven unfulfilled orders, not one. Even stockouts due entirely to the manufacturer (caused, say, by production problems) were counted against the 95% goal.

Harvard Business School Case 9-187-041. This case was written by Professor David E. Bell. Copyright © 1986 by the President and Fellows of Harvard College.

Every weekday morning David examined the current stock level for each of about 1,500 items under his care and made a recommendation about reordering. In the afternoon he met with sales representatives from manufacturers who would try to convince him to carry new items or offer special discounts on existing items for a limited time to encourage sales, often with a requirement that the product be advertised or discounted at retail.

"Exhibit 1 shows a fairly simple example of the kind of printout I look at. You can see that we stock a product, Amcol Beef Strips, that is delivered to us by Amcol Pet Products. Over a year our average weekly sales to all supermarkets is 65.8 cases. This is not a seasonal item, so we can expect similar sales to all supermarkets right now. The exact numbers of cases we have shipped out in the last four weeks are 62, 58, 55 and 53. We have 162 cases on hand, enough probably to last us about 2 1/2 weeks. The lead-time is 14 days, which means I can expect delivery from the vendor within 14 days of the day I make an order.

"I can see that the actual delivery time for the last 13 orders has been 9, 10, 13, 8, 8, 5, 15, 12, 9, 16, 10, 11 and 7 days, so they usually come in well under 14 days. The computer uses 14 days when it calculates whether we need to make an order, so, as you can see, a safety factor is already built in. The computer recommends that I do not make an order and that makes sense. Remember, if I don't order today I can always order tomorrow. In fact, in this case, I'll probably wait another few days.

"Fortunately, the computer knows enough about the basics of this job that I really only have to check its recommendations to make sure that they are consistent with all current information. If I was ill for a day or two my secretary could do a pretty good job simply by typing "A" to accept each of the computer's suggestions. After about a week, though, I think you'd find the situation was deteriorating pretty rapidly. There are just too many considerations for the computer to keep track of. I do it mainly by instinct; if I stopped and thought about what I was doing, I'd never get done. On a typical day I probably make up about 30 to 40 orders, so I can't dawdle!

"Exhibit 2 shows the computer recommendation for ten products delivered by Herb Ox Sales. The computer has indicated it would like to have deliveries of three items, in each case recommending the minimum order size permitted by the vendor. Unfortunately, the vendor also has a constraint on the minimum and maximum total size of an order. Some vendors go by volume, others by weight, still others by constraints on both. They have to make sure the trip will be worthwhile and that there isn't more than a truckload. Herb Ox Sales goes by weight and requires that the total be at least 1,100 pounds. The rightmost column of the printout shows the weight of one case of each item. The suggested order only weighs $20 \times 13 + 30 \times 4 + 17 \times 2$, or 414 pounds. If I were really anxious to avoid a stockout on these items, I could build the order up to 1,100 pounds, but I'd prefer to wait. Soup seasonings are not a fast-selling item in the summer, and once again the vendor delivery times (6, 7, 8, 5, 8, 5, 6, 7, 8, 11, 9, 4, 8) average less than the 10 days the computer's using. I can't see shoppers being incensed if one or two items in this line are stocked out. Mind you, my customers are the supermarkets, not the individual shoppers; the store manager will call me whether it's a bouillon cube or a popular breakfast cereal.

"Finally, Exhibit 3 shows the nine brands of iced tea mix supplied by Nestle. The computer has recommended a purchase order, costing $37,942.40 and weighing 4,104 pounds—just above the minimum. We probably don't need all of these items; we have 241 cases of the Tropical Ice Teasers and sell only 94 a week, but iced tea is a fast mover this time of year and I don't want to take a chance on being short. You have to be a weather forecaster in this job—from what I've heard, this next week will be a warm one and that means lots of iced tea and few bouillon cubes.

"One more complication I have to keep track of are the discounts. Nestle has been giving me $4.80 a case off the diet mix (Item 1) for most of this year (March–September) so it's not a factor in my decisions today. But if I knew a discount was to begin July 14, say, I might try to hold off until then. Similarly, if a discount is to end soon I might want to place an unusually large order. Of course I have to figure out whether the discount is worth the added holding costs (20%); fortunately, a few keys on my console will tell me the Net Present Value and Internal Rate of Return of any forward purchase I'm considering.

Exhibit 1 _____

6/30/86

VENDOR: AMCOL PET PRODUCTS

LEAD-TIME: **14** DAYS LAST **13** DELIVERIES: **9, 10, 13, 8, 8, 5, 15, 12, 9, 16, 10, 11**

TRUCK LIMITS: MIN = **75** CASES MAX = **5,500** CASES

Item #	Tier Size	Pallet Cases	Item Pack	Item Size	Item Description	Available Currently	Order Quantity	Order Min	Weekly Demand	Seasonal Demand
1	10	40	12	502	Amcol Beef Chew Strips	162	0	40	65.8	65.8

Last Four Actual					Allowance			
1	2	3	4		Start	End	Amount	Weight Factor
62	58	55	53		—	—	—	1

Items Ordered: 0   Order Total: $0.00

Exhibit 2

6/30/86

VENDOR: HERB OX SALES

LEAD-TIME: 10 DAYS LAST 13 DELIVERIES: 6, 7, 8, 5, 8, 5, 6, 7, 8, 11, 9, 4, 8

TRUCK LIMITS: MIN = 1,100 LBS., MAX = 3,600 LBS.

Item #	Tier Size	Pallet Cases	Item Pack	Item Size	Item Description	Available currently	Order Quantity	Order Min	Weekly Demand	Seasonal Demand	Last Four Actual 1	2	3	4	Start	End	Allowance Amount	Weight Factor
1	10	30	24	8 env	Herbox Inst Bf Broth	38	0	20	20.0	13.6	17	17	13	13	8/30	9/26	2.52	4
2	10	30	24	4 oz	Herbox Bf Ins Bou Jars	35	0	20	17.3	11.8	9	11	18	9	8/30	9/26	4.5	13
3	10	80	24	4 oz	Herbox Ch Ins Bou Jar	19	20	20	19.5	13.3	12	16	15	12	8/30	9/26	0	13
4	15	150	24	8 env	Herbox Inst Ch Broth	39	30	30	38.5	26.2	31	32	26	18	8/30	9/26	2.52	4
5	15	180	24	1.55 oz	Herbox Beef Bul Cubes	38	0	15	22.3	15.2	16	22	17	12	8/30	9/26	2.46	3.5
6	15	180	24	1.6 oz	Herbox Chick Bul Cubes	42	0	15	24.9	16.9	17	20	17	14	8/30	9/26	2.46	3.5
7	25	300	12	3.25 oz	Herbox Beef Bul Cubes	89	0	50	58.4	39.7	45	36	43	41	8/30	9/26	2.28	2
8	17	51	12	8 s	Herbox Ls Bf Broth	25	0	17	20.3	13.8	7	8	15	18	8/30	9/26	2.04	2
9	17	85	12	8 ct	Herbox Ls Ch Broth	20	17	17	20.2	13.7	13	11	20	17	8/30	9/26	2.04	2
10	22	264	12	3.33 oz	Herbox Chick Bul Cubes	85	0	44	63.9	43.5	52	36	44	45	8/30	9/26	2.28	3.5

Items Ordered: 3   Order Total: $0.00

Exhibit 3

6/30/86

VENDOR: NESTLE COMPANY

LEAD-TIME: 10 DAYS LAST 13 DELIVERIES: 6, 8, 7, 7, 8, 12, 4, 8, 5, 7, 9, 10, 9
TRUCK LIMITS: MIN = 4,000 LBS., MAX = 34,000 LBS. ORDER = 4,104 LBS

Item #	Tier Size	Pallet Cases	Item Pack	Item Size	Item Description	Available Currently	Order Quantity	Order Min	Weekly Demand	Seasonal Demand	Last Four Actual 1	2	3	4	Start	End	Allowance Amount	Weight Factor
1	15	75	12	3.3 oz	Nestea Ice Tea Fr	218	0	15	28.7	61.1	21	29	40	55	3/26	9/29	4.8	10.6
2	10	100	12	26.5 oz	Nestea Iced Tea 10 qt.	596	0	100	73.4	156.3	108	137	115	145	3/21	9/20	6.8	20
3	10	30	12	40 oz	Nestea Iced Tea 15 qt.	409	00	30	27.4	58.4	39	30	42	75	3/26	9/29	4.5	34
4	8	32	12	4.9 oz	Nestea Free Ice Tea	102	40	32	19.2	40.9	27	26	36	24	3/26	9/29	5.42	13
5	10	70	6	53 oz	Nestea Iced Tea 20 qt.	397	0	40	64.3	137.0	50	153	92	103	3/21	9/20	6.66	22.4
6	20	60	24	1.7 oz	Nestea Ice Teas Cit 8	269	80	40	45.7	97.3	14	10	19	32	3/20	10/31	4.32	5.6
7	20	60	24	1.7 oz	Nestea Ice Teas Orange	149	180	40	43.8	93.3	11	15	19	30	3/20	10/31	4.32	5.6
8	20	60	24	1.7 oz	Nestea Ice Teas Lemon	156	280	40	50.9	108.4	18	23	25	54	3/20	10/31	4.32	5.6
9	20	60	24	1.7 oz	Nestea Ice Teas Trop	241	100	40	43.9	93.5	18	15	15	28	3/20	10/31	4.32	5.6

Items Ordered: 5   Order Total: $37,942.40

MARSH & McLENNAN (A)

Marsh & McLennan are international insurance brokers[1] and employee benefit consultants. The firm is an independent contractor remunerated on a commission or fee basis. Its principal function is to assist its clients in placing risks in the insurance market at conditions and premiums equitable to both insured and insurer, as well as to provide consulting, actuarial, and communication services for its clients' employee benefit plans. Marsh & McLennan's services are primarily purchased by corporate and institutional organizations that require specialized and professional counsel to assess their exposures to risk and to fulfill their insurance and employee benefit requirements.

Aircraft Insurance

Early in 1969, in preparation for the renewal of coverage for a three-year policy term, Marsh & McLennan began reviewing the insurance program for one of its clients, Eastern Airlines, Inc.

Aircraft insurance received little attention until after World War I. There were no special forms to cover aviation risks, and the few policies that were issued made use of the ordinary fire and automobile forms. Initially, underwriting was characterized by a considerable element of trial and error. The volume of business was small, and values in a single risk were great. Experience upon which to predict rates was lacking. Early insurers charged high premiums, imposed heavy deductibles, and used some complicated policy conditions.

For a long time, insurance companies were organized into underwriting syndicates to handle the growing volume of aircraft business. Such syndicates still account for a substantial part of the business, especially the protection for the large airline transportation and aircraft manufacturing companies.

At first glance, the aircraft coverages seem to parallel the familiar automobile coverages. Each is divided into two classifications: direct loss and liability coverages. However, compared with automobile risks, aircraft insurance involves huge sums for each accident; direct loss insurance, depreciation, and obsolescence become important factors.

Hull Insurance

The specific insurance policy under study by Marsh & McLennan was hull insurance for Eastern's entire jet fleet (Exhibit 1). Premiums for aircraft hull insurance are often determined retrospectively, based on the amount of loss during the coverage period. There is an upper limit on the premium amount, which transfers some risk to the insurer, but generally the insurer is directly reimbursed for losses paid under the contract. There are many alternative reimbursement formulas, giving the insurer varying margins for expense and risk premiums, but Eastern was considering only two hull insurance proposals submitted by Associated Aviation Underwriters. A third alternative, self-insurance, was not being considered by Eastern at this time.

Harvard Business School Case 9-171-303, revised August 26, 1992. Copyright © 1971 by the President and Fellows of Harvard College.

[1]From *The Marsh & McLennan Story:* "The responsibility of the [insurance] broker is to provide for his client, through quality service by technical, administrative, and executive personnel, an expert appraisal of his insurance requirements, development of custom-made policy conditions to provide proper insurance protection, and the purchase of such coverage in the insurance markets of the world. Additionally, the broker provides technical advice and assistance on a continuing basis during the policy term to assist the client and all related problems."

Loss Conversion Plan

Eastern had been utilizing a Loss Conversion formula. Under this plan, annual premiums are equal to 135% of all losses incurred within that year, subject to a maximum annual rate of $1.05 and a minimum rate of $.50 per $100 insured value. With this method of premium calculation, an incentive credit equaling 10% of total three-year premiums in excess of total three-year losses is given the insured if the plan runs for the full three-year term.

Profit Commission Plan

John Lawton, Marsh & McLennan's Account Executive, suggested that Eastern modify its insurance program to utilize a cumulative three-year Profit Commission method of calculation. Annual premiums under this plan equal losses plus $.25 per $100 insured, subject to a maximum annual premium of 1% of insured value. The incentive credit refunded at the end of the policy was equivalent to the excess, if any, of (a) premiums paid over (b) total losses plus $.20 per $100 value per year.

When the Profit Commission plan was suggested to Mr. Peter Mullen, Eastern's Director-Insurance, he expressed some concern that it could be more expensive than the Loss Conversion plan. He pointed out that Eastern had 206 jet aircraft with a total fleet value of nearly $1 billion and an average value of $4.6 million per aircraft. If the assumption were made that one "average aircraft" was lost each year, the Loss Conversion plan would produce significant savings when compared to the Profit Commission plan. In addition, of the 206 aircraft in the Eastern jet fleet, all but two were presently valued at amounts that, in the event of loss, would produce lower costs under the Loss Conversion plan.

Mr. Lawton thought there were other factors that should be considered. Mr. Mullen was correct in pointing out that Eastern's annual insurance premium could be less under the Loss Conversion plan provided that losses were "average." However, the alternative Profit Commission plan would cost less if there were no losses or if two or more losses occurred in a given year. Considering various possible combinations of losses over a three-year term, the Profit Commission plan produced a lower cost in eight out of ten sample adjustments. See Exhibit 1 for the sample adjustments submitted to Eastern.

In order to prepare for an upcoming conference with Mr. Mullen and other Eastern executives, Mr. Lawton asked a Marsh & McLennan actuary, Charles Porter, to evaluate the relative merits of the two alternative plans and to prepare his recommendations prior to the meeting.

Additional Information

A variety of industry-wide statistics were available. Losses could be studied in detail as they related to type of aircraft and cause of loss, the number of flights, revenue miles, flying hours, etc. In an attempt to estimate the probability that an aircraft would be lost in the course of a calendar year, Mr. Porter had found a research report of the FAA. This statistical survey had shown that the accident rate per cruise hour was essentially identical for all types of aircraft. To adjust for increased exposure during takeoff and landing, 3.7 hours of cruising were added to each flight. Thus, a flight between New York and San Francisco (flight time six hours) would be equivalent to 9.7 hours of cruising; however, a flight between New York and Boston (flight time 45 minutes), although only one eighth as long in terms of flight time, would be equivalent to 4.45 hours of cruising.

To determine the "equivalent hours" of exposure for all jets flown by domestic trunk carriers, Mr. Porter found detailed data for both 1967 and 1968. During this period of time 15,660,000 "equivalent hours" were recorded, with total losses of jet aircraft numbering ten. While Eastern's recent experience had been much better, data relating solely to Eastern would be too scanty to provide a meaningful basis. In addition to total losses, partial hull damage (e.g., minor aircraft damage on a landing or a takeoff) might be estimated from Eastern's experience as $500,000 to $1 million per year.

Information on future fleet expansion and flight schedules was not firm; but for the purposes of his analysis, Mr. Porter was told to base his evaluation of alternative plans upon the current fleet size (Exhibit 2) and an annual estimate of 10,060 "equivalent hours" per jet. The recent congestion along the Eastern Seaboard would eliminate any possibility of significantly higher utilization.

Armed with these data, Mr. Porter prepared to make his evaluation of the two plans.

Exhibit 1

EASTERN AIRLINES HULL INSURANCE—COMPARISON OF COSTS BASED ON CATASTROPHIC LOSSES

	Losses	Loss Conversion Plan	Profit Commission Plan
1.	$ 1,000,000	$ 5,000,000	$ 3,500,000
2.	1,000,000	5,000,000	3,500,000
3.	1,000,000	5,000,000	3,500,000
Total	$ 3,000,000	$15,000,000	$10,500,000
Incentive credit		1,200,000	1,500,000
Net cost		**$13,800,000**	**$ 9,000,000**
1.	$ 1,000,000	$ 5,000,000	$ 3,500,000
2.	1,000,000	5,000,000	3,500,000
3.	6,000,000	8,100,000	8,500,000
Total	$ 8,000,000	$18,100,000	$15,500,000
Incentive credit		1,010,000	1,500,000
Net cost		**$17,090,000**	**$14,000,000**
1.	$ 1,000,000	$ 5,000,000	$ 3,500,000
2.	6,000,000	8,100,000	8,500,000
3.	6,000,000	8,100,000	8,500,000
Total	$13,000,000	$21,200,000	$20,500,000
Incentive credit		820,000	1,500,000
Net cost		**$20,380,000**	**$19,000,000**
1.	$ 6,000,000	$ 8,100,000	$ 8,500,000
2.	6,000,000	8,100,000	8,500,000
3.	6,000,000	8,100,000	8,500,000
Total	$18,000,000	$24,300,000	$25,500,000
Incentive credit		630,000	1,500,000
Net cost		**$23,670,000**	**$24,000,000**
1.	$ 1,000,000	$ 5,000,000	$ 3,500,000
2.	1,000,000	5,000,000	3,500,000
3.	11,000,000	10,500,000	10,000,000
Total	$13,000,000	$20,500,000	$17,000,000
Incentive credit		750,000	0
Net cost		**$19,750,000**	**$17,000,000**
1.	$ 1,000,000	$ 5,000,000	$ 3,500,000
2.	6,000,000	8,100,000	8,500,000
3.	11,000,000	10,500,000	10,000,000
Total	$18,000,000	$23,600,000	$22,000,000
Incentive credit		560,000	0
Net cost		**$23,040,000**	**$22,000,000**
1.	$ 1,000,000	$ 5,000,000	$ 3,500,000
2.	11,000,000	10,500,000	10,000,000
3.	11,000,000	10,500,000	10,000,000
Total	$23,000,000	$26,000,000	$23,500,000
Incentive credit		300,000	0
Net cost		**$25,700,000**	**$23,500,000**
1.	$ 6,000,000	$ 8,100,000	$ 8,500,000
2.	6,000,000	8,100,000	8,500,000
3.	11,000,000	10,500,000	10,000,000
Total	$23,000,000	$26,700,000	$27,000,000
Incentive credit		370,000	0
Net cost		**$26,330,000**	**$27,000,000**
1.	$ 6,000,000	$ 8,100,000	$ 8,500,000
2.	11,000,000	10,500,000	10,000,000
3.	11,000,000	10,500,000	10,000,000
Total	$28,000,000	$29,100,000	$28,500,000
Incentive credit		110,000	0
Net cost		**$28,990,000**	**$28,500,000**
1.	$11,000,000	$10,500,000	$10,000,000
2.	11,000,000	10,500,000	10,000,000
3.	11,000,000	10,500,000	10,000,000
Total	$33,000,000	$31,500,000	$30,000,000
Incentive credit		0	0
Net cost		**$31,500,000**	**$30,000,000**

Exhibit 2

EASTERN AIRLINES JET FLEET (JANUARY 1, 1969)

Aircraft	No.	Book Value Plane Value	Book Value Fleet Value	Insured Value Plane Value	Insured Value Fleet Value
DC-8-61	17	$ 8,709,000	$148,053,000	$ 9,000,000	$153,000,000
DC-8-63	2	11,100,000	22,200,000	11,300,000	22,600,000
	19		$170,253,000		$175,600,000
DC-9-14	15	$ 3,310,000	$ 49,650,000	$ 3,400,000	$ 51,000,000
DC-9-21	14	2,772,000	38,808,000	3,000,000	42,000,000
DC-9-3	62	3,825,000	237,150,000	3,900,000	241,800,000
DC-9-31	5	3,825,000	19,125,000	3,900,000	19,500,000
	96		$344,733,000		$354,300,000
720	15	$ 2,455,000	$ 36,825,000	$ 3,200,000	$ 48,000,000
	15		$ 36,825,000		$ 48,000,000
727	50	$ 3,854,000	$192,700,000	$ 4,200,000	$210,000,000
727-225	1	6,092,225	6,092,225	6,200,000	6,200,000
727-QC	17	5,710,000	97,070,000	5,900,000	100,300,000
727-QC	8	5,710,000	45,680,000	5,900,000	47,200,000
	76		$341,542,225		$363,700,000
TOTALS	206		$893,353,225		$941,600,000

▼   ▼   ▼

 CASE

DMA, INC.

"Everyone loves this software package," said Lee Rautenberg, president of DMA, Inc., in January 1988 as he introduced *PC MacTerm*, the company's latest product, to visitors. Pointing to the two personal computers in front of him, Lee continued, "As you see, the Mac is running Lotus 1-2-3 directly from the hard disk of the IBM PC. All you need to achieve this feat is *PC MacTerm*, *pcAnywhereIII*, and a $15.00 serial cable. Nothing else.

"Developing software is what we are good at," Rautenberg added. "Now we must decide on a marketing strategy. And the most important decision is whether to market the product ourselves or to go with a publisher."

Background

Dynamic Microprocessor Associates (DMA) was founded in 1979 by Rautenberg to develop software for the emerging microcomputer industry. By 1988, the company had grown to twelve people, divided between a technical development group in Long Island and a sales and marketing group in New York. Projected sales for the year were approximately $4.2 million. (See Exhibits 1 and 2 for DMA's latest income statement and balance sheet.)

Harvard Business School Case 9-189-188, revised March 29, 1994. This case was written by Najib Hashem under the supervision of Professor Anirudh Dhebar. Some data has been disguised. Copyright © 1989 by the President and Fellows of Harvard College.

Since its founding, DMA had produced eight software packages for a variety of computer systems. Three of these packages had been selected by *PC Magazine* for its "Editor's Choice" award. The company prided itself on the technical excellence of its products.

DMA's best-selling product was *pcAnywhereIII*, which allowed an IBM personal computer (IBM PC) to access another IBM PC via a modem and a telephone line. *PC MacTerm*, the company's latest offering, enabled an Apple Macintosh computer (Mac) to operate an IBM PC with equal ease. Early reactions from critics indicated that *PC MacTerm* was set to win wide acceptance.

The estimated installed base of personal computers in U.S. businesses (i.e., excluding households and educational establishments) in 1987 was 15.12 million units, and was expected to grow at 11% per annum for the next five years. These personal computers were based on many hardware standards, the two most common being the IBM PC and the Apple Macintosh.

The IBM PC and the Mac differed in many ways. The most striking difference involved the Mac's interface, which relied heavily on the use of icons and a "mouse"; the Mac also operated in a "what you see is what you get," or WYSIWYG, mode: text and graphics appeared on the screen exactly as they would on paper. The IBM PC and the Mac differed in their internal architecture as well. For example, they were designed around different microprocessors (Intel for the IBM PC and Motorola for the Mac), they relied on different protocols and connectors to send data to printers and other devices, and they saved data on diskettes in different formats. These and other differences made the two standards incompatible with one another.

The IBM PC was the accepted business standard. IBM PCs and compatibles held over 75% of the installed base in offices (versus 5% for the Mac). It was generally accepted that the Mac was the more user-friendly machine, and the number of Mac users was growing.

Connectivity—the ability to link computers together for the purpose of sharing information—was a major problem in dealing with systems from more than one vendor. There were three levels of connectivity: (1) limited ability to exchange data files, (2) added capability to run programs, and (3) full connectivity to a host computer with unlimited access to hardware, files, programs, and peripherals (e.g., printers). *pcAnywhereIII* provided the third level of connectivity between IBM computers. *PC MacTerm* promised the same between an IBM PC and a Mac by allowing the Mac to control the IBM. "Given the increasing popularity of the Mac, such a product was waiting to be developed," said Brad Farkas, the creator of *PC MacTerm*.

The Market for *PC MacTerm*

PC MacTerm was created for the 300,000 or so customers who used both an IBM PC and a Mac. Rautenberg was unsure about the proportion of this market that *PC MacTerm* might capture: companies with mixed computer environments had managed with only limited connectivity for quite some time, and, in any case, most individuals used one system or the other, but not both. Would they appreciate the added flexibility that *PC MacTerm* offered? Experts and critics who had tried *PC MacTerm* thought it a very useful product. Would corporate customers react the same way? Rautenberg was also uncertain about the size of the market itself. The number "300,000" was just an estimate. The true number could range anywhere between 200,000 and 1 million.

One of Rautenberg's other worries was the emergence of a competitive product. Many software and hardware firms were working on connectivity issues, and could introduce a more effective or cheaper product. Even if a competitor did not emerge, Rautenberg estimated that product obsolescence in the fast-paced computer industry would limit *PC MacTerm*'s life expectancy to four years at most. After that, either a competitive product (possibly developed by DMA) would become available, or, conceivably, hardware manufacturers might themselves devise methods to overcome the connectivity problem altogether, thus eliminating software solutions.

Marketing

Rautenberg had budgeted $200,000 for a marketing campaign to launch *PC MacTerm*. Much of that money would be spent upfront to generate consumer excitement and raise awareness. He realized, however, that advertising alone would not be enough. Dealers would have to be educated about the benefits of *PC MacTerm*. This would not be easy. Most dealers specialized in either IBM or Apple products, and even those who carried both systems tended to locate them in different parts of their showrooms. In spite of a fairly aggressive marketing plan, Rautenberg was not very optimistic about the market share that *PC MacTerm* could capture in the first and subsequent years. He estimated that market share in the first year could range anywhere from 2% to 5% of the potential market; the share in subsequent years would be a direct function of how well the product sold in the previous period.

The retail price for *PC MacTerm* was to be set at $99, a little lower than the price of many specialist data exchange programs, and comparing favorably with the company's $145 *pcAnywhereIII*. Both *PC MacTerm* and *pcAnywhereIII* would be required to connect an IBM PC with a Mac. Wholesalers typically paid half the retail price. In this case, they would purchase the product from DMA for $50. The company would incur $6 per copy of *PC MacTerm* for program disks, printing manuals, and packaging. A specialist subcontractor would perform these manufacturing operations. Product support would be offered using DMA's existing marketing and program development staff. Exhibit 3 gives the proposed advertising copy for the new product.

The Catalina Deal

DMA intended to market the new software on its own. Just before the company went to market, however, it was approached by Catalina Computing,[2] a $30-million firm specializing in the development and marketing of a line of network communication utilities. Catalina proposed to acquire exclusive marketing rights for *PC MacTerm* and sell the software under its own brand name. In return, DMA would receive a signing bonus of $50,000 plus a royalty of 15% of gross sales (based on $50/unit). Most software publishing contracts also included commitments to spend a minimum number of advertising dollars. This was not possible in the case of *PC MacTerm*: because Catalina planned to combine it with its own product line, it would be difficult to identify the proportion of advertising dollars spent on *PC MacTerm* as compared to the whole line. Therefore, Catalina had proposed minimum royalty payments of $15,000 per month for the first six months, followed by minimum payments of $10,000 per month for up to two years. The minimum payments were an incentive for Catalina to exercise "due diligence" in the promotion of *PC MacTerm*.

---

[2] "Catalina Computing" is a disguised name.

Catalina was a large and established distributor of Mac software and had good name recognition among Mac users. Rautenberg knew Catalina could secure many more outlets and generate far better sales than DMA. Still, was 15% a reasonable royalty rate? Would Catalina be equally affected by the entry of a competitive product? Were there other benefits to turning over the marketing of a DMA product to a company with an established presence in the Mac software market?

Perhaps he was wrong to think simply in financial terms. DMA was a developer of IBM PC software and relatively unknown in the Mac community. The association with Catalina would give the company a valuable "stamp of approval." The Catalina deal would also free DMA from the task of marketing and supporting *PC MacTerm;* the company would be able to devote its scarce resources to what it did best—developing new software programs.

Making a Decision

DMA's culture was strongly focused on product development, and Rautenberg was acutely aware that sales performance had suffered in the past as a result of the company's narrow technical focus. DMA needed to place greater emphasis on marketing if its products were to achieve their full potential. *PC MacTerm* appeared a winner by all accounts, which made the decision on how to sell it all the more difficult. Teaming up with a well-known software publisher would ensure wide distribution and ease the entrée into the Mac world; it would also be a valuable learning experience. On the other hand, if the product was a success, DMA would be forfeiting the chance to gain direct recognition and substantial monetary gain. Was *PC MacTerm* the right product to experiment with? Would there ever be a right product?

Rautenberg had prepared a chart listing his expectations about the market and his uncertainties surrounding many of the sales projections (see Exhibit 4). He wanted to review the numbers and understand the financial implications before making a final decision.

Exhibit 1

INCOME STATEMENT FOR 1987

Sales	$ 3,692,130
Cost of Sales	184,774
Research & Development	558,524
Marketing & Product Support	534,078
Administration Expense	261,095
Depreciation	166,760
Net Income before Tax	$ 1,986,899

Exhibit 2

BALANCE SHEET AS OF DECEMBER 31, 1987

Assets		Liabilities	
Cash	$ 215,848	Accounts Payable	$ 177,484
Accounts Receivable	719,348	Owners' Equity	5,058,315
Investments	2,059,690		
Net Fixed Assets	2,240,913		
Total Assets	$ 5,235,799	Total Liabilities	$ 5,235,799

Exhibit 3

Exhibit 4

MARKET EXPECTATIONS FOR *PC MACTERM*

Assumptions	Best Guess	Range Low	High
Market			
Initial market size (units)	300,000	200,000	1,000,000
Market growth rate	11%	8%	14%
Years to obsolescence	2	0	4
Distribution by DMA			
Promotion budget	$200,000		
Price to wholesalers	$50.00		
Variable costs[a]	$15.00	$12.00	$20.00
Initial market share	3.5%	2.0%	5.0%
Annual market share growth multiplier[b]	1.5	1.2	1.8
Distribution by Catalina			
Signing bonus	$50,000		
Royalty rate	15.00%		
Minimum yr 1	$150,000		
Minimum yr 2	$120,000		
Variable costs	None		
Initial market share	10.0%	5.0%	15.0%
Annual market share growth multiplier[b]	1.5	1.2	1.8

[a] Variable costs included $6 for manufacturing and $9 for anticipated product support costs.

[b] If the share of the unsatisfied market is 10% in Year 1, an annual market share multiplier of 1.5 implies that share of the unsatisfied market in Year 2 will be 15% (= 10% × 1.5), in Year 3, 22.5%, etc.

▼   ▼   ▼

GREAT WESTERN STEEL CORPORATION

The Great Western Steel Corporation operated a dock at a port on the West Coast of the United States at which it unloaded iron ore coming by ship from Venezuela. The dock had facilities for unloading two ships at one time. The ships were all of about the same size and type. The time required to unload a ship was at least one 24-hour day, but on occasion equipment breakdowns would result in longer unloading times, as shown in Exhibit 1. Labor was readily available. When there was no ship to unload, the company did not pay for a crew's time. On the other hand, the company could go on a three-shift, seven-day basis when this was required by the number of ship arrivals.

This arrangement had worked out very well for several years. The ships radioed their arrival far enough in advance so that a crew was always found ready when a berth became available. Not infrequently an arriving ship found both of the dock positions occupied and had to wait before being unloaded, but it was very rare that the delay amounted to more than a few hours. In September 1955, however, management became concerned about the fact that the approaching completion of its new steel mill would increase ore requirements and therefore ship arrivals. About 500 shiploads of ore would be required per year instead of the previous 250, and management was afraid that the ships, for which the company paid a charter rate of $1,400 a day, would sometimes have to wait a very long time before being unloaded.

A study had been made of the possibility of making the arrivals more regular, but it appeared that the variety of conditions encountered during the voyage made this impossible. (Ships could, of course, be instructed to proceed at slow speed when normal speed would have led to arrivals producing congestion in the harbor.) A study of past records showed that ships arrived with complete unpredictability—equally often at all hours and on all days throughout the year, with no apparent pattern. Exhibit 2 indicates the worksheet used in gathering observations on arrivals and dock utilization. From past observations, the best estimate of the time between arrivals of ships with the increased traffic was thought to be as shown in Exhibit 3, where the mean value of the distribution is, of course, equal to $365 \div 500 = 0.73$ days.

A study was then made of the possibility of extending the dock or of building a new dock nearby. The study showed that, using the most economical location available, the company would be obliged to spend about $1.3 million to build a one-berth dock and install all necessary equipment, such as cranes, rail spurs, etc. Maintenance of the new facilities would cost about $28,000 a year; operating expenses could be neglected because they depended on the number of ships arriving and not on the number of berths available. (No premium was paid to dock crews for working nights or holidays.) The life of the proposed new facilities was estimated at 25 years, and the company's policy was to make no investments that did not earn 15% on the investment after taxes. The construction of the dock and installation of the facilities could not be completed by the time the new mill was in operation unless it was begun almost immediately.

Harvard Business School Case 9-175-128. This case was written by Professor Basil A. Kalymon.
Copyright © 1975 by the President and Fellows of Harvard College.

Exhibit 1

UNLOADING TIMES

Hours	Percentage of ships
24	4
25	9
26	18
27	13
28	10
29	5
30	4
31	4
32	6
33	8
34	11
35	6
36	2

Exhibit 2

WORKSHEET

Time of arrival	Time spent unloading	Berth No. 1		Berth No. 2	
		Time in	Time out	Time in	Time out

Exhibit 3

THE ZECKENDORF COMPANY

CASE

William L. Zeckendorf stared at the spreadsheet displayed on his personal computer. "We have a budget of $6 million for interest payments on our building at 68th and Broadway. Interest rates being where they are, we should get away with a million or so less than that. Things would have to get pretty bad for the payments to go above budget. You may be surprised to hear it, but even in a $50 million building we can estimate our non-interest costs quite well. That pleases the bank, for they lend us money on practically a line-item by line-item basis. It also pleases the partners (Japanese in this case), who regard cost over-runs, at best, as a sign of incompetence. Despite the million dollar cushion I still worry that things could go wrong. It could be very profitable for us to have an ongoing relationship with these partners, but that would go up in smoke if we ran over our budget. That's why I've asked our bank to quote me a fixed interest rate and a floating rate with a cap. End of problem!"

Company History

William Zeckendorf Senior had founded the company after the Second World War and acted as developer in the construction of many North American landmarks, including the United Nations Plaza in New York City, Mile High Plaza in Denver, and Place Ville-Marie in Montreal. One of only a handful of major developers in Manhattan, by July 1985 the Zeckendorf company may well have had more active projects than any other Manhattan developer.

Harvard Business School Case 9-186-135, revised March 29, 1994. This case was written by Professor David E. Bell. Copyright © 1985 by the President and Fellows of Harvard College.

William L. Zeckendorf (HBS MBA, 1984), grandson of the founder and a son of the current owner, discussed his family's history. "My family have always been entrepreneurs. My great-great grandfather took thirty thousand dollars worth of goods, in twelve wagon trains, from New Mexico to Tucson; he was immediately bought out by the local shopkeepers for sixty-five thousand dollars. Since that time there always seems to have been a William Zeckendorf finding creative ways to make money. My grandfather got into real estate in 1925 when, by aggressive salesmanship, he managed to rent every floor of a Manhattan building that his uncle owned. Grandfather went from strength to strength. He sold, resold, and rented properties even through the Depression. By the 1960s I'd say that he had amassed a couple of hundred million dollars in personal wealth. But he lost it all, partly due to the rise in interest rates in the mid-sixties. His highly leveraged positions were disrupted when one bank foreclosed and the rest followed in domino fashion. You can see why we are especially cautious when it comes to interest rates!"

The Project at 68th and Broadway

Construction was due to begin in late summer 1985 on a 28-story condominium containing 163 apartments and a new 20,000 square foot A&P supermarket at the base. The Great Atlantic and Pacific Tea Company then owned the 22,000 square foot site, where it operated a store. It had agreed to sell the site and move back in on a long-term lease after the new building was completed.

There would be 22 studio apartments averaging 540 square feet; 64 one-bedrooms averaging 820 square feet, 58 two-bedrooms averaging 1,155 square feet and 17 three-bedrooms averaging 1,690 square feet. There would also be two penthouse suites. Selling prices of around $350 to $400 per square foot were expected. The building would also include a health club of about 8,000 square feet and a garage for 57 cars.

Zeckendorf, as developer, brought in a major Japanese construction firm as a partner, secured the land needed, hired an architectural firm to design the building, and would administer the construction.

Estimating Loan Payments

Although interest rates might be uncertain, the pattern of outstanding loans over time could be predicted with reasonable accuracy. There would be an immediate drawdown of credit for the purchase of the land, followed by further drawdowns as construction began. After eighteen months, as the building became complete, revenues from apartment sales would be used to pay back the loan. Since this project carried a healthy profit margin, there was less danger than usual that revenues would fall short of the loan total. The anticipated loan balances, by month, are shown in Exhibit 1.

"If our interest payments *did* exceed $6 million, the Zeckendorfs would probably dip into their own pockets for the first few hundred thousand, but as you can imagine we don't like doing that. The only reason we would do it is to preserve our reputation with the partners that we can stick to our budget. Believe me, they are concerned about every last dollar; they check my figures down to the last detail," continued William L. Zeckendorf. "Beyond that point we'd have to demand additional funds from the partners, as the partnership agreement allows us to. But they probably wouldn't work with us again. In any event this is all moot since our bank will be responding within a week to my request for quotes. Normally we pay about 2 1/4 points above the commercial paper rate and that floats around of course. I've asked for a fixed rate quote and one for a floating rate with a 13% cap."

Alternative Loan Agreements

In early August 1985 the Bankers Trust Company responded to Zeckendorf's request for a fixed rate quote and for the cost of a 13% cap. The fixed rate would be 10.35% (plus 2 1/4 points, or 12.60%). This rate would hold on all borrowings based on the schedule in Exhibit 1. The bank also offered three periodic caps. Under this procedure, at the beginning of each month Zeckendorf Company would borrow an amount of money for a three-month period at 2 1/2 points above the going three-month commercial paper rate. In this way Zeckendorf Company would effectively have three loans outstanding, each rolled over every three months. If Zeckendorf were to pay for a cap, however, the rate charged for any one three-month period would be the minimum of the commercial paper rate and the cap rate, plus 2 1/4 points. The total cost for three possible caps (again, based on the schedule in Exhibit 1) is shown in Table 3.3.

Table 3.3

Cap	9%	11%	13%
Fee	$808,000	$456,000	$265,000

"These caps are a useful idea, but with a fixed rate of 10.35% I really can't go wrong, since the guaranteed total interest payment of $5,966,535 is under my budget. Mind you, interest rates have been fairly steady lately. With the current commercial paper rate at 8.2% (see Exhibit 2) maybe I shouldn't be so conservative on this deal."

Exhibit 1 _____

	LOAN SCHEDULE	
	Total Loans **Required**	**3-Month** **Loan Size**
September '85	$ 9,060,883	$ 9,060,883
October '85	9,703,531	642,648 [1]
November '85	10,110,873	407,342
December '85	10,635,298	9,585,308
January '86	11,480,026	1,487,376
February '86	12,308,554	1,235,870
March '86	13,495,551	10,772,305
April '86	16,182,114	4,173,939
May '86	18,941,661	3,995,417
June '86	22,639,474	14,470,118
July '86	26,075,966	7,610,431
August '86	28,933,574	6,853,025
September '86	31,671,109	17,207,653
October '86	34,337,160	10,276,482
November '86	36,726,143	9,242,008
December '86	39,580,010	20,061,520
January '87	41,718,766	12,415,238
February '87	43,839,800	11,363,042
March '87	45,732,122	21,953,842
April '87	39,056,031	5,739,147
May '87	30,609,923	2,916,934
June '87	21,884,678	7,943,271 [2]
July '87	12,786,586	0
August '87	731,564	0

[1] 642,648 = 9,703,531 – 9,060,883. This is the amount Zeckendorf's would need to borrow in October to meet their cash flow needs.

[2] This would actually be a 3-month loan of $731,564, a 2-month loan of $9,138,088, and a 1-month loan of $3,358,945 for a total of $13,228,597. However, since we are ignoring Net Present Value, we can estimate the interest payments based on $7,943,271 = $731,564 + $(\frac{2}{3})$ (9,138,088) + $(\frac{1}{3})$ (3,358,945).

Exhibit 2

INTEREST RATES*

Jan-77	6.025	Mar-79	10.050	May-81	17.525	Jul-83	9.750
Feb-77	5.900	Apr-79	10.150	Jun-81	17.650	Aug-83	9.800
Mar-77	5.900	May-79	10.300	Jul-81	18.025	Sep-83	9.900
Apr-77	5.900	Jun-79	10.150	Aug-81	17.900	Oct-83	9.525
May-77	5.900	Jul-79	10.400	Sep-81	15.900	Nov-83	9.525
Jun-77	5.775	Aug-79	11.350	Oct-81	14.900	Dec-83	10.250
Jul-77	5.775	Sep-79	12.150	Nov-81	12.025	Jan-84	9.650
Aug-77	6.275	Oct-79	14.650	Dec-81	13.275	Feb-84	9.950
Sep-77	6.650	Nov-79	12.850	Jan-82	14.150	Mar-84	10.550
Oct-77	6.900	Dec-79	13.900	Feb-82	14.400	Apr-84	10.750
Nov-77	6.750	Jan-80	13.650	Mar-82	15.400	May-84	10.950
Dec-77	7.050	Feb-80	15.100	Apr-82	14.775	Jun-84	11.650
Jan-78	7.000	Mar-80	17.525	May-82	14.025	Jul-84	11.600
Feb-78	6.900	Apr-80	13.400	Jun-82	15.275	Aug-84	11.775
Mar-78	7.000	May-80	9.775	Jul-82	12.025	Sep-84	11.275
Apr-78	7.250	Jun-80	9.400	Aug-82	10.400	Oct-84	10.050
May-78	7.550	Jul-80	9.275	Sep-82	10.525	Nov-84	9.150
Jun-78	8.150	Aug-80	11.525	Oct-82	9.525	Dec-84	8.650
Jul-78	8.100	Sep-80	13.275	Nov-82	9.275	Jan-85	8.600
Aug-78	8.350	Oct-80	13.900	Dec-82	9.525	Feb-85	9.150
Sep-78	8.950	Nov-80	17.025	Jan-83	8.900	Mar-85	9.200
Oct-78	9.500	Dec-80	18.650	Feb-83	8.650	Apr-85	8.600
Nov-78	10.400	Jan-81	17.275	Mar-83	10.025	May-85	7.950
Dec-78	10.800	Feb-81	15.650	Apr-83	8.800	Jun-85	7.950
Jan-79	10.250	Mar-81	14.650	May-83	9.150	Jul-85	8.200
Feb-79	10.250	Apr-81	16.400	Jun-83	9.650		

* Commercial paper rates as of the end of the given month.

▼   ▼   ▼

4 ▼ The Value of Information

Wouldn't it be great if you could get a peek today at tomorrow's newspaper? How much would you pay for a 60-second look at tomorrow's edition of your local daily paper? In answering this question, did you imagine exactly how you'd spend the 60 seconds and what you'd do with the information you gained? Managers often spend money to get information that they need to make good decisions. They conduct surveys of customers, they do patent searches, they wait for a competitor to make the first move. But often they decide to obtain information without thinking through what exactly they intend to do with the information. In this chapter, you'll learn how to recognize and calculate the value of information. Although there are no cases in this chapter, the exercises are challenging and diverse. By the end of the chapter, you should be able to use decision trees to solve information problems; but more than that, you should be educated about the general question of how to revise your opinions in the face of new evidence.

THE VALUE OF COLLECTING INFORMATION

Collecting information is a valuable tool for decision makers. Information is sometimes collected to aid general understanding, and often purely out of curiosity, but on occasion information is collected to aid in making a particular decision. For example, a consumer products company might survey customers about the design of a new product that is still not finalized for production. A purchasing manager might learn about the costs other industries face before putting pressure on her suppliers to lower their prices.

Information is usually obtained only at some cost. Marketing research costs money and time: test markets are expensive to conduct and (often more important) they can delay the introduction even of successful products. The decision to collect information can be analyzed to see if the *expected value* of the information exceeds its *cost of collection*.

Information is seldom perfect. Sample information may be inaccurate for several reasons: pure sampling error, measurement bias (what respondents say is not necessarily what they will do), and selection bias (the sample is not representative of the population). The results of a test market, for example, may not be a perfect indicator of the outcome of a new-product introduction for any or all of the above reasons.

Michelle's Movers

QUESTION 1

Assuming there are no other ramifications to her decision, should Michelle's rent a large truck or a small truck?

QUESTION 2

What would it be worth to Michelle to know for sure whether a small truck would be adequate for the job? (For example, she might send someone a day in advance to examine the job.)

Michelle's Movers rents out trucks with a crew of two on a daily basis, usually to homeowners who are moving or to companies with delivery problems. On one particular day Michelle is a truck short and intends to hire one from a local truck rental firm. The question she faces is, how big a truck should she hire? A large truck costs $200 per day (including insurance, fuel, etc.), a small truck $130 per day. However, if the load is too large, the crew may have to make two trips, which could offset the advantage of hiring the small truck. Michelle assesses the additional cost of making two trips (overtime and truck mileage) at $150. She assesses the probability that two trips will be necessary as 0.40.

To answer Question 1 (see left-hand margin), we can draw the tree shown in Figure 4.1:

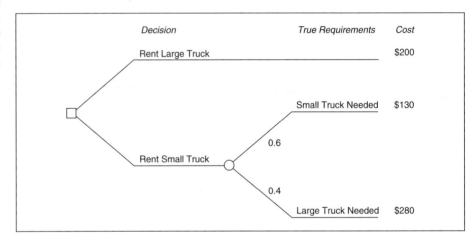

Figure 4.1

The expected cost of renting a small truck is 0.6 × 130 + 0.4 × 280 = $190. Thus she should rent a small truck.

To answer Question 2, let's first assume that the information Michelle gets suffers from none of the possible inaccuracies discussed above: it is "perfect" information. To analyze Michelle's problem, we must draw a more complex tree, as shown in Figure 4.2:

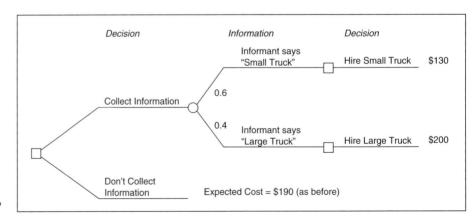

Figure 4.2

Harvard Business School note, revised April 6, 1994. This note was prepared by Professor David E. Bell.

The expected value of the "Collect Information" decision is $0.6 \times 130 + 0.4 \times 200$ = \$158. This is \$32 cheaper than the expected cost without the information. Thus the expected value of information is \$32. If the cost were less than \$32, Michelle would be better off first getting the information, then deciding what to do. However, if the cost exceeded \$32, she would be better off to just go ahead and rent a small truck.

You can see this directly by noting that if the large truck is needed, we will save \$80 by having collected the information. Since the probability of needing the large truck is 0.4, the expected value of the information is 0.4×80 or \$32.

The Value of Imperfect Information

Our example assumed that the information, once obtained, would be perfectly accurate. This is not always the case.

Suppose that the person sent in advance to inspect the job is known to make mistakes. Michelle believes that, even if this person reports "Large Truck Needed," the probability that a large truck is indeed needed is only 0.80. Similarly if the person reports "Small Truck Needed," there is still only an 80% chance that a small truck is needed. How much is advance information of this nature worth?

Before proceeding with the analysis, note that the information will certainly be worth less than \$32. We can solve this problem with the tree shown in Figure 4.3:

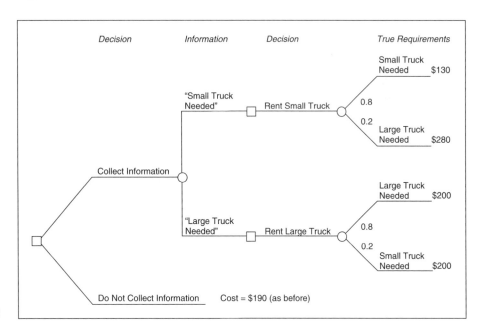

Figure 4.3

This tree is almost complete. However, it lacks one piece of probabilistic information: how likely is our informant to say "Small Truck" versus "Large Truck"? You may think that the appropriate probabilities ought to be 0.6 and 0.4 respectively because these are the probabilities that a small or a large truck is needed. But this is not entirely consistent. Consider the tree shown in Figure 4.4.

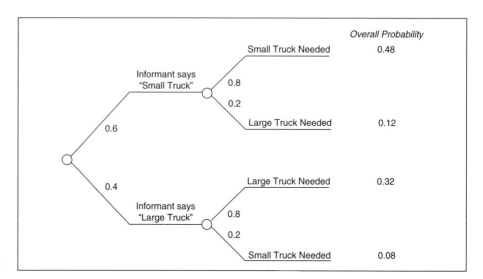

Figure 4.4

According to this tree there is a 0.56 probability that a small truck will in fact be needed (0.48 + 0.08) and a 0.44 probability that a large truck will be needed (0.12 + 0.32). These aren't quite the same as 0.6 and 0.4 respectively. To see this problem more clearly, suppose our informant is right half the time and wrong half the time; then even if we almost certainly needed a large truck, our informant is just as likely to *say* "Large" as "Small."

To find the correct probability, *p*, that our informant will *say* "Large Truck Needed," we need to solve the following equation:

$$p \times 0.8 + (1 - p) \times 0.2 = 0.4$$

or in words:

> *Probability informant says "Large Truck" × Probability this is correct*
>
> + *Probability informant says "Small Truck" × Probability this is wrong*
>
> = *Overall Probability of Large Truck.*

The solution to this equation is *p* = 1/3.

Placing this information in Figure 4.3 we can fold back the tree to find the expected value of the "Collect Information" branch:

$$\tfrac{2}{3}(0.8 \times 130 + 0.2 \times 280) + \tfrac{1}{3} \times 200 = \$173\tfrac{1}{3}.$$

This means we would be prepared to pay up to $16.67 (the $190 expected cost of acting without further information, less the $173.33 cost of acting with imperfect information) for this "imperfect" information.

Bayes' Rule

Information is not always provided in just the format you need for a decision tree. For example, you might know the probability that a successful entrepreneur has an MBA, when what you'd really like to know is the probability that a person with an MBA will be a successful entrepreneur. The thinking process by which one converts probabilities of one type into the other is known as **Bayes' Rule** (because Bayes invented the rule!)

Let's suppose that 60% of all successful entrepreneurs have MBAs (and 40% don't). Let's suppose further that 20% of *unsuccessful* entrepreneurs have MBAs and 80% don't. To find the answer we want, we still need to know what proportion of entrepreneurs are successful. Let's say 5%. Now we draw the tree shown in Figure 4.5:

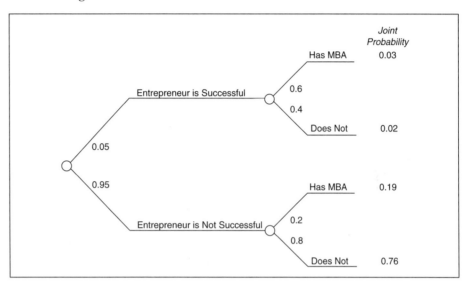

Figure 4.5

Instead of payoffs, we write down the joint probabilities; for example, the probability that an entrepreneur is successful *and* has an MBA is 0.03.

The question we want to answer is, "What proportion of MBAs who are entrepreneurs are successful?" From the tree we see that 0.22 of entrepreneurs have MBAs (= 0.19 + 0.03). Of this 0.22, 0.03 are successful, so 0.03/0.22, or 13.6%, is the answer we seek. (These numbers also suggest that entrepreneurs without an MBA have only a 0.02/0.78 = 2.6% chance of success.)

There is a substantial discrepancy between the number 60% (proportion of successful entrepreneurs who have MBAs) and 13.6% (proportion of entrepreneurs with MBAs who are successful), yet a lay audience often views the two statements as interchangeable!

EXERCISES ON THE VALUE OF INFORMATION

1. In a certain game, payoffs depend on the roll of a die, as described in the following table.

	1	2	3	4	5	6
A	100	200	300	400	500	600
B	600	200	500	200	200	200
C	700	500	400	400	200	100

For example, if the roll is "1," then you win $100 if you choose A, $600 if you choose B, and $700 if you choose C.

Harvard Business School note 9-893-006, revised April 6, 1994. This note was prepared by Professor George Wu.

a. Using an expected value criterion, what should you choose?

b. What is the most you would pay for perfect information on the die roll?

2. Suppose you can earn a little bit of spending money selling falafel sandwiches in a busy square on Saturday afternoons. On a normal Saturday, a day's worth of effort nets you $150. Unfortunately, there is a 30% chance of rain. If it rains, you will make only $50 (a few desperate souls will buy soggy falafel sandwiches!). Suppose you can rent an extra large umbrella for $25/day. In the event it rains, your falafel sandwiches will not be soggy, and you can expect to make $100 (exclusive of umbrella costs).

a. Should you rent the umbrella? You must decide to rent before you find out whether it will rain. Furthermore, you must pay for the umbrella whether or not it rains.

b. What is the most you would pay for a perfectly accurate weather forecast?

3. You are brand manager of Krusty cereal. In spite of the current $1,000,000 in annual profits for the brand, your boss thinks that you can do even better with a new and improved cereal. She estimates that annual profits for such a cereal are equally likely to be $500,000, $1,100,000, or $1,800,000.

a. Should you introduce the new and improved Krusty cereal?

b. Suppose that a test market would inform you perfectly about the future profitability of the improved cereal. What is the most you would pay for such a test market?

4. An oil wildcatter has rights to a piece of land. If she drills, there is a 20% chance that she will strike oil, in which case the payoff is $200,000. The cost of drilling is $20,000.

a. Should she drill?

b. What is the most you would pay for the services of a geologist who can assess the oil prospects with perfect accuracy?

5. ABC company makes 10,000 blenders per year. It must decide whether to make or buy the blender motor. Unfortunately, ABC does not presently have motor technology. Motor development is a two-stage process. The first stage has a 75% chance of success and will cost $10,000. The second stage has a 90% chance of success and will cost $5,000. If development is successful, then the variable cost of producing a motor is $6/motor. If either development stage is unsuccessful, ABC must purchase motors outside at a cost of $10/motor.

a. Should ABC purchase the motor outside or begin development?

b. What is the most ABC would pay to know, before making the first decision, whether the first stage would succeed? the second stage?

EXERCISES ON THE VALUE OF IMPERFECT INFORMATION

1. Read the following excerpt from the *Boston Sunday Globe* (Exhibit 1). The ELISA test for AIDS antibodies declares each person tested either positive (has the antibodies and therefore the disease) or negative (does not have the

Harvard Business School note 9-189-048, revised October 17, 1994. This note was written by Professor David E. Bell.

disease). If a person does not in fact have the disease, ELISA will nevertheless give a "positive" result 5% of the time. For those people who do have the disease ELISA will give a "negative" reading 10% of the time. It is estimated that among low-risk groups in Massachusetts the prevalence of AIDS is 0.002 or 0.2%. Given you are a typical low-risk person, and you have had this test and the result was positive, how likely is it that you have AIDS?

If a person tested positive on the ELISA test, what is the probability that person will *also* test positive on the Western Blot test? If this person has tested positive on *both* tests, what is the probability that he or she has AIDS?

Exhibit 1 _____

Chances of Unreliable Test Results High

The current AIDS-antibody tests are among medicine's most reliable diagnostic tools. But when they are used on a population at low-risk—where only one among thousands of blood samples actually carries the antibodies—the chances of unreliable results are amplified. This has important implications, for individuals and for screening of low-risk populations.

Two tests are commonly used to detect antibodies to the AIDS virus, an index of presumed infection. Initially a blood sample is run through a test called an ELISA. If the ELISA calls it positive, the result is routinely confirmed by a technique called a Western blot.

Under ideal laboratory conditions, the ELISA is 99 percent accurate and the Western blot perhaps 95 percent accurate. But when the U.S. Centers for Disease Control recently sent "blind" test samples to various labs, the ELISA missed 10 percent of samples known by the CDC to contain antibodies and it gave a positive result in five percent of samples known to be negative.

Massachusetts health officials applied this "real world" reliability rate to see what would happen in testing a low-risk population: the 100,000 Bay State residents who get married each year. They found the ELISA plus the Western blot would yield more false-positive results than it would find people truly positive for AIDS virus antibodies.

Thus, Massachusetts state epidemiologist George F. Grady warns that widespread testing of low-risk population is "fraught with all sorts of mischief" because of the currently unavoidable problem of false positives—which have the potential to wreck people's lives needlessly.[1]

2. At the end of the TV game show "Let's Make a Deal!" a contestant is shown three doors. Behind one of them is a major prize (for example, a car). There is no prize behind either of the other two doors. The contestant is asked to select a door. The host, Monty Hall, then selects one of the remaining two doors, opens it, and reveals that nothing is behind it. The contestant is then permitted to stick with his or her original choice of door or to switch to the other remaining unopened door.

You are the contestant. Should you stick or switch (and does it matter)?

You may rest assured the prize is not moved during these proceedings. You may also assume Monty Hall knows where the prize is (the prize is *never* behind the door he opens).

_____

[1] *The Boston Sunday Globe*, May 17, 1987, p. B14. Reprinted courtesy of The Boston Globe.

3. Jack Grayson was a wildcatter who drilled for oil in unproven areas. Developers were a different breed entirely: they merely drilled in known oil-producing areas. But Jack was having second thoughts about the tract where he had set up his rig. Jack figured that there was only a 10% chance of finding oil on this spot; these odds had seemed worth taking, given the cost was only $70,000 to undertake the drilling and the payoff (from a developer) for finding oil would be around $1,000,000. Jack knew that the chance that there was oil under his rig depended heavily on whether there was a geological formation known as a structure. If there was a structure, the odds of finding oil were about 50-50. If there was no structure, the odds of finding oil would drop to 1 in 30.

    Sadly, there was no way, short of drilling, to find out whether a structure existed. However, for $10,000 he could commission a seismic test of the tract. Jack's daughter, who was studying for a master's degree in petroleum engineering at the University of Houston, said that when a structure did exist, the test had an 80% chance of confirming this fact; but even when there was no structure, the test had a 10% chance of suggesting that there was one. Jack wondered if buying the seismic test was a good idea.

4. An investment banker was arrested last night by Portland (Oregon) police on suspicion of assault. The facts are these: An elderly man was walking to his car in a downtown parking lot yesterday evening at about 5:30 P.M., when he was accosted by a tall young man with blond hair who demanded money. The old man gave him a crumpled 50 dollar bill that he always kept in his shoe in case of such an attack. The young man fled into the street.

    The old man flagged down a passing police car, which drove him in the general direction taken by the assailant in the hope of spotting him. Within two minutes the police pointed out a tall, blond young man who was leaning against the wall of an office building, panting. The old man cried out, "That's him, that's the man!" The police questioned the suspect, who agreed to turn out his pockets. The only contents were a key and a crumpled 50 dollar bill. The suspect protested his innocence, explaining that he was an investment banker who had been out jogging; he had talked to no one since leaving his apartment.

    There is no way to tell definitely whether the suspect is guilty or not guilty in this story. (Not least because the story is hypothetical.) However, you should think about the *probability* that the suspect is guilty. The dilemma for you is how to trade off the basic implausibility that an investment banker would be out mugging people with the strength of the circumstantial evidence.

5. You are shown two envelopes, each containing cash. One envelope contains twice as much cash as the other.

    a. You pick one of the envelopes at random and find that it contains $10. Would you prefer to keep the $10 or swap it for the contents of the other envelope?

    b. You pick one of the envelopes at random but do not open it. Would you prefer to keep the contents of that envelope or swap it for the contents of the other envelope?

5 ▼ BIDDING

With this chapter we begin the second half of the book and enter a slightly different realm of analysis. So far, the "opponent" making your life difficult has been either "nature" (such as unpredictable weather, for example) or some sort of good or bad luck (the R&D project worked or it didn't; sales were high or they weren't). But with many problems, life is a little more complicated. In this chapter we'll begin to examine problems where some of the uncertainties stem from our lack of knowledge of what our competitors will do next. For example, our competitors might not sit still while we lower our prices; they might take some action of their own.

In this chapter we look at bidding problems, especially those in which interested parties must submit sealed bids. It's a tricky process: Clearly you don't want to bid more than necessary; on the other hand, there's no sense losing the bid by bidding too conservatively.

AUCTIONS AND COMPETITIVE BIDDING: AN INTRODUCTION

In November 1981 the auction house of Sotheby Park Bernet conducted a very unusual auction. The objects for sale were not art collections or antiques but the rights to use relay devices on RCA's new SATCOM IV satellite. In the space of less than an hour the seven devices, called transponders, were sold for a total price of more than $90 million.[1] This was by far the largest sale in the history of Sotheby's, a firm that had been conducting auctions since 1744.

Auctions have been used since antiquity for the sale of a variety of objects. Herodotus reports that auctions were used in Babylon as early as 500 B.C. In 193 A.D., having killed the Emperor Pertinax, the Praetorian Guard proceeded to auction off the whole Roman Empire. The winning bid was a promise of 6,250 drachmas per man to the Guard. The winner, Didius Julianus, was duly declared emperor but lasted for only two months before being beheaded himself. No refund was offered.[2]

Today the range of objects sold in auctions has increased greatly and the total amounts transacted have grown to staggering proportions. Art objects

Harvard Business School case 9-187-161, revised April 1, 1994. This case was prepared by Professor Vijay Krishna. Copyright © 1987 by the President and Fellows of Harvard College.

---

[1] The details of this auction appear in: *RCA Transponder Auction (A)*, later in this chapter.

[2] For an entertaining account of the history of auctions, see: *Auctions and Auctioneering* by Ralph Cassady, Jr.; University of California Press, 1967.

and antiques have always been sold at the fall of the auctioneer's hammer. But that is just the tip of the iceberg. Numerous kinds of commodities—ranging from tobacco, fish and fresh flowers to scrap metal and gold bullion—are sold by means of a variety of auctions. Timber rights on public land have long been awarded to the highest bidder. Offshore oil leases on the Outer Continental Shelf are routinely auctioned off by the U.S. Department of the Interior for hundreds of millions of dollars. In an auction conducted by Morgan Stanley, Shell Oil acquired the reserves of Belridge Oil for over $3.5 billion, said to be a record. Bond issues by public utilities are usually auctioned off to investment banking syndicates. Long-term securities are sold in weekly auctions conducted by the U.S. Treasury to finance the borrowing needs of the government, which now run in the neighborhood of $200 billion a year.

The process of procurement via competitive bidding is another form of auction, in which the bidders compete for the right to sell their products or services. The U.S. government makes billions of dollars' worth of purchases in this way, and the practice is widespread if not endemic in business. In this chapter, an auction will be understood to include the process of procurement via competitive bidding. Of course, in this case it is the party with the lowest bid who wins the contract.

Why are auctions and competitive bidding so prevalent? Are there particular situations to which an auction is particularly suited as a selling mechanism as opposed to, say, a fixed, posted price? From the point of view of the bidders, what are good bidding strategies? From the point of view of the seller/procurer, are particular forms of auctions likely to bring greater revenues than others? These and other questions will be the subject of analysis.

In this chapter various forms of auctions are briefly described and a conceptual framework for analyzing auctions and bidding situations is outlined. Further issues will be discussed in the cases and the exercises.

What is an Auction?

The word "auction" is believed to originate from the Latin word "auctus" meaning "to increase." In the most familiar auction format, the auctioneer begins by calling out a low price and then successively raising it until there is only a single interested bidder. We will use the term "auction" in a broader sense. Although familiar, the oral ascending auction described above is not the only kind observed in practice. There is a rich and surprising variety of forms. There are sealed-bid, or secret, auctions, auctions where the price moves downwards instead of upwards, the Japanese simultaneous bidding system, and many others. Sometimes only one item is sold. Often the auction involves the sale of numerous but identical items. Our aim will be to provide a useful classification of the most common auction forms and study the strategic possibilities of each type.

Auctions typically involve the public sale of property by a *single* seller to a *few* potential buyers. The objects for sale are usually "one of a kind" for which established markets are thin, if not nonexistent. Furthermore, the value of the objects is often uncertain and very subjective. There is no such thing as "a going price" for a Rembrandt. Each painting is unique, and its value may differ from that of others by the same artist for a variety of reasons. It may differ stylistically from others, the subject of the painting may be unique, or it may have an interesting history. Similarly, oil fields have unique characteristics: their size, location, accessibility, and potential. Bond issues differ because of the differing risks involved in the investment projects to be financed. It is clear that in such circumstances it would be difficult to post a "take it or leave it" price. What price tag would one attach to a newly discovered masterpiece by da Vinci? Auctions serve to determine prices for "priceless" objects.

Uncertain Values and Auctions

From these examples, it is clear that uncertainty about the value of the object sold is a crucial aspect of the problem. Let us first look at the problem from the buyer's point of view. If you are bidding on a rare painting, you may not know, its exact quality. Is it by the master or one of his pupils imitating the style? Is it a fake? Are there many like it? If you are bidding for the right to drill for oil, the potential value of the field is unknown to you. How deep will you have to go? How much oil can you recover? If you are bidding for the right to build a plant in a foreign country, you may be uncertain about the cost of building such a plant, and hence the worth of the contract. Equally important, you may not know the value of the object to your *rival* bidders. This will determine their bidding strategy and affect *your* optimal bid in response. It is useful to develop a rough classification of these situations.

In some situations, you may know the exact value of the object to yourself or your company, but may be unaware of its value to competing bidders. Such a situation is said to involve **private-values**. As an example, suppose you are bidding for the right to build a plant for another company. From your past experience, you know the costs involved quite well. Costs have run close to $10 million for similar plants, and this seems like a good figure for the current plant. On the other hand, you are facing a competitor from abroad. It is very difficult for you to know exactly how much it would cost your competitor to build such a plant. Their bid may involve a slightly different specification because they may use a different technology or design. You can only estimate that their costs lie somewhere between $8.5 million and $12 million. At the same time your competitor, while sure of his own costs, is equally unsure of *your* costs. In such a situation, the costs and the resulting values of the obtaining the contract are *private*.

In contrast to the private-values setting, there may be situations in which you are uncertain of the value of the object you are bidding for, but are quite certain that whatever its eventual worth, it will be the same for all bidders. Such a situation is said to involve a **common-value**. The oil field example is a good one. The extent of the reserves (if any), how deep one needs to drill, the future price of oil, etc., all make it very hard to assign a particular value to an oil tract. However, whatever this value eventually turns out to be, it is not unreasonable to assume that it is the same for all bidders. Drilling technologies are more or less identical. The market price of crude oil will affect the value of the reserves equally for all bidders. In this case it is a good approximation to assume that the value of the object, though unknown, is *common* to all bidders.

The distinction between private and common-values is very important, as it has consequences for both the bidding behavior of the buyers and the revenues that accrue to the seller.

While the exact value of the object may be unknown to bidders in a common-value setting, it is not unreasonable to assume that they have some information about the value of the object (an **estimate**); moreover, this information is exclusive. You may have your favorite expert look at the painting being sold to give you confidence about its authenticity. You may have access to geological information about the oil field being sold, which can give you a better idea of the extent of the reserves. Naturally, it is possible that your competitors may have different sources of information. For example, let's say your rival owns an adjacent oil tract and so is reasonably sure about the value of this one, while you may have no such information. These informational advantages may be strategically exploited in an auction to scare off other bidders or modify their bidding behavior.

To summarize: in a private-values situation, bidders go into the auction knowing the exact worth of the object to themselves (that is, its **value**); in a common-value situation they go in armed only with their **estimate** of the object's value.

Private-Value Auctions

We will first look at four major types of private-value auctions: (1) the familiar open ascending-bid auction; (2) a first-price sealed-bid auction; (3) an open descending-bid auction; and (4) a second-price sealed-bid auction. Types (3) and (4) are not as common as the first two. The general rules for each type are described in the following sections.

Open Ascending-Bid (or English) Auction

The word "auction" conjures up images of a crowded room full of eager buyers bidding back and forth under the direction of a cajoling auctioneer. Typically, the auctioneer will begin by inviting buyers to bid at a relatively low level, the intention being to involve as many of the bidders as possible. As long as there are interested bidders, the price keeps rising until only one interested bidder—the winner—remains. Since this format has been used in England for a long time, it is sometimes known as an "English auction." While the general rules are familiar to all, it is worthwhile looking at some variations.

In a Japanese variation, the gradually rising price is displayed on a screen and all bidders are asked to keep pressing a button to indicate their continued interest. When the price gets too high for a particular bidder, he removes his finger from the button, indicating that he is no longer interested. Once only one active bidder remains, the auction is over. The price at which the second last bidder dropped out and the identity of the one remaining bidder, the winner, are then displayed on the screen. While the format is quite different from traditional open auctions, it is easy to see the important similarities between the two. The cajoling auctioneer has been replaced by an electronic device, but that is not important when bidders are sophisticated.

When auctioneers are present, they can sometimes play a significant role. Often, buyers who wish to remain anonymous during the bidding prearrange signals with the auctioneer ("When I scratch my left ear, it means I raise the bid by $100."). Sometimes buyers get agents to bid on their behalf in order to preserve anonymity.

To see how one might decide on a bidding strategy, it is important to once again make the distinction between a situation involving private-values versus one involving a common but unknown value among all bidders. Optimal bidding strategies can differ drastically in each case.

In a private-values setting, each bidder is sure of the value of the object to himself but uncertain about its value to competing bidders. As an example, suppose you are bidding for a piece of furniture for which the potential for resale is slim. You are prepared to pay up to $50 for this, as it catches your fancy.

Thus your private valuation for the object is $50. There is one other bidder in the room interested in this piece of furniture, but you have little idea how much he is willing to pay. How much should you bid for this item? In the context of the auction, your "bid" is the level at which you decide to drop out of the bidding as the price rises. It can be argued that it is best to bid exactly your valuation. To explore that, let's look at some hypothetical situations.

Clearly, it makes little sense to stay in the bidding once the price rises above $50. For in that case you run the risk of paying more than $50 for an object whose value to you is only $50. Can it be in your interest to drop out of the bidding at a price lower than $50? Again the answer is no. To see why, suppose you were to decide to drop out at $40. If your competitor were to drop out at $35, you would obtain the object at a price of $35 (this is important!) and you would have gained the difference between how much you value the object and what you paid for it. This difference is $15. But if you had decided to stay in until the price was $50 instead of $40, you would have won anyway and your gain would still have been $15. Next suppose your opponent were to bid more than $50. In this case you lose whether you bid $40 or $50, and it makes little difference to you. Your gain is zero in either case. The only time underbidding your true value makes a difference is when your opponent bids somewhere between $40 and $50, say he bids $45. If you bid $40, you end up losing the auction and gaining nothing. On the other hand, if you had bid $50, you would have obtained the object for $45 and ended up gaining $5.

We have just argued that it is a dominant strategy to bid your valuation. The argument is a little tricky, and it is worthwhile making sure that you understand it. The overall message is: *in an open ascending-bid auction with private-values the best strategy is to bid your true valuation.* It does not pay to bid above your private-value, as you run the risk of winning when you do not want to (that is, when the price exceeds your valuation). It does not pay to bid below your private-value, as you run the risk of not winning when you want to. Notice that bidding your true value does not mean that your expected gain is zero. Remember, in an oral auction the bidding ends when you are the only bidder left. Thus, if you win, you end up paying a price equal to the *second* highest bid. In that case, your gain is equal to the difference between your valuation and the second highest bid.

First-Price Sealed-Bid Auction

In a sealed-bid auction, interested parties are invited to bid. As the name implies, the bids remain secret until a preannounced date and are then opened simultaneously. As usual, the highest bidder is awarded the object. In a first-price sealed-bid auction, the highest bidder is asked to pay the amount he had bid for the object (we will examine an interesting variation of this later). These auctions are used almost exclusively for procurement. In that case, of course, the contract is awarded to the bidder who bids lowest and the winner receives the amount bid for the contract. Most large financial transactions (sales of securities, bond issues, etc.) carried out by auction usually employ the sealed-bid method. Once again, to analyze the bidding problem, it is useful to distinguish between private and common-values.

Let us return to the simple example given above and suppose that now the format is that of a first-price sealed-bid auction. How much should you bid if you value the object at $50? Clearly, it makes no sense to bid above $50 since you may end up getting the object for a price above the value you attach to it. Remember, in a first-price sealed-bid auction, if you win, you pay what you bid. It makes no sense to bid $50 either since if you win, your net gain is zero, and you may as well not participate. Thus, in a first-price sealed-bid auction, it makes sense to bid *below* the value you attach to the object. How much should you shade your bid? Once again, there is no dominant strategy. It depends on your estimate of your competitor's behavior. Since you are unaware of the exact value of the object to your competitor, your estimate must be probabilistic at best. ("I think my rival may bid anywhere between $35 and $60; as far as I know, any of these bids is equally likely.") In response to this, you can compute your best bid, one that maximizes the expected gain to you. (Exactly how this is done will be seen in the cases and exercises to follow.) The general rule turns out to be: *in a first-price sealed-bid auction with private-values, bid your estimate of the second highest valuation among the bidders, assuming yours is the highest.*

As you can see, the rule is not as simple as it was in the case of the open ascending-bid auction. But let us examine the rule further to see that it makes sense. Suppose that, among those bidding, you value the object most. You want to bid as low as possible and still get the object, that is, win at the lowest possible price. Since other bidders' valuations are unknown to you, the best that you can do is to bid the expected value of the second highest valuation, which is what the rule prescribes. Again while a complete argument is a little more complicated, reflecting on the rule gives an intuitive feel for its plausibility. (If you are confused by the reasoning, don't blame yourself. It is rather involved. For the time being it is sufficient to understand what the rule says. The exercises and class discussions will help to convince you further.)

While the first two auction formats described above are familiar and commonly observed in practice, the next two are special and not so common. Nevertheless, they are very helpful in increasing our understanding of the process of bidding.

Open Descending-Bid (or Dutch) Auction

In an open descending-bid auction, the auctioneer begins by calling out a very *high* price for the object—typically one that exceeds any conceivable bid by the bidders. This price is then gradually reduced until one of the bidders stops the bidding by crying out "mine." The auction is then over and the winner is asked to pay the price at which he or she stopped the auction. This format is routinely used in Holland (hence the name "Dutch auction") for the sale of fresh flowers. Auctions are regularly held in Aalsmeer, and the flowers are then flown all over the world from the nearby airport. The auctioneer has once again been replaced by a mechanical device. A giant clock is installed in the room. An initial high price is set, and as the clock ticks down the price decreases. Each bidder is provided with a switch that can stop the clock. Once the clock is stopped, the price and the identity of the winner are automatically displayed.

What bidding strategy should one use in a Dutch auction? The answer turns out to be surprisingly simple. From the point of view of the bidders, *a Dutch auction is identical to a first-price sealed-bid auction.* In a Dutch auction, a "bid" is just the level at which you decide to stop the clock. Again, the winner pays what he or she bid. So in both the private-values case and the common-value case, a Dutch descending-bid auction is identical to a first-price sealed-bid auction. It is worthwhile to be a little skeptical of this argument. Suppose you are in a common-value situation, that your estimate of the value of the object is $100 and that you decide to bid $80. As the clock winds down and you see that no one has stopped it, can you infer something about the true value?

Once the clock has reached $85, should you be tempted to revise your strategy and keep it going until $75 instead? The answer is no, but test your understanding by thinking about why this is so.

Second-Price Sealed-Bid Auction

As the name suggests, this is also a sealed-bid auction, but with an interesting twist. As before, the winner is the party who submits the highest bid; but now, instead of paying the amount he or she bid, the winner is asked to pay the amount of the *second highest* bid. As an example, suppose three bids of $35, $50, and $60 are received at such an auction. The object is awarded to the person who bid $60 but he is asked to pay only $50 for it. Although this sounds a little strange, this is exactly what happens in an open ascending-bid auction. Recall that the open auction ends when there is only one bidder left. In the example above, once the price reaches $50 (or just above $50), there would remain just one active bidder, the one prepared to remain until the price reaches $60, and he would pay $50 for the object. The second-price auction is the sealed-bid version of the open ascending-bid auction.

When values are private, the analogy between the English auction and the second-price sealed-bid auction is exact. Hence, bidding strategies in the two are also the same: *in a second-price sealed-bid auction with private-values, it is optimal to bid your valuation exactly*. The reasoning for this is the same as was given in an open ascending-bid auction and once again implies that bidding your valuation is a dominant strategy. This is because, in both cases, the price paid upon winning is independent of the winner's bid.

Common-Value Auctions

We now turn to a brief discussion of common-value auctions, in which the object being sold has the same value for all bidders.

Open Ascending-Bid (or English) Auction

While the optimal bidding strategy in an open ascending-bid auction is straightforward in a situation involving private-values ("bid your valuation"), things are not so simple once we move to a common-value situation. To see this, let us once again consider a simple example. Suppose the drilling rights to an offshore oil field are for sale. It was argued earlier that a common-value specification is appropriate here. Suppose that you have access only to publicly available information. You have seen the geological charts and seismic data, and have arrived at some estimate of the present discounted value of the oil reserves. Your competitor, however, owns an adjoining tract and so has access to more accurate information regarding the field's potential. In an open auction, it may be possible to update your estimate of the value by observing your competitor's behavior. If you see him bid beyond your original estimate, you may infer that the field is in fact more valuable than you had thought and then decide to stay in the bidding. On the other hand, your rival bidder, knowing that you are watching him, may try to mislead you by pretending that the field is not so valuable. As you can see, the strategic interaction is more subtle and involved. There is no dominant strategy, and although equilibrium bidding strategies can be derived for specific forms of the underlying uncertainty, there is no simple way to describe these. In general, these depend on the structure of information among the bidders (i.e., who knows what) and the possibilities for learning additional information during the auction. The important distinction between the private-values and common-value situations is that, in the latter, there is the possibility of learning during the auction something about the potential common-value. In the private-values case, there was nothing to be learned about the value of the object from observing a competitor's bidding behavior, as each bidder was sure of the value of the object to himself.

First-Price Sealed-Bid Auction

In a common-value situation, even though the value of the object to be sold may be the same for all bidders, bidders typically come with differing estimates of this value. The differences in their estimates may arise because of the various pieces of exclusive information they have access to, or because of their different assessments of the same publicly available information. If all bidders bid their estimates, the bidder with the most optimistic estimate will bid the highest and will win the auction. Typically, the most optimistic estimate will overestimate the *true* value of the object. Hence, the winner will find that the object is actually worth less than he had thought. This phenomenon is known as "the winner's curse." ("If you lose, you lose and if you win, you also lose.") Obviously, to avoid the winner's curse, you must bid below your estimate. Once again, no simple rule can be given in a common-value situation. The answer hinges on the exact nature of the uncertainty and the information available to the bidders. You will see examples later.

Open Descending-Bid (or Dutch) Auction

Earlier in this chapter, we argued that a Dutch auction was equivalent to a first-price sealed-bid auction. This equivalence continues to hold in a common-value situation. You should check your understanding of this by verifying that the argument given earlier did not rely on the values, being private.

Second-Price Sealed-Bid Auction

In a common-value situation, the analysis is more complicated, as always. First of all, it is *not* the case that bidding strategies in the English auction and a second-price sealed-bid auction are still the same. An English auction is open, with bids being made publicly. In a common-value situation, observing other people's bids (that is, observing when other bidders drop out of the bidding) can yield valuable information to you. In a sealed-bid auction the possibility of observing other bids does not exist, as the bids are made in secret. So what do optimal bidding strategies look like in a second-price auction? They are not unlike those in a sealed-bid first-price auction. The general rule is: *bid the expected value, conditional on your own estimate and conditional on the event that your estimate just exceeds the highest estimate among other bidders*. The rule is complicated. Let us try to make some sense of it. Because of the winner's curse, it is incorrect to bid the expected value conditional on your estimate alone. As before, one must also take into account that winning implies that yours is the highest estimate. It can be argued that optimal strategies in a second-price auction advocate more aggressive bidding than in a first-price auction. This also follows from the fact that, in a first-price auction, your bid can determine whether you win or not, while in a second-price auction the amount you pay when you win is determined by the second highest bid. This fact generally leads to higher bids in a second-price auction than in a first-price auction.

Caveat Emptor

One of the purposes of formal analysis is to help you avoid pitfalls that intuition and "gut feelings" can lead you to. For instance, it is important to understand that the purpose of bidding is *not* always to win, but only to win when it is worth your while. If the optimal bid is one where your chances of winning are only one in five, you should resist the temptation to raise the bid. If you bid higher than you should, you could end up as the accursed winner! If you win too often, you will end up losing money. Optimal strategies serve to avoid this mistake.

As always, the prescribed rules and strategies must be used with care. First, one must decide whether a private-values analysis or a common-value analysis is appropriate. In reality, some hybrid form may occur. Next, one must have a good idea of the underlying uncertainty and be able to get good probability assessments. That is asking for a lot. Usually you will develop a good understanding of the various factors as you grow familiar with the sorts of bidding situations you are involved with. The rules should not be viewed as hard and fast, but rather as guides for developing a sensible bidding strategy. Their virtue is to help you focus on the factors and considerations that are important in particular situations, where raw intuition can lead you astray. When used in this way, they are a valuable and systematic guide.

BIDDING EXERCISES

1. You are responsible for submitting a bid on an electricity generating plant that is being sold by a bank after foreclosure. You are acting on behalf of Waterfall Parks, Inc., a Florida-based company that owns and operates a number of theme and amusement parks. The generating plant will be used to provide electricity backup facilities for one of the parks. You have estimated that the net present value of the contribution from this facility to your company (energy savings less operating costs, discounted at 15%) is $800,000. You have heard that the only other bidder is a mining company from Canada. Given the disparate potential locations and uses of the facility, you have little idea how much your opponent is likely to bid. What bid would you make on behalf of Waterfall Parks? (Note: There is no uniquely correct answer to this question; just think hard what you would do in a situation like this and be prepared to defend your recommendation.)

2. Your grandmother's will ordered that her possessions be sold by auction and the proceeds divided equally among her living grandchildren. There are three grandchildren, including yourself. You are attending the auction in order to buy one of the items, a tapestry for which you have a great sentimental attachment. The auction house has appraised the tapestry at $3,600—a sum that is far in excess of the amount you would be willing to pay for it, were it not for its sentimental value.

   The auction is to be in open-ascending (English) style. Both buyer and seller must each pay 10% of the bid price to the auction house as commission. (To make this clear, if you were to win the tapestry with a bid of, say, $1,000, you would pay the seller $1,000 and the auction house $100. In addition the seller would also pay the auction house $100.)

Harvard Business School Case 9-191-133, revised October 17, 1994. These exercises were prepared by Professor David E. Bell. Copyright © 1991 by the President and Fellows of Harvard College.

To help you think about how much you would be willing to bid for the tapestry, you contemplate easier circumstances. If the tapestry were for sale in an antique store and had no sentimental value, you would be prepared to pay at most $1,000 for it. If your grandmother had sold *her* tapestry to the antique store, you would be prepared to pay at most $3,000 for it—the additional $2,000 reflecting your appraisal of its sentimental value. Of course you hope that on this item, at least, bidding will be slow. But if bidding is active for the tapestry, and assuming there are no tax implications in this situation, what is the highest bid you would be prepared to make?

3. You are to submit a sealed bid for the rights to drill for oil in a large tract of ocean off the coast of California. The owner of the tract (the U.S. government) has published geological information about the site, and experts generally agree there is a 20% chance of finding oil. In addition to purchasing the drilling rights, a buyer would have to spend approximately $10 million making exploratory drill holes in a search for oil. If oil were found, the estimated value of the tract would jump to about $150 million. (The owner would either develop the field or sell it to someone else.) If no oil is found, the drilling rights become worthless.

   There is only one other serious bidder for this tract. You have studied their past bidding tactics and have concluded that there is a 25% chance they will submit a "low" bid of about $5 million, a 50% chance they will submit a "medium" bid of $10 million, and a 25% chance they will submit a "high" bid of $15 million.

   Assuming you represent a large company to whom this is a routine decision (it has no long-term strategic implications, nor is it viewed as especially risky), what is the appropriate bid to make?

4. You are one of two architectural firms bidding for the right to design a new skyscraper in Seattle. The fee has already been fixed; it is simply a question of which of the two of you will win it. It is apparent to both of the bidding firms that the client is likely to be impressed more by a scale model than a simple design drawing. There is no limit, however, to the amount that might be spent in constructing the scale model. Clearly it would make no sense to spend more on the model than the *contribution margin* to be expected from gaining the contract; however, since the losing bidder will gain nothing, there is considerable downside to overspending on the model. Assuming that the firm that spends more on the model wins the job, and that the net profit to be made, if awarded the job, is $300,000 (less the cost of the model), how much should you spend? How does your analysis change if each of the firms gets to see the other's model as it progresses?

5. In bidding for the rights to televise the 1992 Olympic games in Barcelona, the three U.S. television networks (ABC, CBS, and NBC) each submitted sealed bids to the International Olympic Committee. On opening the envelopes and announcing the amounts of the bids, the IOC declared that the bids did not meet the IOC's minimum expectations, and invited the networks to resubmit higher and final bids in one hour (which they did).

   Presumably, if the networks had known that the IOC would conduct a second round, they might well have acted more strategically with their first bids. In particular, there would be no reason, in round 1, to submit any amount higher than necessary to establish oneself as a serious player.

Suppose then that the rules of the auction had been announced, in advance, as follows. In round 1 each of the three networks submits a sealed bid. In round 2, the two *higher* bidders are invited to submit new sealed bids, each to be higher than their round 1 bids. The highest bidder in round 2 gets to televise the games. What bidding strategy should you, representing one of the networks, use?

PORTSMOUTH PAPER COMPANY

Bernard Sheldon, one of Portsmouth Paper Company's three partners, settled down at his desk for some planning. His bid to the State of New Hampshire's Division of Purchasing and Property was due in about six weeks, on October 15, 1982, and he had not yet decided what prices Portsmouth Paper Company (PPC) would offer for the four classes of bags the state was seeking.

New Hampshire permitted the sale of hard liquor only in its 73 state-owned liquor stores, whose low prices often attracted buyers from neighboring Massachusetts as well as local residents. The state required bids every six months for the contract to supply its stores with four sizes of paper bags: the quart liquor size ($4\frac{1}{2}''$ x $16\frac{1}{4}''$, with a $2\frac{1}{2}''$ tuck); 10-lb. heavy-duty grocery bags ($6\frac{1}{2}''$ x 13-5/16″, with a 4-1/6″ tuck); 20-lb. heavy-duty grocery bags (8-3/16″ x 16″, with a $5\frac{1}{4}''$ tuck); and 1/8 barrel sacks ($10\frac{1}{4}''$ x 14″, with a $6\frac{1}{4}''$ tuck). PPC and its competitor had to provide a price per thousand for each of the four bag sizes. The New Hampshire Division of Purchasing and Property indicated in its request for bids just how many bundles of each type of bag would be required, and how many of each size bag were to be packaged in a bundle. The Division determined its supplier by adding up the full cost of the contract as bid by each potential supplier, and awarding the contract to the overall low bidder.

The Division required that bidders submit samples of their products. Prices were F.O.B. locations listed in the proposal, namely the 73 liquor stores situated throughout the state. The vendor was obligated to meet a monthly shipping schedule which reached him at the beginning of each month. The date of delivery was about the fifteenth of the month; following each delivery, the vendor would invoice the State Liquor Commission.

Portsmouth Paper Company Background

Portsmouth Paper Company was one of New England's largest distributors of paper and plastic packaging materials, custodial supplies, and maintenance equipment. The company bought materials from more than 40 manufacturers and made them available to factories, businesses, hospitals, and government facilities. Packaging and wrapping materials, including tapes, accounted for about half of a typical year's business, while office products represented another 10%. Materials and tools for cleaning and maintenance accounted for a further 10%, and another 20% of PPC's business was food-related (paper plates, cups, napkins, and the like).

In 1981, about 2% of PPC's sales had come from contracts, like the one for the New Hampshire liquor stores, which were awarded on the basis of competitive bids.

Harvard Business School case 9-183-086. This case was prepared by Professor William Krasker.
Copyright © 1982 by the President and Fellows of Harvard College.

Portsmouth Paper's Costs

Bernard Sheldon began his deliberations about the size of his bid by determining how much it would cost PPC to provide the required bags. Table 5.1 shows the number of bundles of each type of bag specified in the contract, the number of bags per bundle, the total bags, and PPC's cost per thousand bags.

Table 5.1

Bag Type	Number of Bundles	Bags per Bundle (000)	Total Bags (000)	PPC cost (per 000)
Quart liquor bags	2,193	3	6,579	$7.83
10-lb. heavy-duty grocery bags	3,321	1	3,321	$11.81
20-lb. heavy-duty grocery bags	2,919	0.5	1,459.5	$17.07
1/8-barrel sacks	2,500	0.5	1,250	$16.22

From this table, Mr. Sheldon determined that PPC's cost for the full contract would be $135,923.

Additional costs, beyond the cost of goods sold, also had to be considered. In order to meet the specifications of the contract, Portsmouth Paper would have to maintain a substantial inventory of all four types of bags. Mr. Sheldon estimated that PPC would have to keep an additional $25,000 worth of inventory during the six months of the contract. There would be no significant increase in labor, administrative, or clerical costs. However, there would be some minor additional trucking costs: in a few instances PPC would have to send its fleet to areas of the state where it currently had no need to travel. The route extensions, Mr. Sheldon estimated, would cost PPC a total of about $600.

Mr. Sheldon decided that he would apply an 8% discount rate to the cash flows associated with this contract. In 1982, PPC faced a tax rate of 46%.

Assessing the Distribution for the Competitor's Bid

Mr. Sheldon next thought about the possible bids his competitor could make. He compared his estimated costs with the size of the winning bid for several previous contracts similar in type to this one. As a result of this analysis, Mr. Sheldon decided that his competitor's bid was as likely to be above $160,000 as below. Having determined the median of the distribution for his competitor's bid, Mr. Sheldon proceeded to evaluate other bids against that median.

There was only a 0.25 probability, he thought, that his competitor's bid would be lower than 97% of the median. On the other side, he felt there was a 0.75 probability that his competitor's bid would be less than 103% of the median. His competitor's bid was almost certain to lie between 91% and 111% of the median. Using these assessments, Mr. Sheldon felt that he could choose an appropriate bid for Portsmouth Paper Company to present.

▼   ▼   ▼

THE SS *KUNIANG*

On April 9, 1981 the SS *Kuniang* ran aground off the Florida coast during unseasonably severe weather conditions. Captain McIver of the Pennsylvania Shipping Company telephoned Ed Brown, Chairman and CEO of the New England Electric System, suggesting that they turn this unfortunate accident to their mutual advantage.

The British owners of the *Kuniang* intended to declare the vessel a total loss. This meant that New England Electric System and Pennsylvania Shipping might have an opportunity to acquire the ship, repair it, and then use it to haul coal.

The management of New England Electric System had been wrestling for some time with how to transport coal to their generating plants. New England Electric and Pennsylvania Shipping Company had recently entered into a joint venture to have General Dynamics construct and operate a self-unloading collier with a capacity of 36,250 tons—a ship they all referred to as the GD-I. McIver was proposing a similar type of joint venture for the *Kuniang*.

New England Electric System

New England Electric System (NEES) was a public utility holding company that owned four electric operating subsidiaries: Massachusetts Electric Company, serving 750,000 customers in Massachusetts; Narragansett Electric Company, serving 265,000 customers in Rhode Island; Granite State Electric Company, serving 25,000 customers in New Hampshire; and New England Power Company (the generating subsidiary). In addition, NEES owned a service subsidiary, New England Power Service Company, and a fuel exploration company, New England Energy Incorporated.

As an aftermath of the energy price shocks of the early 1970s, New England Electric's long-range plan incorporated the goals of reducing dependence on foreign oil and diversifying the fuel mix for the system's generating plants. NEES sought to achieve an energy mix of 39% coal; 25% nuclear; 18% domestic oil; 10% imported oil; and 8% hydro, wind power, and other alternatives. This plan called for the conversion of more than half of the utility's oil-fired capacity to coal. After full conversion, NEES plants would require 4 million tons of coal each year: 3.0 million tons at Brayton Point, Massachusetts; 0.75 million tons at Salem Harbor, Massachusetts; and 0.25 million tons at the Providence, Rhode Island generating plants.

The New England Power Service Company (NEP) subsidiary of NEES had been given responsibility for the annual transportation of the 4 million tons of coal. As the company had no experience in shipping, they had entered into the joint venture with the Pennsylvania Shipping Company.

Transportation

Existing Arrangements

The GD-I was being built by General Dynamics Ship Building Division, in Quincy, Massachusetts. The vessel, the first coal-fired transport ship to be ordered in 25 years, would carry 2.25 million tons of coal per year from Virginia to Brayton Point, Massachusetts. Delivery of the vessel was set for April 1, 1983.

Harvard Business School case 9-190-014, revised August 2, 1994. This case was prepared by Professor David E. Bell. Copyright © 1989 by the President and Fellows of Harvard College.

Current requirements for coal were being met by the vessel *Marine Electric*, which had been chartered by NEP from the beginning of 1981 until April 1982. Beyond that, NEP had the option of continuing with the charter indefinitely. In addition to the *Marine Electric*, a consecutive-voyage charter had been signed with Universal American Barge Corporation (UABC) to provide any further coal-carrying capacity that might be required. The UABC charter was split into two phases, determined by the date the GD-I became available. Once the GD-I began operation, the UABC charter could be terminated or could carry the remaining tonnage not carried by GD-I.

Options Under Consideration

The following options had been singled out by NEES for active consideration:

Null Option   Continue to charter ships with UABC (or on the open market) for all coal not carried by the GD-I.

GD-II   Order a second ship from General Dynamics. Under the terms of the shipbuilding contract, General Dynamics was obligated to offer a series production right to build a second ship. This new ship would be available six months after GD-I. After accounting for inflation, the cost would be essentially the same as the sister ship ($70 million) and would have the same freight capacity (36,250 tons of coal).

This provided NEES with more capacity than needed, but there was a virtually guaranteed demand for the excess. Two principal classes of customer were (i) other utilities requiring coal haulage and (ii) the U.S. government for grain transportation. This latter business was derived from Public Law 480, by which American grain was donated to Third World countries. NEES was confident that there would be enough demand from both of these sources to ensure that any additional capacity would be kept occupied. As a result, Ed Brown's analysts had estimated that the GD-II option would provide NEES with a net benefit of $2.1 million in present value over the null option.

SS Kuniang   Bid for the SS *Kuniang*. In addition to the cost of the bid, NEES, if it won the bidding, would have to pay for repairs to the *Kuniang* to make it seaworthy once more. These were estimated to cost $15 million.

The *Kuniang*, however, had a potentially significant drawback. Under the Jones Act of 1920, only American-built, American-owned, and American-operated ships could trade between two U.S. ports (coastal trade). But the SS *Kuniang* was not American built, and NEES would need the ship primarily for U.S. coastal trade. Nonetheless, there was a possible resolution to this potential problem. A long overlooked law (U.S. Code Title 46, Section 14, enacted December 23, 1852) permitted a foreign-built ship to be regarded as American for the purposes of the Jones Act if (i) the previous owners declared the ship a total loss (which the owners of the *Kuniang* were going to do) and (ii) the cost of repairs was at least three times the salvage value of the ship.

This latter provision created a dilemma. The U.S. Coast Guard was responsible for determining the salvage value of the ship. Since there were no rules governing salvage values and few precedents to guide them, it was not clear if they would base their assessment on the ship's scrap value, its auctioned price, or on some other basis. The Coast Guard was not going to rule on this matter until after the sealed-bid auction of the *Kuniang*. A decision on this question would obviously affect its value.

Acquiring the *Kuniang* would present another decision. The *Kuniang* had no self-unloading capability. The installation of a self-unloader would greatly reduce the time the *Kuniang* would need to unload, and therefore effectively increase the yearly capacity of the ship. It was possible to install a self-unloading capability into the *Kuniang*. This could be done at any time for a cost of $21 million. At a total repair cost of $36 million, the *Kuniang* would then easily qualify as a Jones Act vessel, given any conceivable Coast Guard valuation.

If NEES won the *Kuniang* in bidding, its estimated present value without a self-unloader was estimated to be $41.75 million higher than the null option. This figure did not include repair costs or the amount of the bid. With a self-unloader, the present value of the *Kuniang* was estimated to be $46 million, not including repair, self-unloader, and bid amount.

What to Do?

Ed Brown valued Pennsylvania's many years of experience in the shipping business and was encouraged by their enthusiasm for the *Kuniang* alternative. However, it was not clear what to bid for the *Kuniang*, much less whether to bid at all.

Bidding for the SS *Kuniang*

Captain McIver of Pennsylvania Shipping Company had recommended a bid of $3 million, the value of the *Kuniang* as scrap. But Ed Brown was concerned that other companies, including other utilities, might enter the bidding and raise the price needed to win. Since the auction was by sealed bid,[3] NEES would not know the identity of the bidders until the envelopes were opened. Brown was sure that NEES could win the *Kuniang* with a bid of $10 million, but such a bid could make conversion under the Jones Act very expensive since NEES would have to find ways to *increase* the cost of repairs.[4] At the same time he thought it very unlikely that the ship could be had for $3 million. Brown assessed the chances of NEES' winning with various bids as shown in Table 5.2.

Table 5.2

NEES Bid	Chance of Winning
$3 million	0.05
$4 million	0.15
$5 million	0.25
$6 million	0.40
$7 million	0.55
$8 million	0.70
$9 million	0.85
$10 million	1

The viability of the *Kuniang* would depend on the price for which it could be purchased at the auction and on the Coast Guard's appraisal of its salvage value for the purposes of the Jones Act. Brown thought the odds were against the Coast Guards' valuing the *Kuniang* at its scrap value, estimating this probability at around 30%. Brown also felt that if the Coast Guard did not value the *Kuniang* at scrap, they would value it at the winning bid price. This all served to complicate the question of whether and how much NEES should bid on the *Kuniang*.

▼   ▼   ▼

---

[3] In a sealed-bid auction, bidders write the amount they are prepared to bid in separate envelopes that are submitted individually but opened by the seller at an agreed time. The highest bid is accepted.

[4] For example, if the Coast Guard valued the ship at the bid amount, rather than at scrap, and if NEES won with a bid of $10 million, repair costs would have to be at least $30 million.

MAXCO, INC. AND THE GAMBIT COMPANY

Background

Maxco, Inc. and the Gambit Company were fully integrated, major oil companies—each with annual sales over $1 billion and exploration and development budgets over $100 million. Both firms were preparing sealed bids for an oil rights lease on block A-512 off the Louisiana Gulf coast. Although the deadline for the submission of bids was only three weeks away, neither firm was very close to a final determination of its bid. Indeed, management at Maxco had yet to decide whether to bid at all, let alone how much to bid. Although Gambit was virtually certain to submit a bid, the level of Gambit's bid was far from settled. This uncharacteristic hesitancy in the preparation of both firms' bids was a direct result of certain peculiarities in the situation surrounding the bidding for block A-512.

Block A-512 lay in the Alligator Reef area immediately to the south of a known oil-producing region (see Exhibit 1). Just to the north were blocks A-497 and A-498, both of which were already under lease to the Gambit Company. On its leasehold Gambit had two completed wells that had been in production for some time. In addition Gambit had an offset control well in progress near the boundary between its leasehold and block A-512. When this well was completed, Gambit would have access to direct information concerning the value of any oil reserves lying beneath block A-512. Maxco's nearest leasehold, on the other hand, was some seven miles to the southeast. Therefore, any bid submitted by Maxco would necessarily be based solely on indirect information.

The Role of Information in Bidding for Oil Rights Leases

In any bidding situation, information concerning either the object of the bidding or the notions of competing bidders is highly prized. This is especially true in bidding for the rights to oil reserves lying perhaps thousands of feet below the surface. There are, of course, various kinds of information available to bidders for oil rights. Such information falls into one of two categories: direct or indirect.

Information obtained by drilling on a parcel of land is called **direct information**. Obviously this is the most precise information that can be obtained about the subsurface structure. From core samples taken up during the drilling operation, and from careful laboratory analysis of these samples, considerable information may be accumulated—not only about the presence or absence of oil, but also about the type, thickness, composition, and physical properties of each of the various geological strata encountered. Such information then provides the driller with a relatively accurate estimate of the oil reserves lying beneath the parcel. Direct information concerning adjacent parcels may be obtained by drilling offset control wells. (Offset control wells are offset from the principal producing areas, but adjacent to the boundaries of the leased parcel. Such wells may provide precise and valuable information about the leased parcel.)

Harvard Business School case 9-174-091, revised April 1, 1994. This case was prepared by Research Associate Donald L. Wallace under the supervision of Professor John S. Hammond. It was developed from a study by Professor Donald H. Woods, Georgia State University. Copyright © 1974 by the President and Fellows of Harvard College.

Indirect information is obtained from sources other than drilling and may be roughly divided into two kinds: scouting and nonscouting. **Scouting information** is gained by observing the operations of other drillers. By counting the sections of drill pipe—each of known length—introduced into a hole, an observer may infer the depth of the hole. By observing the quantity of cement (required by law) used to plug the various porous strata that are encountered, the thicknesses of these strata may be determined. Normally, however, this type of scouting information does not yield nearly the precision available to the driller himself. It can help to determine whether or not oil reserves exist at a particular location, but it is much less useful in determining the size of the reserves.

More definite scouting information may sometimes be obtained by more clandestine means. Eavesdropping on conversations in public places, subtle forms of bribery and interrogation, even forcible entry onto a competitor's drilling site may provide much more detailed—and more valuable—information. An extreme anecdote tells of two men caught while inspecting a competitor's drilling log, the source document of a driller's direct information. The men were reportedly held at gunpoint for several days in anticipation of the approaching deadline for the submission of bids. Managing to escape the day before the deadline, the two men were able to report back what they had seen in the log. As a result, the operator whose log had been compromised was forced to raise his bid by $7 million.

Less melodramatic, but highly significant, sources of indirect information are available through means other than scouting. **Nonscouting information** is obtained, first, from published sources such as government geological and geophysical surveys, and reports of previous explorations. Second, nonscouting information may be obtained from local seismic surveys conducted by either in-house personnel or private contractors. A third source of nonscouting information is found in the trading of dry hole information. Drilling operators have a tradition of sharing their dry hole experiences. The feeling seems to be that there is far more to be gained from the reciprocal exchange of dry hole information than can be gained from watching a competitor pour a considerable investment into a site that is known to be barren. Finally, nonscouting information may also be obtained from independent prospectors, promoters, and traders who may have become familiar with certain tracts in the past and are willing to trade this information, again on a reciprocal basis.

As might be suspected in an environment where information has such a high (and immediate) value, internal security presents a clear and ever-present problem. Bank-type vaults, armed guards, and electrified fences are commonplace. On occasion, entire drilling rigs have been encased in canvas to thwart the efforts of prying eyes. (This can create substantial slowdowns in operations, however, as well as almost unbearable working conditions.) A blanket of security must also be placed over the derivation and submission of bids: information on the level of a particular bid can be even more valuable than information on the value of reserves. When bids were being prepared for the tracts surrounding Prudhoe Bay on Alaska's North Slope, one company packed its entire bidding organization onto a railroad train and ran it back and forth over the same stretch of track until bids had been prepared and submitted and the bidding deadline had passed!

Finally, because information is such a prime concern, bidding parties often attempt to circulate false information. If an operator is successful in leaking false negative information about a particular parcel, he may be able to later "steal" the parcel with a relatively low bid. Or, to divert attention from a particular parcel, an operator may feign interest in another one by seeming to conduct tests there.

Maxco's Bidding Problem

Mr. E.P. Buchanan, Vice President for Exploration and Development, had primary responsibility for preparing Maxco's bid. As indicated previously, Mr. Buchanan's information about block A-512 was indirect in nature. Although some scouting information on Gambit's offset control well was available to him, the primary basis of his information was a private seismic survey, together with published government geological maps and reports. Maxco had acquired the survey data, in a jointly financed effort with Gambit, through the use of a private contractor. The contractor, Noble and Stevens, had prepared a detailed survey of the entire Alligator Reef area several years earlier when blocks A-497 and A-498 had been up for bid. Under the joint financing arrangement, identical copies of the completed report had been submitted to both Maxco and Gambit. Such an arrangement, while unusual, was not without precedent in known oil-producing areas. Exhibit 1 represents an updated version of a subsurface map included in Noble and Stevens' report.

Based on all the information available to him, Mr. Buchanan's judgment concerning the monetary value of the oil reserves under block A-512 was essentially captured by the probability mass function given in Exhibit 2. Furthermore, Mr. Buchanan held that Maxco's bid should be based solely on this monetary value of the oil reserves. Since it was known that no nearby blocks were to be put up for bid for at least 10 years, Mr. Buchanan did not ascribe any informational value to owning a lease on block A-512.

Mr. Buchanan also felt—for the present at least—that Gambit's uncertainty was virtually identical to his own. He was sure, however, that Gambit's offset control well would be completed by the deadline for the submission of bids. At that time Gambit would know the value of the reserves, up to perhaps ±5% or ±10%.

For the past several years, Mr. Buchanan had refused to bid on any parcels of land where he felt he was at a distinct disadvantage to a competing bidder. If a competitor had superior (direct) information about a parcel while Maxco had only indirect information, then Mr. Buchanan preferred not to bid at all.

However, less than five months ago, in an area not far from Alligator Reef, Mr. Buchanan had *lost* a bid on a block adjacent to a Maxco leasehold. Maxco had gone to the expense of drilling an offset control well on its own block and had found a reasonably large oil reserve. Maxco had then lost the bid, however, to a competitor who was operating solely on the basis of indirect information. In addition, the competitor's winning bid had still been low enough to provide a substantial profit on the venture.

Thus Mr. Buchanan was considering a change in his policy. While he very much doubted that anyone else would enter the bidding for block A-512, he was beginning to feel that he himself should do so. If he did decide to bid, he needed to determine what sort of bid might be reasonable.

Gambit's Bidding Problem

Mr. Buchanan's counterpart in the Gambit Company was a Mr. K.R. Mason, who had primary responsibility for preparing Gambit's bid. Until Gambit's well on the Alligator Reef leasehold was completed, Mr. Mason's information concerning block A-512 would be indirect in nature. The primary basis of that information was still the private seismic survey (for which Gambit had contracted jointly with Maxco), together with published government geological maps and reports.

Although Mr. Mason also had detailed production logs on the two producing wells on Gambit's leasehold, he felt that this information was not relevant to the problem of assessing the potential value of block A-512. There was almost certainly some cross-faulting in the Alligator Reef area (see Exhibit 1). Since this cross-faulting would probably terminate the producing area, the principal uncertainty surrounding the value of block A-512 was the precise location of the northernmost cross-fault. Thus, Mr. Mason's judgment was also essentially captured by the probability mass function given in Exhibit 2. Although Mr. Mason's judgment certainty did not coincide precisely with Mr. Buchanan's, the facts available to the two men and the economics in the two companies were largely similar. Therefore, neither man's estimate of the situation differed significantly from Exhibit 2.

This would, of course, change dramatically when Gambit's offset control well was completed. At that time Mr. Mason would be able to reevaluate the property with a much higher degree of precision.

Normally Mr. Mason would then be in a position to submit a bid relatively close to the true value of the block, while still allowing a generous margin for profit. Other bidders, not knowing the true value of the block, would be unable to adopt such a strategy. If they bid at all, they would have to either bid relatively low or risk the possibility of "buying in high" to a disastrously unprofitable situation.

Over the past year, however, several operators in the Louisiana Gulf Coast had narrowly lost out when bidding for blocks on which they had direct information. Granted that in no case were extremely large reserves lost; nevertheless, operators bidding with nothing but indirect information had been able to "steal away" substantial reserves from operators who were basing their bids on direct information.

With a view toward reassessing his approach to this kind of situation, Mr. Mason thought that it might be useful to prepare a whole schedule of bids. For each possible "true value" of the reserves, Mr. Mason felt that he should be able to establish an appropriate bid—given that value of the reserves. Thus, Mr. Mason felt that he ought to be able to complete a bid schedule similar to that given in Exhibit 3. He was wondering, however, what a reasonable schedule of bids might be like.

Exhibit 1 _____

SUBSURFACE MAP OF THE ALLIGATOR REEF AREA

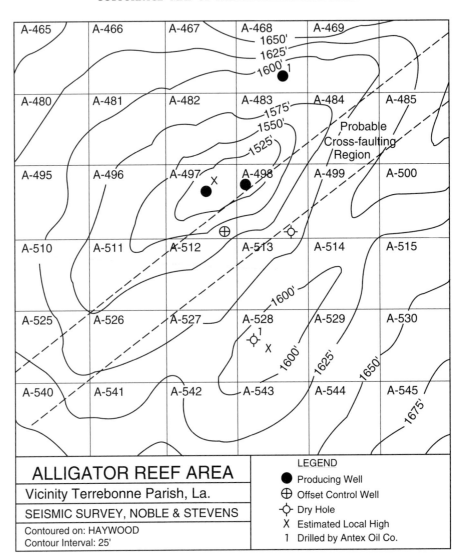

ALLIGATOR REEF AREA

Vicinity Terrebonne Parish, La.

SEISMIC SURVEY, NOBLE & STEVENS

Contoured on: HAYWOOD
Contour Interval: 25'

LEGEND
● Producing Well
⊕ Offset Control Well
⋄ Dry Hole
X Estimated Local High
1 Drilled by Antex Oil Co.

Exhibit 2 _____

PROBABILITY DISTRIBUTION OF MONETARY VALUES

Monetary Value of Oil Reserves* ($ millions)	Probability
$1.7	0.03
2.7	0.06
3.7	0.10
4.7	0.17
5.7	0.28
6.7	0.18
7.7	0.08
8.7	0.04
9.7	0.02
10.7	0.01
11.7	0.01
12.7	0.01
13.7	0.01
	1.00

Mean Value = $5.83 million
*Net Present Value at 10%

Exhibit 3 _____

GAMBIT'S BID SCHEDULE

If the true value of the reserves is:	Then Gambit's bid should be:
$1.7 million	$____million
$2.7 million	$____million
$3.7 million	$____million
$4.7 million	$____million
$5.7 million	$____million
$6.7 million	$____ million
$7.7 million	$____million
$8.7 million	$____million
$9.7 million	$____million
$10.7 million	$____million
$11.7 million	$____million
$12.7 million	$____million
$13.7 million	$____million

▼   ▼   ▼

RCA TRANSPONDER AUCTION (A)

On November 9, 1981, Sotheby Park Bernet held one of the most unusual auctions in its history. On sale were not Cezannes but satellite transponders—each worth in excess of $10 million. The concept was as radical for the communications industry as it was for Sotheby's.

Orbiting communication satellites have revolutionized personal and business communications, as well as other fields such as meteorology and broadcasting. The satellites are owned by a number of companies, including RCA, Hughes Aircraft, Western Union, Comsat, Satellite Business Systems, and others. In one particularly lucrative application, the satellites are widely used to transmit cable TV programming.

Each satellite contains a number of separate **transponders**—packets of circuitry, not much larger than a cigarette carton, that receive radio signals from ground stations, amplify them, and beam them down to receiving dishes scattered around the country. In recent years, the lease and sale of these transponders has become a large business.

In order for a cable operator to receive signals, it must install a dish costing $25,000 to point at the satellite. Once in place, the dish can receive programming from all the transponders on the satellite, but monitoring another satellite requires a separate dish aimed at that satellite. Understandably, then, some satellites have more sought after locations than others. The most popular was RCA's Satcom III-R, launched in 1981. A strong programming line-up meant that many dishes were pointed at the bird, which in turn made other programmers eager to get on board. Satcom III-R featured Home Box Office, Showtime, Spotlight, Ted Turner's Cable News Network, and Getty Oil's Entertainment and Sports Network. In total, 90% of the country's 27 million cable TV households received programming from the satellite.

Unfortunately, RCA and other satellite owners could not charge nearly as much as the market would bear—because they had been licensed by the FCC as "common carriers," entitled only to a regulated fee for its services, like a railroad or trucker.

Hughes Aircraft, however, changed the rules of the game. Clay Whitehead, a former special assistant to Nixon, later director for the U.S. Office of Telecommunications Policy, and then president of a Hughes subsidiary, convinced the FCC to go along with a creative redefinition of the industry. Instead of leasing transponder space, he would *sell* the transponders to customers. Hughes quickly signed up a stellar cast for its first satellite, Galaxy I.

In the wake of the Hughes decision, RCA and Western—although still classed as common carriers—were allowed by the FCC to sell their leases for whatever the traffic would bear, provided that they did so in a "nondiscriminatory" way. And so RCA found itself as the seller in an auction at Sotheby's. Exhibit 1, the text of an article from the *New York Times* of November 10, 1981, tells what happened.

Exhibit 1

New York Times   November 10, 1981

Sotheby's Satellite Auction

By Eric Pace

In a hushed Sotheby Park Bernet auction hall, as tense cable television executives signaled with paddles, a sale of communications satellite facilities for their booming industry brought $90.1 million in winning bids yesterday.

The high total, a record for a Sotheby auction, reflected keen competition for use of the facilities, which are to be carried by an RCA satellite to be launched on Jan. 12.

Auctioned off, at Sotheby's York Avenue galleries, were seven-year leases for seven devices called transponders, which are used for relaying signals from the earth's surface back down to earth and, indirectly, to television screens and other recipients. Demand for transponders is intense, largely because cable television programming has been proliferating.

The seven high bidders at the auction, the first of its kind, included such prominent cable television programming companies as Home Box Office, a Time Inc. unit, which won a lease for $12.5 million, and the Warner Amex Satellite Entertainment Company, which got one for $13.7 million.

The highest bidder, whose lease cost $14.4 million, was identified as the "Transponder Leasing Company, c/o Satellite Systems Corporation." An RCA spokesman said he had no knowledge of the corporation, but an executive of D.H. Blair & Company, the investment banking firm, which has ties to satellite systems, said he understood the auctioneer, John L. Marion, Sotheby's president, said smilingly after the auction, "At those prices, it would be terrific to have these people come back again."

His organization's previous record total for a single auction sale was $34 million for art work collected by Robert von Hirsch, at Sotheby in London in June 1978. The previous record bid for a single item was $6.6 million, for a pair of large diamond earrings sold in Geneva late last year. A Turner painting sold by Sotheby in New York last year brought in $6.4 million, its record for a single art work.

Fifty companies and individuals took up Sotheby's black-and-white bidding paddles to participate, despite the fact that the Federal Communications Commission has not ruled whether the auction is permissible—and despite a legal challenge to the proceedings that was lodged last week by a major cable television programming company.

A further question mark over the outcome is the ability of some of the seven winning bidders to pay. RCA did not check the participants' financial standing before the auction, and an RCA spokesman said the company had no details about another winner, identified as UTV Cable Network, in addition to Transponder Leasing. He said it was assumed that both "would represent cable programming interests."

Transponder Leasing placed the winning bid for the first lease offered. The six subsequent winners, and the prices they bid, were, in chronological order: Billy H.Batts, identified by RCA as affiliated with Faith Broadcasting, a Protestant Evangelical group, $14.1 million; Warner Amex, which lodged last week's challenge, $13.7 million; RCTV, a pay cable television channel formed recently by Rockefeller Center and RCA, $13.5 million; Home Box Office, $12.5 million; the Inner City Broadcasting Corporation, $10.7 million, and UTV Cable, $11.2 million.

The winners will be required now to demonstrate their financial capability, RCA executives said, but they will not have to pay until late in January. The FCC has until Jan. 15 to disallow the auction if it decides to do so.

Andrew F. Inglis, president of RCA American Communications Inc., the RCA subsidiary that owns the satellite and is selling the leases, said the $90.1 million total was about $20 million more than RCA Americom, as his company is known, stood to take in under a previously announced schedule of rates, payable over time, which it hopes to supersede with the auction prices.

Referring to Transponder Leasing and UTV Cable, John S. Reidy, media analyst with Drexel Burnham Lambert, said after the auction that "the two mystery bidders" are "in a good position now to raise money, via either debt or equity," to pay for their leases, since demand for leases is so high.

And he added that, "if the auction is upheld by the FCC, RCA Americom is the beneficiary of the value imputed to transponders above and beyond" the earlier announced prices. "Previously, that value often went to middlemen leasing out transponders they had acquired."

Heavy Demand Underscored

The lively interest in the auction, said J. Kendrick Noble, an analyst at Paine Webber Mitchell Hutchins, "underscores the heavy demand for transponders; there's a shortage right now, and demand will continue to rise." But he added that the shortage might ease in the three years after additional satellites are sent into the skies.

An RCA Americom spokesman reported that only four or five other satellites were now being used to relay signals for the cable television industry. The winning bidders have to "demonstrate their financial capability," he said, but they do not need to pay the money until after the satellite is launched.

Weeks ago, RCA Americom informed the FCC of its plans for the auctions, but the commission has not said whether it approves of this form of sale and of the sale's complex ground rules. Commission sources recently declined to predict when the FCC might take a position on the matter, but they emphasized that the agency still had the option of, in effect, declaring the auction null and void—as long as it acts before Jan. 15.

The legal challenge to yesterday's proceedings was lodged last week by Warner Amex Satellite Entertainment, known as Wasec, which is a 50-50 joint venture of Warner Communications Inc. and the American Express Company. It owns three cable television programming services: the Movie Channel, Nickelodeon, and Music Television.

Illegal Action Charged

Wasec filed a complaint with the FCC, contending that RCA Americom had acted illegally in putting one of the seven transponders, known as transponder 11, up for auction. All told, there are to be 24 on board the satellite, each roughly the size of a cigarette carton. Executives of Wasec argued that RCA Americom had previously, through a body of correspondence, promised transponder 11 to their company.

Theodore D. Kramer, acting chief of the FCC's enforcement division, said, in an interview last week, that RCA Americom had until Dec. 1 to respond to Wasec's contentions. The commission is to rule on the complaint after that.

Essentially, a transponder is an electronic package that receives a signal from a ground facility known as an uplink earth station, amplifies it, shifts the frequency, and redirects it back down to earth.

The RCA Americom spokesman said that to build and launch a satellite of the Satcom IV type required an investment of about $65 million.

LIST OF WINNING BIDS

Transponder	Bid
2	14,400,000
3	14,100,000
4	13,700,000
11	13,500,000
15	12,500,000
16	10,700,000
23	11,200,000

▼   ▼   ▼

CONTRACTS AND INCENTIVES

Lawyers were one of the first professional groups to use decision trees, because the method is helpful when considering what to do in case of various eventualities. One law firm devised a decision tree for a certain proceeding, tacked it on the wall, and consulted it regularly over the next two years of the suit! A decision tree is also useful in thinking through the nature of a contract between two parties. Instead of fighting a lawsuit later, why not agree at the outset how potential contingencies are to be treated? The cases in this chapter will teach you the kinds of thinking needed to be successful in this process.

CONTRACTS AND INCENTIVES

Two people may fully intend to cooperate in a venture, but the association may flounder if the incentives of each are different. Sometimes, but not always, a legal contract can correct this problem. Here we review some of the problems, discuss some guidelines for their solution, and establish some terminology.

Incentive Compatibility

Rule: Each party should have the incentive to act in the interest of the group as a whole.

Two partners in an entrepreneurial business venture each do a lot of traveling between Boston and Chicago. Each partner would, as an individual, be prepared to pay up to $100 for the privilege of flying first class rather than coach. The actual premium is $150 and so each "should" fly coach. But, as partners in the business venture, and thus sharing all costs equally, a decision by either of them to fly first class has an effective cost to themselves of only $75, since the non-flying partner will also be paying $75. If the partners fly together, this incentive problem becomes readily apparent. If only one partner does all the flying, this distortion of incentives may be disguised. One solution to this problem that corrects the incentives is for the partners to agree that the partnership will reimburse the flier only for coach fare. Any premium must be paid individually.

The lack of incentive compatibility is a widespread problem that can rarely be solved effectively. Employees have little financial incentive to save energy in the workplace or to be conservative in their use of the copying machine.

A fairly simply system exists to check for a lack of incentive compatibility: simply express the joint problem as a decision tree.

Rule: In a decision tree all parties should agree on the preferred alternative at each decision point (including contingent decisions) and each party should agree on the preferred outcome of each uncertainty.

The need to agree on all decisions is clear, since otherwise conflict can arise. The need to agree on the outcome of uncertainties stems from the ability, in practice, for people to influence the outcome of uncertainties by suitable direction of their effort. If the decision tree does not satisfy this condition, the contract should be rewritten with contingent side payments so as to create incentive compatibility.

Asymmetries

One difficulty to be surmounted in multiple-party agreements is that people may have different beliefs and preferences about the problem at hand.

As a simple example, suppose you and I are siblings who have been left $1,000 cash and an oil painting by a recently deceased uncle. The oil painting was painted by the uncle when he was a young man and has little or no market value. His will expresses the desire that we split his estate "equally." How should we do this?

Let us suppose that you are very sentimental and would enjoy hanging the oil painting in your home whereas I would, at best, hide it in the attic. The noble thing to do would be for me to let you have the painting and then for us to split the cash equally. But I might propose that a fair way to divide the estate is to let you pick either the painting or the $1,000. If you pick the painting, it must be because you value it at least as much as the cash, so you are getting at least half of the estate. Of course you may argue that since I find the painting worthless, I have, in effect, received the entire value of the estate. In solving problems like this, two guiding principles are:

▸ The negotiating procedure should induce honesty (or non-strategic behavior) in the parties involved.

▸ The negotiated solution should maximize the total value received by all parties. It is clear that I should not end up with the oil painting (which I might if we draw lots, or if I lie about its value to me).

Asymmetries can also occur if two people disagree on the likelihood of certain events (i.e., if I think an event is quite likely to happen and you don't) or if one person is more risk-averse than the other.

The following examples illustrate typical incentive problems. It is difficult to solve them precisely. They are presented to promote discussion.

1. You have seen some houses for sale that you like. They vary in price. In order to decide how much you can afford, you need a fair estimate of the value of your current home. You cannot wait until you sell your current house before selecting another house because the one you want may disappear in the interim. The local realtor will charge you a commission for selling your current house equal to 6% of its sale price. You must rely on the realtor for a fair estimate of your home's worth.

    a. Is it in the realtor's interest to tell you what the house is worth?

    b. Suppose the commission is charged as follows:

      (i)   The realtor provides an estimate, E thousand dollars, the house's worth.

      (ii)   The realtor sells the house for S thousand dollars

      (iii) The realtor's commission is $E(S-\tfrac{1}{2}E)$.

For example, if the realtor estimates \$120,000 and the sale price is \$100,000 the commission will be:

$$120(100 - 60) = \$4{,}800 \ .$$

What are the advantages and disadvantages of this commission arrangement?

2.   The CEO of a company is trying to decide whether to spend \$10 million on a new computer networking system to bring the company into the 1990s. The CEO is 64 years old, has never touched a computer in his life, and doesn't really understand the extent of the benefits that computing power can bring. The company's two major divisions are headed by Alice and Bernard. It is generally agreed that Alice's division stands to benefit from the computer system more than Bernard's, and so the question has arisen of how the expense of the computer system will be charged to the divisions. Alice and Bernard both receive bonuses that are tied closely to divisional performance. Alice has little idea what the system is worth to Bernard, and Bernard has little idea what the system is worth to Alice. The CEO has little idea about the value to either.

Devise a procedure for deciding whether the computer system should be bought and how it should be charged to the divisions.

3.   The CEO of a company is reflecting on appropriate bonuses to be paid to key employees for the calendar year just ending and the level of salary increases for the coming year. These amounts are not made public, but word inevitably gets around; employees who feel unjustly treated may leave or be made unproductive through discontent. Even the task of determining the relative effectiveness of key employees is hampered by the different kinds of business they are in. Consider the example of an investment bank sales and trading department. Both salespeople and the traders have identifiable and quantifiable productivity measures (sales and trading profits/losses, respectively). Nevertheless, it is unclear how the incentive structures should be designed. Should salespeople be paid on commission and traders on a percent of annual profits, or should both be paid according to a more subjective evaluation process? Whatever system the CEO uses for distributing salaries and bonuses should achieve at least two goals:

▸   A person should be paid at least his or her "market value" so long as the person is worth that amount to the company.

▸   A person should find his or her bonus and salary increase "fair" relative to the amounts received by other people within the company.

How should the CEO accomplish this?

C. K. Coolidge, Inc. (A)

On Sunday afternoon in mid-September 1993, Christine Schilling was in the office of Ralph Purcell, president of C. K. Coolidge, Inc. (CKC). Schilling, recently hired as Purcell's analyst, was presenting the details of an analysis she had prepared on Saturday. Purcell hoped that by the end of the afternoon, aided by Schilling's insights, he would be able to establish a course of action that might hasten the final settlement of a patent suit brought against CKC three years earlier by the Tolemite Corporation and its licensee, Barton Research and Development (BARD).

The Contenders

CKC was founded in Milwaukee, Wisconsin, in 1932 as a commercial outlet for the inventive genius of Dr. Charles K. Coolidge, an astute organic chemist. The company had weathered the Depression and then participated in the prosperity associated with World War II and the postwar years. By 1970, annual sales were in the neighborhood of $3 million.

Dr. Coolidge owned and managed the company until 1980, when, desiring to retire, he sold it along with all its patents and products to Arrow Industries, a small Chicago-based conglomerate. CKC continued to prosper as an Arrow subsidiary and by 1993 had annual sales of $10.5 million[1]—14% of the Arrow total. About 10% of CKC's sales in 1993 were derived from a chemical component called Varacil, whose manufacturing process was the subject of the patent suit. The remainder of its sales included a wide range of specialty organic chemical products sold, in relatively small volume, primarily to the pharmaceutical industry.

Tolemite, also headquartered in Chicago, was a large chemical and pharmaceutical manufacturer with estimated 1993 sales in excess of $300 million. In 1984 Tolemite had been awarded a patent covering various aspects of a new, low-cost method for synthesizing Varacil. The techniques covered by the patent had been discovered at Tolemite's research facility in 1979 as an offshoot of another project. Since Tolemite was neither a user nor a producer of Varacil, it had decided to offer the use of the patent, under license, to BARD, the principal Varacil producer in the United States.

BARD, located in Evanston, Illinois, had begun as a small research company. By 1984, however, it had dropped all research and was involved solely in the production of Varacil. To maintain its position as industry leader, BARD had accepted Tolemite's licensing offer and had at once begun conversion of all Varacil production to the new process. In return for the use of the patent, BARD had agreed to pay Tolemite a 4% royalty on all sales of synthetic Varacil. In addition, BARD had received rights to sublicense any other Varacil producers who became interested in the process and to work out individual royalty agreements with producing firms. Under these sublicensing agreements, royalties of 4% would go to Tolemite, and any excess would accrue to BARD.

In 1989, five years after Tolemite had received its patent, a research chemist at CKC had, quite independently, discovered a very similar process for synthesizing Varacil. The CKC researchers, however, had not felt that the new

Harvard Business School case N9-894-017, revised November 17, 1993. This case was prepared by Research Associate Donald L. Wallace under the supervision of Senior Lecturer Dr. John S. Hammond III.

---

[1] Based on actual sales for January–August and an estimate for September–December.

processing techniques could be patented. Thus, no patent search had been initiated and production facilities had simply been converted to the new process. At the time, no one at CKC had suspected the degree to which its new process was similar to the one originated by Tolemite and covered by Tolemite's patent. It was with some surprise then that CKC management learned that it was being sued by Tolemite and BARD for patent infringement.

Varacil

Varacil was a chemical substance sold almost exclusively to pharmaceutical manufacturers. Although it appeared in a variety of drug preparations, it represented only a minor fraction of any one drug. The economics of its manufacture, however (high fixed and low variable costs, plus economies of scale), suggested that it be made in relatively long runs involving substantial volume. Thus the major drug companies themselves were not involved in its preparation.

Before 1984 Varacil had been processed from naturally occurring organic chemicals found in animal tissue. As a result of the high cost of these natural chemicals, the cost of Varacil itself had been relatively high. With the advent of synthetic Varacil, this situation was dramatically changed. Variable costs in the manufacture of synthetic Varacil represented only about 15% of sales, so the synthetic soon drove the natural product virtually out of the market. (A few Varacil users still specified the natural product in the belief that it had certain superior properties.)

In 1993 the national market for synthetic Varacil amounted to some $9 million in sales. On a unit basis this market had been relatively stable for several years. As drugs requiring Varacil had been phased out, new ones requiring similar amounts of the compound had always seemed to appear. Furthermore, there was no reason to believe that this stability would be lost over the next several years. Industry unit sales projected thus tended to be quite flat as far as five and ten years out.

On the dollar value side, however, the story was quite different. Prices for Varacil, and industry dollar sales as well, had been in decline for several years. When converting to the synthetic process, each competitor in the industry had tooled up to supply an optimistic share of the market. Then, when market share objectives were not met, prices were slashed in an attempt to keep manufacturing facilities operating at efficient levels and to bring in as much contribution as possible toward fixed costs. This situation was expected to continue for at least five years. Exhibit 1 shows industry unit and dollar sales of synthetic Varacil for the period 1984-1993, as well as projections for 1994-2004.

In 1993 there were seven principal competitors in the synthetic Varacil market. BARD, with $6 million in sales, took 67% of the market. CKC, with $1,050,000 in sales, was the second largest operator and held a 12% share. The remaining five competitors, none of whose Varacil sales exceeded $570,000, constituted the remaining 21% of the market. By 1990 all seven of the principal competitors were manufacturing synthetic Varacil by nearly identical processes. Only BARD, however, was paying royalties to Tolemite.

Background on the Litigation

On June 12, 1990, Tolemite and BARD had jointly filed suit in the Superior Court of the Fifth District of Wisconsin, charging CKC with having infringed on Tolemite's patent on the manufacturing process for synthetic Varacil. To remedy the infringement, Tolemite and BARD were seeking a royalty payment of 10% of all of CKC's future sales of synthetic Varacil over what remained on the 17-year life of the patent, as well as a lump-sum indemnity to cover past sales.

When confronted with the suit, Purcell had immediately discussed the matter with Aaron Mantiris, general counsel for Arrow Industries. Both men had felt there was considerable evidence indicating that Tolemite's process might not be patentable. At Mantiris's suggestion, CKC had obtained the services of Evans and Blaylock, a well-known and highly reputable firm of patent attorneys in New York. These attorneys agreed with Mantiris on the potential weakness of the Tolemite suit. Thus, in 1990, Evans and Blaylock had begun to prepare a case for CKC's defense.

Tolemite's patent contained 12 claims of originality. To obtain the patent, Tolemite, like all successful applicants, had had to demonstrate to the patent examiners that there was no "prior art" and that there was invention. Prior art could consist of previous patents, covering the applied-for patents, or processes in the public domain—unpatentable but generally known—that were similar. To show invention, it was necessary to demonstrate that the applied-for process was not obvious to a person reasonably knowledgeable about related chemical processes.

Any patent was always subject to later challenge in the courts. All or part of a patent could be overturned on the basis of prior art or absence of invention. As a practical matter, it was sometimes possible to argue the absence of invention years later. Ideas that had seemed novel at the time of the invention often seemed far more obvious at a later date. The patent holder, in defense, attempted to reemphasize the novelty of the ideas at the time of the invention. Nevertheless, there were many instances of patents being successfully challenged. In the matter of synthetic Varacil, Mantiris argued that Tolemite had not, in fact, introduced any novelty. It had merely observed and harnessed a naturally occurring process that, in itself, was not patentable.

From 1990 to 1993 a partner in Evans and Blaylock worked intermittently in liaison with Mantiris researching and preparing the case. CKC considered the suit to be little more than a nuisance and was content to drag its feet in hope that Tolemite's case might simply collapse from inertia. Late in 1992, however, a tentative trial date was set for January 1993. Before a firm date could be set, Purcell and Mantiris decided, with the concurrence of the patent attorneys, to make at least a token effort at a pretrial settlement. Their offer amounted to the payment of all future liabilities at a royalty rate of 2 1/2% of sales. This offer was rejected out of hand by Tolemite and BARD. Eventually, the case reached the court docket and a trial date in October 1993 was set.

By September, Purcell was becoming uneasy over the high—and increasing—level of attorneys' fees. These fees had already reached a total of $300,000 and if the trial were to take place as scheduled, they would surely loom large in comparison with the total value of any successful defense. Furthermore, these legal fees and any future ones would not be recoverable, even if CKC won its case.

In response to this uneasiness about both the progress of the suit and the alarming accumulation of the attorneys' fees, Purcell decided on two immediate actions. First, through Mantiris, he arranged for a meeting in New York City to review the case thoroughly with the patent attorneys. Second, he asked his new analyst, Schilling, to review the case, in the hope that she would bring a fresh viewpoint to bear.

Schilling's Analysis and the Meeting with the Patent Attorneys

Christine Schilling was a recent graduate of the Harvard Business School. While pursuing her studies she had become interested in the application of formal, quantitative frameworks to decision problems. Thus, her approach to this particular problem took the form of a decision tree. This analysis recognized two options open to CKC:

▮   Go to court and contest the patent, which would cost an additional $150,000 in legal fees and lead to winning the suit with probability X or losing it with probability $1–X$; or

▮   Settle out of court for an amount $Y\%$ of past and future sales. She summarized these options in the decision diagram shown in Figure 6.1.

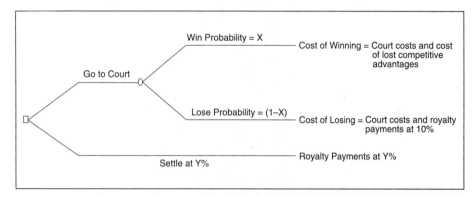

Figure 6.1

The purpose of her analysis was to determine for any given out-of-court settlement offer Y, how large the probability X of winning the suit would have to be to justify rejecting the offer. To do this break-even analysis she solved the following equation for X, given various values of Y:

$$[Cost\ of\ Winning]\ (X)\ +\ [Cost\ of\ Losing]\ (1\text{–}X)\ =\ [Cost\ of\ Settlement\ at\ Y\%]\ .$$

This resulted in the break-even curve shown in Figure 6.2. For all offers above the curve it was preferable to go to court. Offers below the line were worthy of consideration. For example, if CKC personnel felt that the probability of winning was 0.6, then settling up to a 7.5% royalty rate (shown by the dotted line in Figure 6.2) could be justified.

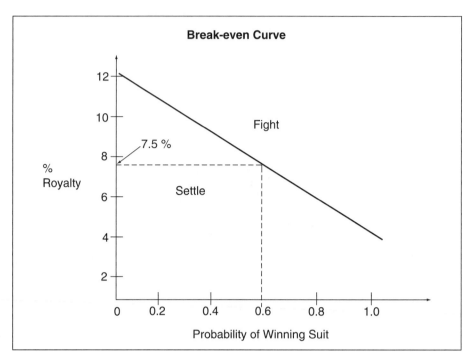

Figure 6.2

Schilling's principal conclusion from this analysis was that unless the odds of winning the suit were extremely good, any reasonable pretrial settlement was preferable to paying the additional costs and taking a chance on going to court. Purcell, a chemical engineer, was himself well attuned to quantitative analysis and, in fact, liked to support his own arguments with numerical data whenever possible. He was intrigued by Schilling's presentation, and invited Schilling to join him and Mantiris on the trip to New York City to meet with the patent attorneys. At that meeting Purcell intended to confront the attorneys with Schilling's analysis and then to obtain their opinion on the benefits of pursuing the case to trial.

In New York the patent attorneys began the meeting by presenting an outline of their case. Everyone attending agreed that the case was indeed a strong one with a high probability of success in the trial phase. The attorneys demurred, however, when asked to give a precise figure for their probability of success in court. At that point, Purcell sketched out Schilling's analysis. He then asked the patent attorneys if they still felt that their probability of success was high enough to merit going to trial. The attorneys were visibly uncomfortable with Schilling's approach. Although they remained convinced of the merits of their case, they agreed that some rethinking was probably necessary before proceeding to trial.

On the flight back to Milwaukee, Purcell discussed with his general counsel and his analyst what had happened at the meeting. As a result of that conversation he decided that Schilling should pursue her analysis further and take into account such things as potential appeals and to appraise the sensitivity of the analysis in the underlying assumptions. All three agreed that settlements well in excess of 2.5% would, in all probability, be preferable to a court fight.

Final Analysis

The next day, Saturday, Schilling broadened her analysis as Purcell had requested. The expanded analysis took into account the possibility of appeals by Tolemite or CKC and the additional legal expenses in the event of such appeals. The result was the revised break-even curve shown in Figure 6.3, which strengthened the conclusion that any reasonable settlement would be preferable to going to court. (The complete analysis is presented in the appendix.) On Sunday afternoon Schilling presented her findings to Purcell in an informal meeting and they began to map a strategy for resolving the suit.

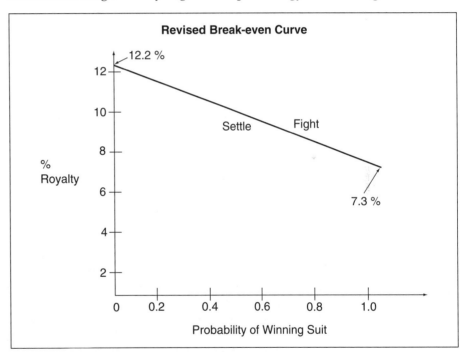

Figure 6.3

Exhibit 1

	UNIT AND DOLLAR SALES OF SYNTHETIC VARACIL BY COMPANY					
	BARD		Coolidge		All Others	
Year	lbs.	$	lbs.	$	lbs.	$
1984	1,000	153,000	0	0	0	0
1985	5,000	738,000	0	0	0	0
1986	20,000	2,676,000	0	0	0	0
1987	60,000	6,569,000	0	0	0	0
1988	68,000	8,022,000	0	0	0	0
1989	76,000	9,045,000	0	0	0	0
1990	83,000	9,624,000	1,000	111,000	0	0
1991	89,000	9,546,000	6,000	576,000	2,000	213,000
1992	94,000	7,899,000	11,000	936,000	19,000	1,608,000
1993[a]	100,000	6,000,000	17,000	1,050,000	35,000	2,100,000
1994	100,000	6,000,000	17,000	1,020,000	35,000	2,100,000
1995	100,000	5,700,000	17,000	969,000	35,000	1,995,000
1996	100,000	5,400,000	17,000	918,000	35,000	1,890,000
1997	100,000	4,800,000	17,000	816,000	35,000	1,680,000
1998	100,000	4,500,000	17,000	765,000	35,000	1,575,000
1999	100,000	4,500,000	17,000	765,000	35,000	1,575,000
2000	100,000	4,500,000	17,000	765,000	35,000	1,575,000
2001	100,000	4,500,000	17,000	765,000	35,000	1,575,000
2002	100,000	4,500,000	17,000	765,000	35,000	1,575,000
2003	100,000	4,500,000	17,000	765,000	35,000	1,575,000
2004	100,000	4,500,000	17,000	765,000	35,000	1,575,000

Source: C. K. Coolidge, Inc.

Note: Total unit sales of Varacil (including the natural product) were roughly 150,000 lbs. annually for the period 1984-1993. Sales for 1984-1993 were actual; sales for 1994-2004 were projected.

[a]Estimated.

Appendix: Christine Schilling's Analysis

Objective

Determine the range of payment Arrow Industries can offer to pay in pretrial settlement relative to future costs and the probability of success in court.

Conclusion

If the likelihood of winning the trial is between 75% and 100% Arrow can pay a pretrial settlement royalty rate of up to 8 1/2% and save money. In fact, Arrow can afford to pay a royalty rate of 7% even if the probability of winning the trial is 100%, because of the magnitude of future attorneys' fees and subsequent appeals. (See Figure 6.3 for the break-even probability curve.)

Assumptions

I. Expected proceedings:

    A. If Arrow wins the trial, there is only a 90% chance that Tolemite will appeal.

    B. If Tolemite wins the trial, there is a 10% chance that Arrow will win the appeal.

    C. If Arrow wins the trial, there is a 75% chance that Arrow will win the appeal.

    D. If Tolemite wins the trial, there is a 75% chance that Tolemite will win the appeal.

II. Future attorneys' fees and court costs will be:

    A. For the trial—$150,000.

    B. For the appeal:

        1. If Arrow wins the trial—$150,000.

        2. If Tolemite wins the trial—$75,000.

III. Exposure to liability:

    A. Past liabilities

        1. If Tolemite wins the trial, it will seek 10% of sales from 1990 to 1993—total liabilities of $267,300.

        2. Tolemite will settle past liabilities prior to the trial at the same royalty rate applied in future sales. (See III.B.2.)

    B. Future royalties

        1. If Tolemite wins the trial, it will seek 10% of future sales.

        2. The Tolemite pretrial settlement royalty requirement is unknown but will be approached in this analysis as that rate at which Arrow Industries would break even in the alternative of facing the costs and risks of trial. (See Figure 6.3.)

IV. Actual royalty costs involved:

    A. C. K. Coolidge will continue to produce 17,000 pounds of Varacil per year for the next seven years (remaining life of the patent).

    B. The price/pound for Varacil will erode as expected and produce the total sales shown in Table 6.1 on the following page.

    C. In this industry of high fixed and low variable costs, resulting in severe pressure upon price, BARD will have a competitive advantage directly proportional to the royalty differential between itself and CKC. The assumption is that it will lower the price rather than simply absorb extra profit. The extent of BARD's use of this advantage and its significance to CKC's profitability will be illustrated in the analysis

    D. The "value of money" to the corporation is approximately 10%.

Table 6.1

PRESENT VALUE OF ROYALTIES AND LOST COMPETITIVE ADVANTAGE ($ IN THOUSANDS)

Year	Discount Factor [a]	Cost of 10% Royalty Payments and Past Liability Claims			Cost of 4% Lost Competitive Advantage		Cost of Settlement at 8% Royalty	
		Sales	Royalty (10%)	NPV [b]	Lost Competitive Advantage (4%)	NPV	Royalty (8%)	NPV
0	1.000	$2,673 [c]	$267.3	$267.3	—	—	$213.9	$213.9
1	.909	1,020	102.0	92.7	$40.8	$37.2	81.6	74.1
2	.826	969	96.9	80.1	38.7	31.8	77.4	63.9
3	.751	918	91.8	69.0	36.6	27.6	73.5	55.2
4	.683	816	81.6	55.8	32.7	22.2	65.4	44.4
5	.621	765	76.5	47.4	30.6	18.9	61.2	38.1
6	.564	765	76.5	43.2	30.6	17.4	61.2	34.5
7	.513	765	76.5	39.3	30.6	15.6	61.2	31.2
				$694.8		$170.7		$555.3

[a] Rate = 10%
[b] Net present value
[c] Past sales (1990-1993)

Analysis

The objective of this analysis is to define, in general terms, the relationship between the future expenses and risks faced in the Tolemite suit with the cost of an immediate settlement. An attempt has been made to break the overall problem into a number of smaller events and action alternatives and to assess reasonable ranges of event probability and consequence; these elements are then related mathematically to obtain a solution.

There can be a substantial advantage in using this approach to illuminate the basic issues, which generally remained submerged in a single assessment of the entire situation. However, there is a potential danger in the quantification and simplification of complex problems: the result is apparently so precise and straightforward that it can be easy to forget that the result is no better than the assumptions on which it is based.

Based on the above assumptions and the decision diagram shown in Figure 6.4; these costs were calculated:

1. Cost associated with End point (1)   (Arrow wins trial, Tolemite appeals, Arrow wins appeal)

Present value of 4% lost competitive advantage (See Table 6.1)	=$170,700
Appeal costs	= 75,000
Trial costs	= 150,000
Total	$395,700

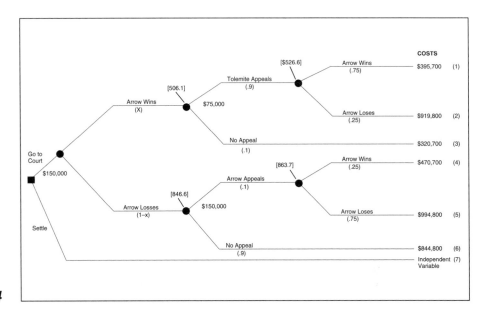

Figure 6.4

2. Costs associated with End point (2) (Arrow wins trial, Tolemite appeals, Arrow loses appeal)

Present value of royalty payments and past liabilities claims at 10% (Table 6.1)	=$694,800
Appeal costs	= 75,000
Trial costs	= 150,000
Total	$919,800

3. Cost associated with End point (3) (Arrow wins trial, no appeal)

Present value of 4% lost competitive advantage	=$170,700
Trial costs	= 150,000
Total	$320,700

4. Cost associated with End point (4) (Arrow loses trial, Arrow appeals, Arrow wins appeal)

Present value of 4% lost competitive advantage	=$170,700
Appeal costs	= 150,000
Trial costs	= 150,000
Total	$470,700

5. Cost associated with End point (5)   (Arrow loses trial, Arrow appeals, Arrow loses appeal)

Present value of royalty payments and past liabilitiesclaims at 10%	=$694,800
Appeal costs	= 150,000
Trial costs	= 150,000
Total	$994,800

6. Cost associated with End point (6)   (Arrow loses trial, Arrow does not appeal)

Present value of royalty payments and past liabilities claims at 10%	=$694,800
Trial costs	= 150,000
Total	$844,800

The next step is to find, for a given settlement rate of $Y\%$ royalty, the probability of winning the trial that will make the expected cost of going to court equal to the cost of the settlement. For example, assuming a settlement rate of 8% royalty payments, the present value of the cost of settlement is $506,100, as shown in Table 6.1. The break-even probability of winning, X, could be calculated from the following equation:

$$\textit{Expected cost of going to court } = \textit{ Cost of settlement}$$

$$\$506,\!100X \; + \; 846,\!600 \, (1\!-\!X) \; = \; \$555,\!300$$

$$\text{To get: } X \; = \; 0.85$$

Solving this equation for different settlement rates resulted in the break-even probability curve shown earlier in Figure 6.3.

▼   ▼   ▼

BROCKWAY AND COATES

Part A

On the morning of March 18, 1991, Tom Coates, President of the publishing company of Brockway and Coates (B&C), met with Vicky Jacobs, Vice President for Marketing and Sales, and Arnie Deakins, Chief Editor for Non-Fiction, to discuss the negotiations under way with Senator Murphy regarding his soon-to-be-written autobiography. Senator Murphy was 82 years old and had served in the United States House of Representatives for 16 years before being named to the United States Senate by the governor of Tennessee to fill the unexpired term of a deceased senator from the state. That was in 1952. Senator Murphy planned to retire before his current term expired in 1992, on the 40th anniversary of his

Harvard Business School case N9-892-002, revised October 23, 1991. This case was prepared by Professor David E. Bell. Copyright © 1991 by the President and Fellows of Harvard College.

becoming a senator. He had approached B&C, as well as two other publishing houses, with a view to publishing his reminiscences, which he had already entitled *Serving Time*.

While Senator Murphy had never been mentioned as a presidential (or even vice-presidential) aspirant, he was widely respected as an influential voice on Capitol Hill. His advice had been sought by friend and foe alike. He was a fixture in the White House, especially during Republican administrations. There had not been a meeting on an important issue in the last 30 years where he had not been either a discussant or the topic of discussion (or so he said). He had kept his friendships in Congress and in Tennessee by being a reliable confidant.

But, as he faced his retirement, he had apparently decided to cash in on the experiences and leave a nest egg for his grandchildren. B&C had probed him about the likely content of *Serving Time*, and while it was clear he intended to tell all about the political intrigues he had known, he also seemed to be well-informed about non-political gossip, the kind that would allow an autobiography such as this to become a best-selling book.

The Senator was very clear about his fee expectations, $500,000 to sign a deal and another $500,000 upon delivery of the manuscript. It was also understood that the manuscript would be ghost-written: the Senator would tell his reminiscences to B&C staff who, would fashion them into a book.

The Meeting between Tom, Vicky, and Arnie

Tom began by asking Vicky about her sales forecasts for *Serving Time*.

Vicky: "I think there's a very real chance that this book could be our big hit of 1992. I'd say sales could be as high as $1 million copies assuming a price of, say, $30 retail."

Tom whistled: "Those are hardback books, right?"

Vicky: "Of course. As I read it, this is first and foremost a political book, not a scandal sheet. There's no point going down-market with a softcover version. But don't get too excited; it seems to me we have to consider the possibility that the Senator's personal appeal, which is sky-high at the moment, might diminish over the next year. We also don't know whether other politicians might publish their memoirs around the same time, thus cutting into our market. On the other hand, 1992 is an election year and Murphy has known most of the presidential hopefuls since they were in diapers.

"Bottom line? I'd say that at $30 retail, there is a 30% chance of sales of around $1 million books, a 40% chance of sales of around 400,000 books, and a 30% chance of sales of around 100,000 books. Those are just representative scenarios for the purpose of our calculations, of course."

Arnie spoke up: "Don't forget that the book has to be written before we can sell it. Murphy has never written a book before, so he doesn't know what it involves. And there's always a chance with someone of his age that death or infirmity might intervene."

Tom: "We're also not entirely sure that his memoirs are going to be as exciting as we are assuming. Let's face it, when our staff start looking at his stories they may find that the book is going to be deadly dull."

Vicky: "I hate to say it, but it wouldn't be the first time we've published a deadly dull book. The real question is, Can we make a profit if we publish it? Thank goodness Murphy's proposal accepts the possibility that we may not wish to publish the book once we get a look at the manuscript!"

Arnie: "That's true, but so long as he delivers a finished manuscript, we'd still have to pay him the second $500,000, whether we publish it or not."

Tom: "It seems to me there is only an 80% chance Murphy will actually deliver a manuscript. Even assuming he does deliver a manuscript, there's a 25% chance that the manuscript would be so poor that we'd choose not to publish it. If we do choose to publish the book, then I'd be prepared to take Vicky's sales forecasts as accurate. I can't see that we'll learn much more about our likely sales before it comes time to make our final decision about going to press."

Arnie: "Why would we sign a contract that hands over half a million dollars to someone who may never deliver a manuscript?"

Tom: "I'd like to avoid that possibility if I can, and I have some ideas in that direction. But before we get into that, Vicky, could you use these sales projections and probabilities and check to see if this deal is anywhere close to making sense?"

Vicky: "Before I do that, let's look over this cost summary sheet I drew up. First of all, there's the cost of editorial services (writing, editing, proofreading, obtaining permissions for photographs, etc.), say, $250,000. This cost will be incurred even if we decide not to publish the book. If we *do* decide to publish the book, then we will also incur the cost of preparing camera-ready proofs; that will cost about $50,000. Printing costs will be $4 per copy."

Tom: "Four dollars per copy is just an average, right? There should be some economies of scale."

Vicky: "Yes, but we'll need to print 100,000 copies no matter what. So, although it would cost much more per copy if we were printing, say, 2,000 copies, for the numbers we are talking about, it's a pretty flat rate. Furthermore, for orders of our size, the printer will allow us to order copies on an 'as-needed' basis, and we'll still get the same rate. This means we won't get stuck with piles of books we can't sell."

Arnie: "We'll get stuck with lots of copies if the retailers can't sell them. As you know, returns can kill you in this business."

Vicky: "Actually, Arnie, my proposed price of $30 retail assumes a wholesale price of $15. For a generous margin like that, we will not permit returns. That's a common enough practice with books of a very topical nature. Distribution costs (shipping to wholesale customers, etc.) will be about 25 cents per copy. Marketing costs usually work out to about 40% of the wholesale price (i.e., 20% of retail)."

Tom: "But much of that marketing cost is fixed. We have a marketing department and sales force whether we sell Murphy's book or not. What are our *incremental* marketing and sales costs?"

Vicky: "We pay 5% of the wholesale price as a commission to the sales force. We would also spend about half a million dollars on advance publicity. There'd be no need to incur the cost of publicity if we kill the book based on our judgment about its content. That's about it for costs."

Arnie: "It occurs to me that if we're only considering incremental expenses, then the cost of editorial services would be more like $100,000 rather than $250,000—since the permanent editorial staff aren't very busy these days. The incremental cost will only be $50,000 if Murphy fails to deliver a completed manuscript."

Part B

The next day, Tom Coates and Vicky Jacobs resumed their discussion about Senator Murphy's manuscript.

Tom: "I can see from your analysis, Vicky, that this book is a viable proposition and that we should press ahead with the negotiations. I've been giving some thought to the incentives involved here. It seems to me we should offer Murphy a deal that more closely resembles a royalty arrangement. What I had in mind is that we offer him a lump sum on completion of the manuscript, representing an advance on royalties, and then pay him a certain amount for every copy we sell. The advantage of this arrangement is that it gives him an incentive to finish the book and to make it as interesting as possible."

Vicky: "So, to be specific, we would not pay him the $500,000 up-front payment for signing the contract, but would give him an advance royalty payment of $500,000 upon completion of the manuscript. Then, assuming we decide to publish the manuscript, we'd pay him a royalty of, say, $2.50 for every copy sold, except that he wouldn't receive the $2.50 per copy until after we'd sold enough copies to pay off his $500,000 advance."

Tom: "Yes, that's right. Another way to think about it is that we pay him so long as he delivers a manuscript, and the amount we pay him is the greater of (i) $500,000, or (ii) $2.50 a copy. Not only is a royalty arrangement more sensible for us than a flat fee, I'd say that if he accepts this deal I'd attach a higher probability to the prospect that he would actually deliver a manuscript, in fact I'd put it at 85%. I'd also raise to 80% the probability that the manuscript, if delivered, will be worth publishing. Even senators sometimes need a little incentive. However, I would not change your sales forecasts, assuming we do print the book."

▼   ▼   ▼

NEGOTIATION

The emphasis in the last chapter was on the satisfactory nature of a contract. In this chapter, we concentrate more on the process by which an agreement is reached. How should you negotiate an agreement in which most of the uncertainty in the problem stems from an incomplete understanding of the other party's preferences and needs? The three cases are examples of very typical negotiating situations. Be prepared to test your own theories about negotiating strategies as you enter the realm of sports contracts, real estate leases, and energy purchases.

THE 1987 NFL STRIKE (A)

On September 22, 1987, two weeks into the 1987-88 professional football season, more than 1,500 players from 28 teams walked off the field and went on strike. As a result, the 14 scheduled games for the following weekend were canceled. The strike had been called by the National Football League Players' Association (NFLPA), the union representing the players, following a breakdown in negotiations between the NFLPA and representatives of the 28 team owners. Those negotiations had been aimed at reaching a new collective bargaining agreement between the players and the owners to replace the old agreement signed in 1982 and due to expire in February 1988.

Both sides expected the strike to be expensive. It was estimated that team owners would collectively lose about $40 million per week and that, on average, a player would forgo a salary of about $15,000 per week.

The National Football League

The National Football League (NFL) is a nonprofit organization whose goal is to promote American football as a professional sport. It consists of 28 teams located in major metropolitan areas all over the United States. Each NFL team, however, is a privately owned, profit-making enterprise, with a primary owner who sometimes represents a group of partners. NFL teams obtain revenues from the sale of stadium tickets, stadium concessions, and broadcast rights for television and radio coverage of the games.

Harvard Business School case 9-189-093, revised June 18, 1993. This case was prepared by Professor Vijay Krishna. Copyright © 1988 by the President and Fellows of Harvard College.

Although professional football developed in the United States in the late nineteenth century, it was only after the formation of the NFL in 1922 that professional football became a major spectator sport. The league standardized the rules of play and set the schedule according to which the teams played against each other. By the late 1950s there were 14 teams in the NFL. With the merger of a rival—the American Football League—in 1966, as well as some expansion, by 1970 the NFL had reached its current size of 28 teams.

Professional football is played in the fall and winter of each year. In 1987, NFL teams played a total of 16 regular season games. The teams with the best win/loss records advanced to the playoffs. The season culminated in a championship game, called the "Super Bowl," which was played in January.

Through the 1970s spectator interest in professional football continued to rise and both stadium attendance and television ratings increased steadily. By the 1980s football had supplanted baseball as the premier spectator sport in the country.

The Players

Each team had 45 active players on the roster. This number had been agreed upon in the old collective bargaining agreement signed in 1982, but one of the current demands of the players was that the size of the roster be increased to 52. Because of the physical nature of the sport and resulting injuries, players' professional careers were rather short. On average, a player played for only three to four years in the NFL.

Almost exclusively, players in the NFL were selected out of colleges by means of a **draft**, an annual procedure according to which players were allocated to the various teams. The purpose of the draft was to ensure that the weaker teams in the league had an opportunity to pick the best players in the current crop. Typically, the team with the worst playing record in the league had the first pick, followed by the team with the next worst record, etc. The selection was carried out in this fashion in many "rounds" with teams exercising their rights in order. However, teams were free to trade these rights, called **draft choices**, in exchange for other draft choices, veteran players, or cash.

Once a player had been drafted by a particular team, the team had exclusive rights to negotiate and sign a contract with that player for the period of one year. If a mutually agreeable contract could not be reached in that period, the player would become eligible to reenter the pool of potential draftees for the next year.

The contracts, once signed, were very one-sided. Whereas a team could release most players at any time with no obligation, a player was bound by the terms of the contract.

While under contract to a team, a player could be traded or sold to any other team at any time in his career. On the other hand, if a player wished to change teams, he could do so only by achieving the status of a **free agent**. The regulations governing eligibility for free agency differed according to a player's experience in the NFL. Players with more than four years in the NFL could become free agents any time after the expiry of their contracts. However, a player with less than four years' experience was obliged to play for his original team for an additional year, called the **option year**. For example, a player who signed a two-year contract out of college was obliged to play for a third year with the team before he became eligible as a free agent.

Once a player became a free agent he was theoretically free to receive offers to play from other teams. However, his old team still had the right of first refusal by matching the competing bid. Furthermore, a player's old team was also entitled to receive significant compensation from the new team in return. This compensation took the form of future draft choices and was governed by strict rules, depending on the player's salary. For instance, a team that desired to sign a free agent currently earning $140,000 would owe his old team a first-round draft pick.

The tight free-agency rules restricted players' mobility significantly. Under the current system, only one player in the last ten years had been able to use this route to change teams.

Although the collective bargaining agreement governed the overall structure of players' compensation and related issues regarding pensions, minimum salaries, free agency and the draft, individual salaries were negotiated on a case-by-case basis between the player (or his agent) and the team. In 1987 the average salary in the NFL was estimated to be around $230,000 per year. Of course, this average hid a wide variation. Top players, usually quarterbacks or running backs, commanded salaries exceeding $1 million, whereas a marginal defensive back in his first year might get as little as $50,000 per year.

The Team Owners and Management

The ownership of an NFL team brought with it substantial status. Teams usually developed loyal followings in the cities in which they were based and team owners were inevitably proud of the accompanying public role. Some teams had been owned by the same family since the early days of the NFL, whereas others were more recent acquisitions. Some of the older owners considered football to be their major business. Others were entrepreneurs with substantial business interests and viewed football mainly as means of attaining a high profile in the community.

The 28 owners constituted an owners' council; all major decisions, including approval of a new bargaining agreement, had to be approved by 21 of the 28 owners. Transfers of ownership had also to be approved by the council and were rare in any case. In the last two major transfers, the Denver Broncos and the San Diego Chargers had been sold in separate transactions for an estimated $70 million each in 1984. The New England Patriots were up for sale in 1988 for a similar amount.

The teams had two major sources of revenues. By far the most lucrative source was sale of broadcast rights to television networks. The broadcast rights were sold by the NFL *in toto*, and television revenues were divided evenly among the 28 teams. In 1987 this amounted to about $17 million per team and represented approximately 60% of the gross revenues.

The other major source was from gate receipts. These were shared according to a 60/40 formula, with 60% of the gate receipts going to the home team and 40% to the visiting team. Receipts from luxury boxes, stadium concessions, parking, etc., were not shared but were retained by the home team.

A team's major expenses, by far, were the salaries and other compensation (pensions, medical coverage, etc.), paid to the players. These amounted to between $10 and $15 million per team in 1987. Other expenses included stadium rentals, travel, salaries of the coaching staff, and cost of equipment.

The owners elected a commissioner and a six-member executive committee that governed the NFL. The commissioner had substantial independent power over many aspects, including negotiating the all-important television rights and arbitrating disputes between owners, coaches, and players.

Labor Relations in the NFL

Although a loose association to look after the interests of the players had existed since 1956, it was only after the merger of the American Football League (AFL) and the old NFL that there was any serious confrontation between the owners and the players. The players went on strike for the first time in 1967, although the strike was short-lived—lasting for only two days during the pre-season. By 1971 the Players' Association had been certified as a legitimate labor union.

In 1974 the players went on strike following a breakdown in talks aimed at reaching a new collective bargaining agreement. During the strike, no games were canceled. The owners were able to employ rookies, a few free agents, and nonstrikers, thereby nullifying the effects of the strike. The players returned to work after 42 days, unable to wrest any concessions from the owners.

A similar scenario was played out again in 1982, when another collective bargaining agreement was being negotiated. The players proposed, among other things, a profit-sharing arrangement according to which 55% of the profits would be pooled in order to pay players' salaries according to a seniority scale and without regard to performance. Teams would be free to pay bonuses out of their share of the profits. The owners refused to even consider this proposal.

On the other side of the table, the owners offered increases in minimum salaries, life insurance, and medical coverage. After rejecting the owners' offer, the union voted to strike on September 25, 1982. This strike lasted 57 days and caused half of the regular season games to be canceled. It was estimated that the league lost about $200 million in television revenues alone. Players lost half their salaries, which were in the neighborhood of $100,000 annually at that time.

In the end, the players abandoned their profit-sharing demands and settled for an agreement that awarded bonuses, had higher minimum salaries, severance pay, and an increase in postseason pay. Free-agency rules remained unchanged. The final pact was very similar to a proposal put forward by the owners before the strike began. The 1982 strike was a bitter defeat for the union.

It was against this background that Gene Upshaw, an ex-football player for the then Oakland Raiders and now executive director of the NFLPA, called another strike in September 1987. A brief chronology of events during the strike is given in Exhibit 1 at the end of this case.

Issues in the 1987 Strike

As in any labor-management negotiation, there were numerous issues at stake. The major issues are described below:

1. **Free agency:** Without a doubt, the predominant issue was that concerning the status of free agency in the league. The 1982 agreement had not addressed this in a manner agreeable to the players: many felt that on this count they had been "sold out" by the union and its then executive director, Ed Garvey.

Although average salaries for NFL players had risen steadily over the last decade, rising from $90,000 in 1982 to $230,000 in 1987, they lagged far behind those of other professional athletes. The lessons from baseball were particularly clear. In 1976 the average salaries in baseball and football were nearly the same, just over $50,000. In 1977, however, as the result of a favorable court ruling, baseball players were able to obtain rather liberal free-agency rules. In 1987, the average salary in professional baseball was over $400,000 per year whereas average salaries in football were $230,000. Basketball players also earned over $400,000 on average. All this, when the professional career of a football player was much shorter than that of other professional athletes.

2. **Guaranteed contract:** According to the current system, if a player did not make the team in a year, he could be "released" by the team. The team was under no obligation to continue to pay his salary anymore. The players wanted teams to guarantee contracts of those players in their second year who were considered good enough to make the team. According to their proposal, a team would be obligated to pay a player who had been signed to a four-year contract even if he did not make the team in, say, his third year. Thus after he made the team for two years, a player's contract would be guaranteed. Such guaranteed contracts were the norm in other sports such as baseball and basketball.

3. **Salary scale:** The players wanted an increase in minimum salaries across the board. This minimum would increase with seniority.

4. **Pensions:** The players wanted a doubling of the NFL's contribution to their pension fund. It was also alleged that the NFL had not been keeping up contributions to the pension fund as mandated by the 1982 agreement.

5. **Roster size:** The union wanted an increase of 7 players in the roster, bringing it up to 52. It was argued that the small roster was a leading cause of injuries to players and, hence, of short professional careers.

6. **Drug testing:** Modify system to mimic drug-testing programs and penalties for drug usage employed in other professional sports.

7. **Union protection:** The union wanted protection for its representatives on each team. The issue had been brought to the forefront after the New England Patriots had summarily traded Brian Holloway, the team's controversial union representative. The union alleged that the Holloway was traded only because the management objected to his union activities.

The major issues at stake in the 1987 strike, together with a summary of the initial positions of both sides, are listed in Exhibit 2.

Exhibit 1 _____

A BRIEF CHRONOLOGY OF THE 1987 STRIKE	
April 20	Union and management first exchange proposals.
September 8	Union negotiators meet in Washington, D.C., to vote on September 22 as a tentative strike date.
September 15	The NFLPA makes a "proposal for settlement" that is termed "significant" by Gene Upshaw, the union's executive director.
September 16	Jack Donlan, head of the management council that is the owners' negotiating arm, characterizes the union's proposal as "discouraging."

Exhibit 1 continued _____

September 22	Strike begins.
September 24	NFL calls off 14 games scheduled for the following Sunday and Monday (September 27 and 28).
September 25	After 17 hours of dialogue over three days, talks between the union and the owners are suspended. The league indicates that replacement teams will play the scheduled games for October 4 and 5.
September 27 & 28	No games are played.
September 29	Television networks announce that they will telecast games played on October 4 and 5 as usual even though these would be played by replacement and nonstriking players.
October 2	86 players cross picket lines to rejoin their teams and meet the deadline set by the owners in order to remain eligible for the week's paycheck. Among the returning players is star quarterback Danny White of the Dallas Cowboys, who is reputed to have lost $45,000 for not playing in last Sunday's game. Fights erupt between players manning picket lines and returning players, who are called "scabs."
October 4	Replacement games are staged while strike continues. Picket lines are quite effective in keeping fans away from the games. Attendance in most cities is quite poor, as are the television ratings. More than 300,000 tickets (35% of all sold) are returned for refunds, estimated to total $5 million.
October 5	Rev. Jesse Jackson offers his services as a mediator.
October 6	Because of the low ratings of the televised games, the NFL is obliged to refund approximately $30 million to the television networks.
October 12	Union offers to return to work if owners will agree to mediation for six weeks on all unresolved issues and leave the remaining issues for binding arbitration.
October 13	Owners agree to protection for union representative for the remainder of the season and offer to keep the 1982 collective bargaining agreement in force.
October 14	Management council accepts the idea of mediation but refuses to submit to arbitration on any issue.
October 19	Strike collapses after the Washington Redskins vote to return to work. Players' Association says that it is calling off the strike. It also files an antitrust suit against the NFL in the Federal District Court in Minneapolis.

Exhibit 2

ISSUES IN THE 1987 NFL STRIKE

Issue	Current System	Union's Proposal	Management's Proposal
Free Agency	If a player's contract has expired, his team has the right to match another team's offer. If another team signs the player, that team must yield draft picks, the number to be determined by the player's salary.	All players would be completely free to move after four years in the league. If a player has less than four years of experience, his team would have only first-refusal rights with no compensation.	To keep first-refusal rights, but to liberalize compensation from new club.
Guaranteed Contracts	Virtually none. Only 4% of NFL contracts are guaranteed, compared with more than 90% for basketball and about half for baseball.	Once a player in his second year makes the team, his contract is guaranteed.	A vested veteran (a fourth-year player) who is cut after the third game of the season.
Salary Scale	Minimum of $50,000 for rookies. League average is $230,000.	$90,000 minimum for rookies, escalating to $320,000 minimum for a 13-year player.	$60,000 for rookies as part of a wage scale for draft picks. The first player chosen, for example, would get a $50,000 bonus.
Pension Contribution	NFL pays $12.5 million annually.	Double that to $25 million.	A 15-year player's minimum would be $200,000. Combined pension and severance of about 17%.
Roster Size	45-man squads.	52-man squads.	47-man squads.
Drug Testing	One mandatory preseason test, but clubs can test further with "probable cause."	Current system can be enhanced with National Basketball Association-type arrangement that provides for treatment and disciplinary action, including expulsion from the league.	Random testing at its discretion.
Union Protection	None specified; subject to grievance procedure.	If a player representative is cut, his club would be fined an amount equal to the average league salary, and that fine would go to the player.	A three-party board, composed of a management representative, a union representative, and a neutral third party would adjudicate grievances.

NOTE ON NEGOTIATION

Negotiating is a pervasive activity. Managers negotiate not only with their peers but also with subordinates and superiors. Managers are often called upon to resolve disputes within the firm by playing the role of facilitator, mediator, or arbitrator.

Any occasion that calls for more than one person to be involved in a decision requires some period of compromise between the potentially conflicting interests of the parties involved. In an extreme case, the parties may have diametrically opposing interests; for example, when haggling over price, every dollar increase takes a dollar out of the buyer's pocket and puts it in the seller's pocket. One of the important lessons of the art and science of negotiation is to get away from viewing negotiation as a zero-sum contest. For example, a buyer and seller may find it difficult to agree on a price for a second-hand car. If the only dimension being negotiated is price, then there may be little chance for agreement. Yet the buyer's principal concern may be the reliability of the car rather than its price. The seller may be holding out for a high price because she knows it has never given any trouble. By offering a guarantee on performance, buyer and seller may easily come to an agreement.

Preparing for Negotiation

The most important step in preparing for a negotiation is to decide what it will take for you to "walk away." You should have a clear understanding of what you will do if there is no agreement and how much you like that outcome. Many people have a tendency to wait and see where the negotiations lead before facing up to the prospect of no agreement. Since you are unlikely to achieve all of your goals in a negotiation, it is necessary to consider the trade-offs that you are prepared to make: will you back off on issue #4 if that's what it takes to have issue #7 resolved in your favor?

It is also important to think through the other party's perspective on the matter to be negotiated. What are they likely to want out of this? What are their expectations? What do they need before they prefer to walk away? What are their trade-offs likely to be?

Finally, it is useful to think of some creative alternatives that can be introduced up front or as needed during the negotiations. Creative solutions are often generated by extending the scope of the discussions to include other issues (your employee may accept a lesser wage increase in exchange for more flexibility in taking vacation time) or conditioning the deal on some related events (such as the second-hand car's performing well, or not).

Negotiating Styles

There are many characterizations of what a successful negotiating style should be. Some advocate the get-tough approach in which one makes a take-it-or-leave-it offer at the outset. Others believe both sides should engage in a certain amount of casual socialization before negotiations begin in order to enhance the amicability of the proceedings.

There is a basic tension in negotiations between revealing too much and letting your opponent take advantage of you, versus "keeping your cards close to your chest" and risking no agreement or a suboptimal agreement. By listening

Harvard Business School case N9-191-154, revised April 6, 1994. This note was prepared by Professor David E. Bell. Copyright © 1991 by the President and Fellows of Harvard College.

to what each side really wants, it is often possible to create a considerable amount of value for both sides. Creating joint gains is the ideal approach to negotiation in which both sides exert their creativity in enlarging the pie. Unfortunately, the process of claiming shares—dividing the pie—takes place simultaneously and one process gets in the way of the other.

It is often tempting to believe that sowing misinformation about one's true goals ("I don't really care about the money") can lead to strategic triumph. While tales along those lines abound, the net effect is often to throw the negotiation into disarray and possibly lead to distrust and therefore to no agreement.

Finally, there is the question of reputation. If you expect to negotiate with this person again or if news of this negotiation is likely to circulate among others with whom you might negotiate later on, then there is some benefit to behaving in a manner that will be advantageous for the future. The best reputation to have is probably one of honesty, fairness, and creativity.

Tactical Issues

A number of factors can affect the dynamics of the negotiation. For example, where will the negotiations be held: your place, their place, or a "neutral" site? Who will be present? Who will do the talking? Who will do the deciding?

Will there be time pressure? If so, which side benefits from this pressure? Does one side have more at stake than the other?

Will the agreement be enforceable? What if the other side changes its mind afterwards? Can concessions be retracted? Can you extract additional concessions after agreement has been reached?

Two factors are worth considering, especially if you are in a weaker negotiating position. The first is to ask the other side to support their position in some objective way. Suppose you have been turned down for a pay raise by your employer; you have no intention of resigning and thus (in a sense) have no leverage. You could still ask the employer how pay raises are determined. Or ask your carpenter how much of his or her estimate is labor versus materials. What labor rate is assumed? Many people feel some obligation to answer these types of questions, and the answers can weaken the resolve of the stronger party.

The second suggestion is that you not make or accept concessions along the way. The difficulty with making small agreements along the way is that flexibility is reduced. As a very simple example, suppose that two people have been given two $5 bills and one ticket to a baseball game. If they each take $5 initially (because the money can be evenly divided), there is an impasse over the ticket. However, one person could have the ticket and the other could have the $10.

The Role of a Third-Party Helper

A neutral third party can be of great value in situations where agreement cannot be reached, especially where there is a lack of mutual trust. The third-party helper can be a mere facilitator who helps bring the disputing parties together and establishes a proper ambiance for negotiations; or he or she can play the role of a mediator who helps the parties find an agreeable compromise; or he or she can play the role of arbitrator who, after fact-finding, is empowered (either voluntarily or involuntarily) to dictate a final agreement.

Properties of an Agreement

A good agreement should be efficient and equitable. An agreement is efficient if it is not possible to find an alternative settlement that is preferred by both sides. If one could graph the value to each side of various possible agreements (the shaded area in Figure 7.1), then the final agreement should be one of those on the top right-hand side of the region. This region is known as the **efficient frontier**.[1] If two parties have come to some agreement, A, and if a third-party helper can later identify a solution, B, that is preferred by both sides to A, then it would make sense for both sides to tear up agreement A and sign a new one based on B. Identifying where the efficient frontier lies may be difficult if the two sides have been less than forthcoming about their true interests.

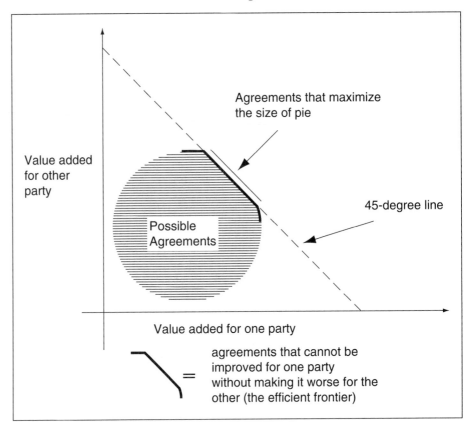

Figure 7.1

An agreement could be efficient but not equitable. Some people think that an agreement is fair if it gives roughly equal shares to both sides. Perhaps it is more appropriate to think of providing equal shares relative to each side's "best alternative to a negotiated agreement." The side that has less to lose by failing to agree is in a stronger bargaining position and "deserves" to get a better deal. A sense of equity and fairness is important, for some people will walk away from an agreement if they feel it is inequitable; they would rather suffer the consequences of no agreement than be a party to inequity.

---

[1] An Italian economist, Vilfredo Pareto, first discussed these solutions; thus efficient agreements are often called "Pareto optimal."

Finally, an agreement should be enforceable. This may often be achieved through the legal process; however, where there are no guarantees of performance other than the goodwill of the participants, it is important that the agreement be structured so as to provide incentives for both sides to fulfill the contract.

Further Reading

Negotiating is an art, not a science. The human element is very important. But the ideas and issues raised in this note are worth recalling before (and during) a negotiation. The following books offer more extended discussions of the subject.

1.   Roger Fisher and William Ury, *Getting to Yes* (Penguin Books, 1983).
2.   Gerard Nierenberg, *Fundamentals of Negotiating* (Hawthorn Books, 1973).
3.   Howard Raiffa, *The Art & Science of Negotiation* (Harvard University Press, 1982).
4.   David Lax and James Sebenius, *The Manager as Negotiator* (The Free Press, 1986).

CASE

THE 1987 NFL STRIKE (B): NEGOTIATING EXERCISE

This exercise is designed to aid in discussion of an accompanying case, The 1987 NFL Strike (A). Although the numbers have been chosen to broadly conform with the facts surrounding that strike, the exercise is completely artificial and there are numerous factors that have been omitted in the interests of simplicity. The goal is to draw attention to some underlying strategic aspects of the situation rather than to carry out a detailed and comprehensive analysis.

The Current Position

The NFLPA and representatives of the team owners have been negotiating for months and have managed to resolve their differences on every issue except free agency and minimum salary scales. The union's proposal is a package that is estimated to result in a rise in average salaries around the league to about $450,000 over the next two years. The management feels that they have already conceded enough on other issues and want to keep the current arrangement. Average salaries currently stand at about $230,000.

It has been estimated that every $10,000 increase in the average salary would result in increased costs of around $30 million to the owners over the next two years, after which a new contract will have to be negotiated.

As a whole the players gain roughly $25 million over the next two years for every $10,000 increase in average salary.

Harvard Business School case 9-189-094, revised April 1, 1994. This case was prepared by Professor Vijay Krishna. Copyright © 1988 by the President and Fellows of Harvard College.

The Costs of a Strike

Both sides realize that a strike would have a negative impact. Each week of the strike that resulted in complete cancellation of all games would cost management approximately $60 million. This figure results from a loss of both gate receipts and television revenues; however, it includes the savings from the fact that players' salaries will not have to be paid during the strike.

From the union's point of view, a week's worth of forgone salaries amounts to roughly $25 million at the current levels. Judging from the experiences of past strikes, players would not be able to sustain a strike for more than seven weeks. At that point the union would have to call off the strike and players would return to the playing field.

Rules Governing the Negotiations

1. You will be asked to represent one of the two sides and will negotiate with your counterpart from the other side.

2. The following rules have been agreed to in order to facilitate the negotiating process and minimize rancor. You must follow these exactly.

3. Negotiations will be conducted by means of an alternating offer arrangement (Figure 7.2). The union will make the first offer next Monday (week 0). Management has two options. It can accept the union's offer and the players will return to the teams immediately. In this case there would be no strike. If it rejects the union's offer, this would prompt a strike but negotiations would continue. In that case, management has one week in which to put together a counteroffer, which will be put on the table the following Monday (week 1). Now the union can either accept management's offer or come back with another proposal the next Monday (week 2) while the strike continues. Negotiations would continue in this way until agreement is reached.

4. For the sake of the exercise, the negotiations are restricted to be over one number only—the average salary of players. Thus all offers and counteroffers should only consist of salary levels demanded or offered. The union's current demand is $450,000 and the owners' current offer is $230,000. All offers and counteroffers are constrained to lie in this range.

5. Both sides understand that the strike cannot last for more than seven weeks. At that time the union would have to accept management's last outstanding offer.

6. If you are a union representative, your goal is to maximize the difference between the gain over the next two years from increased salaries and the costs resulting from the strike. Similarly, if you are representing the team owners, you should try to minimize the sum of the costs to the NFL over the next two years resulting from increased salaries and the loss of revenues during the strike.

7. Your objective, as a union representative, is not to do better than your counterpart who represents the owners but rather to do as well as you can for your own side. The same should be true of the owners' representative.

8. For the purposes of this exercise you should neglect all other factors such as the effects of precedent and the importance of building reputations.

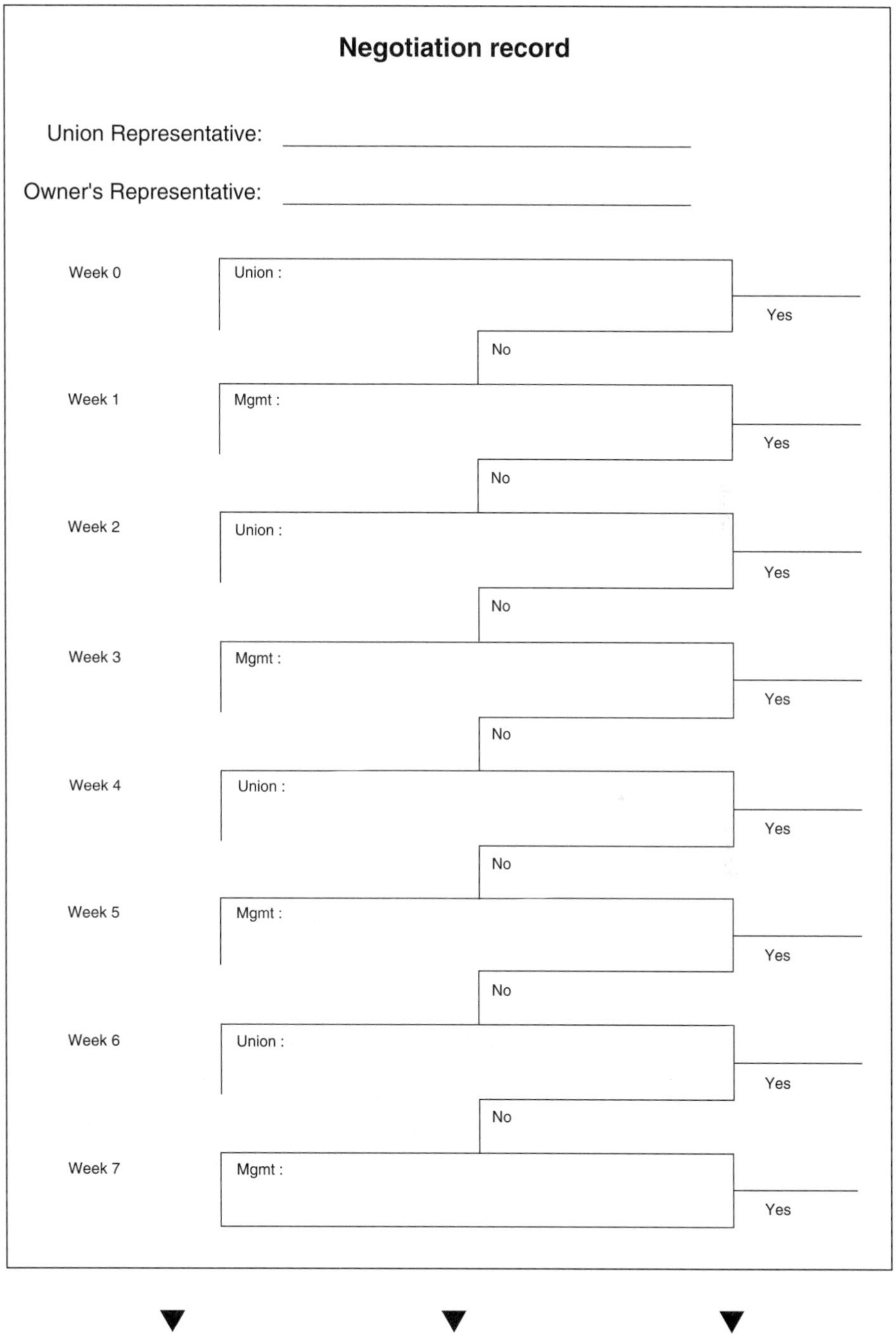

Negotiation record

Union Representative: _____

Owner's Representative: _____

Week 0	Union :	Yes
		No
Week 1	Mgmt :	Yes
		No
Week 2	Union :	Yes
		No
Week 3	Mgmt :	Yes
		No
Week 4	Union :	Yes
		No
Week 5	Mgmt :	Yes
		No
Week 6	Union :	Yes
		No
Week 7	Mgmt :	Yes

Figure 7.2

▼   ▼   ▼

JOAN MITCHELL STORES, INC.

Joan Mitchell Stores, Inc. was a Boston-based women's wear chain composed of four suburban stores and a larger downtown store. Its management was in the process of negotiating a lease for a 15,000-square-foot store in a new suburban shopping center being developed by the real estate developers Brown & Kenney. The new center had a desirable location in an area where Joan Mitchell had no stores. Further, since it was expected that no other major shopping centers would be built in the area for at least ten years, Mitchell management was particularly eager to get into the center.

Management at Joan Mitchell was concerned about rumors that Kerner Stores, a large national women's wear chain, was also interested in locating in the center. Managers feared that Brown & Kenney would either try to drive a hard bargain (because it could lease to Kerner instead of Joan Mitchell) or that it might lease to Kerner in addition to Mitchell. The latter course was considered less likely.

The Brown & Kenney shopping center was on a large tract of land, on which the developers would also build an apartment complex over a ten-year period. Several weeks before the negotiation session, the developers told Joan Mitchell management that four tenants had signed up: a gift shop, a Steve's ice cream parlor, a restaurant, and a Tweeter electronics store. They expected to sign up a video/music shop within the next few weeks. Further, they were in serious negotiations with Sears, which would be the major tenant.

Earlier, the developers had shown the managers studies of population and land development trends, expected apartment occupants, demographics of the surrounding towns, and automobile traffic, all of which indicated that customers would be primarily in the upper-middle income range. While Mitchell managers were impressed and thought the center very likely would succeed, they also recognized that the center could fail.

The contemplated store would be located in a one-story building that would cost approximately $110 per square foot to build. Brown & Kenney had reportedly invested $25 million to date in the new development, primarily for the land and the first phase of the apartment complex.

Setting Objectives

Top management held a series of meetings to discuss the objectives for the upcoming negotiations. The meetings were led by Barbara Levinson, purchasing vice-president, who was selected on the basis of her bargaining skills to handle the actual negotiations.

From the meetings, a near consensus on objectives emerged. Management singled out the rental rate, length of the lease, renewal clause, right to sublet, competing tenant clause, sign clause, and cancellation clause due to fire or acts of God as being of particular interest.

To facilitate making trade-offs among these issues, Levinson and Corporate Treasurer Herbert Bernstein assigned specific dollar values to various potential outcomes to reflect their relative importance and desirability. These amounts could be added together to calculate a net present value (NPV), which would measure the desirability of the deal.

Harvard Business School case 9-190-098, revised October 24, 1994. This case is adapted from a case by Professor John S. Hammond, Bobbi Barker (A2), HBS case #174-109. Copyright © 1990 by the President and Fellows of Harvard College.

Determining Trade-offs

The following statement of objectives was developed to calculate NPV.

Rental Rate: The rental rate in the lease was considered the most important variable. The annual rent could be determined in two possible ways: (1) by using a flat rental rate of so many dollars per square foot per year, or (2) the greater of the annual square foot rental or a percentage of the store's annual gross sales. By tying rents to sales, the latter type of agreement potentially protected the landlord against inflation. For example, suppose the agreement was $16 per square foot, or 5% of gross sales, whichever was greater, and that the store's gross sales in a particular year were $3½ million. Since 5% of these sales is $175,000, which is less than the $240,000 calculated by using the $16 per square foot rental rate, the annual rent charged would be $240,000. If in some other year the store's gross sales had been $5 million, then 5% of the sales would be $250,000. Since this is greater than $240,000, the annual rent charged would be $250,000.

The going annual rate for space in similar shopping centers was $16 to $18 per square foot on 30-year leases. However, lesser rates with a percentage of gross were frequent (for example, $14 per square foot, or 8% of sales, whichever was greater). Levinson had noticed in preliminary discussions about three weeks earlier with David Kenney, the developer's negotiator, that Brown & Kenney thought inflation would be more severe than Mitchell management did. Further, the developers seemed slightly less optimistic about sales per square foot of the new store than their prospective tenants. In estimating the present value cost of the lease, Levinson made certain assumptions about expected sales per square foot, the inflation rate, and an appropriate discount rate (see Exhibit 1).[2] She calculated, for example, that a 15-year lease at $16 per square foot and 6% of sales would cost the firm an effective $2,011,000 in present value terms.[3]

Length of Lease, Renewal Clause, and Right to Sublet: Since the success of the shopping center was uncertain, management preferred a 15-year lease with option to renew under the same terms for another 15 years. (In fact, a shorter lease with option to renew was even more desirable, but Levinson was sure Brown & Kenney would never agree to it.) At an earlier meeting, the developers had pushed for a 30-year lease; they had indicated that if they granted the 15-year lease, they preferred that its terms be renegotiated if the tenant desired to extend the lease after 15 years.

When Levinson had raised the possibility of a right-to-sublet clause, Kenney had said he would consider it only if Brown & Kenney had the right to approve of the subletting tenant or tenants. It seemed to Levinson that having the right to sublet would soften the negative impact of a 30-year lease, if she had to take it. Six combinations of circumstances regarding lease term and right to sublet emerged. These, together with the dollars indicating their desirability to Mitchell management, are shown in Table A of Exhibit 1.

Competing Tenant Clause: Mitchell management desired a clause in the lease limiting the developers to leasing no more than 10,000 square feet to all

---

[2] To preserve confidential information, Exhibit 1 is available only on the data diskette, in file MITCH1.WK4. See your instructor for the password.

[3] In calculating the NPV of the lease amount, Mitchell management used payments only over an initial 15-year period. The additional cost of a 15-year renewable lease or a 30-year lease is accounted for in the "Terms of Lease" trade-off assessment. In effect, these tradeoff costs can be thought of as option values of extending the lease relative to whatever other alternatives would be available at that time.

other women's wear stores. They figured this would keep out another large store such as Kerner's and hold the number of small competing stores to manageable proportions. While they realized that recent edicts from the Federal Trade Commission had cast doubt on the enforceability of such clauses, management felt that such an "understanding" with the developers would be desirable. Their conclusions about the value of this clause in relation to the length of the lease are given in Table B of Exhibit 1.

Sign Clause: Joan Mitchell stores used the same large, though tasteful, sign on each of its five other stores. Brown & Kenney objected, since it had initially planned to keep signs in the center under a certain size. Management felt the sign was the stores' trademark and was anxious to use it. The value Levinson attached to obtaining this desire is given in Table C of Exhibit 1.

Acts-of-God Cancellation Clause: About five years earlier, one of Mitchell's suburban stores had been heavily damaged by fire and the landlord had been very slow in making repairs. Consequently, Mitchell lost considerable sales, as well as its market position in the region. Management had learned its lesson from this experience and wanted to be able to terminate the lease if its store was damaged at least 15% by fire, flood, or other acts of God, or if the shopping center itself was damaged more than 30% (thus reducing traffic). If Mitchell elected to continue to lease, it wanted abatement of rent until repairs were made. The values assigned by Levinson to these clauses are given in Table D of Exhibit 1.

Upcoming Negotiations

While Levinson reviewed her objectives, she wondered how important Brown & Kenney would consider these aspects of the lease. She also began to consider a possible bargaining strategy, using her dollar system as a guide to making trade-offs and as a way of evaluating potential terms offered by the developers. She summarized her various assessments (Exhibit 1) in a Lotus 1-2-3 worksheet and began calculating values for a number of possible scenarios.

As she prepared for the meeting, Levinson recognized that the net present value approach gave her considerable autonomy over the type of deal she might strike because the trade-offs that management was willing to make were explicit. She hoped to strike an aggressive deal in present value terms but acknowledged that Brown & Kenney were also reputed to be tough negotiators. In encouraging her to do as well as she could, management reminded her that she should be able to reach a deal costing *no more* than 25% in excess of the proposed cost of the Nashua, New Hampshire store being considered as an alternative to the Brown & Kenney deal. Her targets for the overall value of the deal she was to negotiate are summarized in Table E of Exhibit 1.

▼   ▼   ▼

CASE

BROWN & KENNEY DEVELOPERS, INC.

Brown & Kenney, real estate developers, invested $25 million in the purchase and partial development of a tract of land in suburban Boston. In addition to allotting land for an apartment complex (to be completed in stages over ten years), the firm set aside a large portion of this tract for development as a

Harvard Business School case 9-190-099, revised October 24, 1994. This case is based on an earlier case by Professor John S. Hammond, Bradley & Hurley Developers, HBS case #174-107. Copyright © 1990 by the President and Fellows of Harvard College.

shopping center. Five tenants were already signed up: a restaurant, a gift shop, a Steve's ice cream parlor, a Tweeter electronics store, and a video/music shop. Negotiations with the anchor tenant, Sears, had just been successfully completed. Among the tenants still being sought were a theater, a large women's wear store, a shoe store, a jewelry store, a card store, a furniture store, and a book store.

Studies of population and land development trends, expected apartment occupants, demographics of the surrounding towns, and traffic indicated to the developers that the prospective customers would be primarily in the upper-middle-class income range and that a shopping center would be likely to succeed.

About three weeks earlier, the developers initiated negotiations with a Boston-based women's wear chain, Joan Mitchell Stores, Inc., regarding leasing a 15,000 square foot store. The chain had four other suburban stores of approximately the same size and a larger downtown store, but no stores in the immediate vicinity of the new shopping center. The contemplated store would be in a portion of a one-story building that would cost about $110 per square foot to build.

Brown & Kenney was quite eager to sign up Joan Mitchell Stores because it believed that the store would draw customers into the center. Further, it felt that with the Sears and Mitchell leases in hand the firm would be in a stronger position to attract other tenants.

Previous negotiations with Kerner Stores, a large national women's wear chain, had fallen through within the past week. This was a disappointment: Kerner's excellent credit rating associated with a long-term lease could have helped obtain more favorable mortgage terms. (The credit rating of Joan Mitchell was considered good, but not as good as Kerner's AAA rating.) Further, Kerner would have been a slightly better draw of customers into the center.

Setting Objectives

Brown & Kenney, partners for a dozen years, made a practice of thoroughly reviewing each negotiation—whether it be with a seller of land, a contractor, a source of financing, or a prospective tenant—before actual bargaining got under way. They would develop a clear statement of objectives and a bargaining strategy. David Kenney, who was in charge of the financial end of the business, usually handled detailed analysis and the actual negotiations.

The planning for this particular negotiation had an added dimension, however. Kenney, a Massachusetts Institute of Technology graduate, had run into Richard Whitelaw at his twenty-fifth class reunion. Whitelaw, a specialist in operations research, had described some work he had done at his company helping negotiators to make trade-offs explicit before entering into negotiations.

The approach involved specifying the important dimensions in a negotiation (such as annual rent, length of lease) and then assigning a dollar value for each potential outcome that indicated its relative importance and desirability. These values could be added together to get a score that was an index of attractiveness for the deal.

Kenney was intrigued and invited his friend to participate in the planning for the upcoming negotiations with Joan Mitchell. Whitelaw met on two successive Saturdays with the partners to develop their objectives and trade-offs.

Determining Trade-Offs

The developers singled out the rental rate, length of the lease, renewal clause, sublet clause, and competing tenant clause as being most important. They also expected that a sign clause and a cancellation clause due to fire or acts of God would be at issue, since the prospective tenants had inquired about them. After considerable discussion, the partners, aided by Whitelaw, stated their objectives as follows:

Rental Rate: The rental rate in the lease was considered the most important variable. The annual rent could be determined in two ways: (1) by using a flat rental rate of so many dollars per square foot per year, or (2) the greater of the annual square foot rental or a percentage of the store's annual gross sales. By tying rents to sales, the latter type of agreement had the potential to protect the landlord against inflation. For example, suppose the agreement was for $16 per square foot or 5% of gross sales, whichever was greater, and that the store's gross sales in a particular year were $3½ million. Since 5% of these sales is $175,000, which is less than the $240,000 calculated by using the $16 per square foot rental rate, the annual rent charged would be $240,000. If the store's gross sales had been $5 million, then 5% of sales would be $250,000. Since this is greater than $240,000, the annual rent charged would be $250,000.

The going rate, based on a 30-year lease, for space in similar centers was $16 to $18 per square foot annually, according to surveys made by the developer. However, lesser per square foot rates with a percentage of gross were frequent (for example, $14 per square foot, or 6% of sales, whichever was greater).

Whitelaw set out to calculate the NPV of a 15-year lease for various combinations of lease and percentage of gross. He made certain assumptions about expected sales per square foot at the store, the inflation rate, and an appropriate discount rate. (These are given in Exhibit 1.[4]) He estimated for example, that a 15-year lease at $17 per square foot or 5% of sales was worth $1,260,000.[5]

In their last conversation with the prospective tenants three weeks earlier, it appeared that Mitchell managers were forecasting a lower inflation rate and that its store sales forecasts were slightly greater than the developers'.

Length of Lease, Renewal, and Sublet Clause: Because of mortgage obligations the partners preferred a 30-year lease; however, at an earlier meeting, Mitchell management expressed interest in a 15-year lease with an option to renew for another 15 years under the same terms. Brown & Kenney had stated that it preferred a 15-year lease to a 15-year lease with a renewal clause (but not, of course, to the 30-year lease). Also discussed was the right to sublet, which Brown & Kenney was willing to consider only subject to its approval of the substitute tenant or tenants. Thus, there were six possibilities under consideration; their dollar values are shown in Table A of Exhibit 1.

The sublet clause was of less concern with the 15-year lease than with the 30-year lease. The developers disliked the renewal clause because it not only gave Mitchell managers an out (as the 15-year lease did) but it also gave them a chance to continue on the original lease terms *if* the terms looked good to Mitchell after 15 years.

Competing-Tenant Clause: Mitchell management was concerned about

[4] To preserve confidential information in the negotiations, Exhibit 1 is available only on the data diskette (BROWN1. WK4). Please ask your instructor for the password.

[5] In calculating the NPV of the lease amount, Brown & Kenney used payments only over an initial 15-year period. The additional value of a 15-year renewable lease or a 30-year lease is accounted for in the "Terms of Lease" trade-off assessment. In effect, these trade-off values can be thought of as option values of extending the lease relative to whatever other alternatives would be available at that time.

the prospect of another women's wear store in the center and desired a clause in the lease prohibiting the developers from leasing more than 10,000 square feet total to all other women's wear stores. It hoped thereby to hold competition from small shops to a minimum and keep out another large women's wear store. Brown & Kenney managers realized that recent edicts from the Federal Trade Commission had cast doubt on the enforceability of such a clause; further, they were reluctant to grant it. Nonetheless, if they did decide to grant it, they intended to keep their word. However, at this early stage in the center's leasing they hated to give up the flexibility of signing up whomever they wanted. The developers felt that the amounts described in Table B of Exhibit 1 represented the cost to them of allowing various competing tenant provisions.

Sign Clause: Joan Mitchell Stores had used the same large, though tasteful, sign on each of its five other stores. Brown & Kenney objected to the Mitchell sign since all other signs were to be under a certain size. Mitchell management felt the sign was its trademark and was anxious to use it; the developers felt that the atmosphere of the center would be slightly diminished if the oversize sign was included. This loss of image was valued as shown in Table C of Exhibit 1.

Acts-of-God Cancellation Clause: About five years previously, one of Mitchell's suburban stores had been heavily damaged by fire and the landlord had been slow in making repairs. Consequently, Mitchell had lost considerable sales, as well as its market standing in the region served by the store. Mitchell management wanted a clause that would offer it the right to terminate the lease if 30% of the center was damaged by fire, flood, or other acts of God (thus cutting traffic in the center) or if at least 15% of its own store was destroyed. If Mitchell elected to continue the lease, it wanted abatement of rent until repairs were made. Because of the fire-resistive nature of the construction, the developers didn't think such an occurrence was very likely. Further, they could buy fire insurance at relatively low rates. The cost to Brown & Kenney of including these various clauses is summarized in Table D of Exhibit 1.

The Upcoming Negotiations

As he reviewed his firm's objectives, Kenney began to wonder how important Joan Mitchell management would consider various aspects of the lease. He also began to consider a possible bargaining strategy. He intended to use his NPV dollar system as a guide to making trade-offs and as a way of evaluating potential terms offered by the tenants. He and his partner had put a lot of thought into the system, and he felt it accurately reflected the relative importance of what he might pursue in the negotiation. Although he had already estimated that the minimum deal value was the minimum required to meet the project's debt burden, he was in fact aiming for a much more aggressive deal value (also given in Table E of Exhibit 1). However, he was also very aware of the Kerner Stores negotiations, during which he had proven intransigent and the deal had fallen through. To facilitate his preparation, Kenney summarized the costs associated with his various objectives in a spreadsheet. He took out his portable computer and began to work on a strategy for negotiations with Barbara Levinson, a Mitchell vice-president, with whom he would meet the next day.

▼   ▼   ▼

SOUTHEASTERN ELECTRIC COMPANY (B)

The following is a simplified business situation in which Southeastern Electric Company is to negotiate with RCI Inc. for purchase of steam during the calendar year 1993. The information in Part I of this case is known to both parties. The information in Part II is strictly internal to Southeastern.[6] As this case is intended as an exercise, please ignore the effects of taxes and the time value of money.

Part I

RCI Inc. is a major diversified company with a 50-year history of investing in long shots, stemming from its initial success with an oil well (long since dried up). Though RCI has no current interests in oil, it does specialize in finding ways of producing energy. Consistent with this strategy, RCI has agreed to build and operate a resource recovery facility for Westborough County. On completion, the plant will receive all of Westborough's residential and commercial refuse, recover any usable materials for resale, then burn the residue—both to reduce it in size for landfill purposes and to produce steam that can be sold.

You have been put in charge of negotiating with RCI for purchase of that steam during the calendar year 1993. On January 1, 1994, Southeastern will convert from oil to 100% nuclear energy and will thus have no further use for the steam. RCI had been unable to obtain a commercial loan for the project but had apparently funded the project internally. This was quite consistent with RCI's reputation for investing in projects with potential. The terms of RCI's contract with Westborough require the county to pay five equal installments of $10 million when the plant is 20, 40, 60, 80, and 100% complete. You share RCI's belief that construction will cost exactly $50 million and take exactly one year (the calendar year 1992). RCI apparently negotiated away any construction profit in return for exclusive title to all by-products of the plant, including steam. When operational, the plant will produce steam with an annual usable energy equivalent of 100,000 barrels of oil.

You have learned that Acme Company has offered to buy all of RCI's steam for the six winter months (November to April, inclusive) of each year at a 20% discount rate from the price of oil prevailing on January 1st of each year. Any deal between Southeastern and RCI for 1993 would not affect this offer for subsequent years.

Acme intends to use the steam directly for its internal heating system, but Southeastern requires electricity and would need to build a generating facility near the RCI plant to convert the steam into electricity. Such a generating facility would take one year to build at a cost of $1 million. The facility's location and design is such that it is of no use to anyone but Southeastern, and will have no salvage value if not needed by them.

Harvard Business School case 9-182-281, revised February 1994. This case was prepared by Professor David E. Bell. Copyright © 1982 by the President and Fellows of Harvard College.

[6] Available only from file SEB.WK4 on the data diskette. Ask your instructor for the password.

Calendar

1 Oct 91	"Now"
1 Jan 92	Construction begins on resource recovery plant and, if necessary, on generating facility.
1 Jan 93	If plant works, steam is supplied to Acme or Southeastern as appropriate.
1 Jan 94	Steam is supplied only to Acme, and then only in the winter months.

▼   ▼   ▼

RCI INC. (B)

The following is a simplified business situation in which RCI must negotiate with Southeastern Electric Company for sale of steam during the calendar year 1993. The information in Part I of the case is known to both parties. The information in Part II is strictly internal to RCI.[7] As this case is intended as an exercise, please ignore the effects of taxes and the time value of money.

Part I

You are vice president of research and development for RCI Inc., a company founded in the 1930s on the basis of one producing oil well. That well has long since dried up and RCI has no current oil-producing facilities, but the money has financed RCI's growth into a large diversified company whose motivation is still to take calculated risks in projects that could produce energy. You recently negotiated a contract to build and operate a resource recovery facility for Westborough County. The plant will receive all of Westborough's residential and commercial refuse, recover any usable materials for resale, then burn the residue—both to reduce it in size for landfill purposes and to produce steam that can be sold.

You are confident that the construction will take exactly one year, starting January 1, 1992 and will cost $50 million. RCI's size had given it a major advantage in bidding for the original contract because smaller businesses had been unable to find commercial loans because of the technological uncertainty surrounding the plant design. RCI had chosen to fund the project out of retained earnings. Westborough is committed to paying five equal installments of $10 million when the plant is 20, 40, 60, 80, and 100% complete. RCI negotiated away a profit on the construction phase of the enterprise in return for exclusive title to the by-products of the plant, the recovered materials, and steam.

When operational (January 1, 1993), the plant will produce steam with an annual energy equivalent of 100,000 barrels of oil. You have identified two possible customers for the steam. Acme Company has agreed to purchase all of your steam output during the six winter months, November to April inclusive, at a 20% discount from the price of oil prevailing on January 1st of each year. They would be happy to commence this agreement on either January 1, 1993 or January 1, 1994.

Harvard Business School case 9-182-278, revised February 1, 1994. This case was prepared by Professor David E. Bell. Copyright © 1982 by the President and Fellows of Harvard College.

[7] Available only from file RCIB.WK4 on the data diskette. Ask your instructor for the password.

The Southeastern Electric Company has expressed a willingness to discuss the purchase of all of RCI's output of steam during the year 1993. On January 1, 1994 Southeastern will convert from oil to 100% nuclear energy and will then have no further use for the steam. If Southeastern agrees to purchase the steam, it will have to build a generating facility near the RCI plant to convert the steam into electricity. Construction of this facility would take one year and cost $1 million. The facility's location and design is such that it is of no use to anyone but Southeastern, and will have no salvage value if not needed by it.

Calendar

1 Oct 91	"Now"
1 Jan 92	Construction begins on resource recovery plant and, if necessary, on generating facility.
1 Jan 93	If plant works, steam is supplied to Acme or Southeastern as appropriate.
1 Jan 94	Steam is supplied only to Acme, and then only in winter months.

▼   ▼   ▼

Strategic Decisions

In this last chapter, you'll encounter situations that require the most sophisticated type of thinking. Whereas negotiations are typically held face to face, most kinds of competition take place at arm's length. How can you reach "win-win" outcomes in complex situations if you are not permitted to communicate with the other party? In this chapter you will learn how to do this: at the very least, you'll become aware of some of the pitfalls that may await you.

THE PRISONER'S DILEMMA AND OTHER GAMES

Jerry Inc.

Jerry Inc. was considering entering an industry in which there was currently one monopoly supplier, Tom Inc. A critical consideration in Jerry's decision was predicting Tom's likely response: Would Tom lower prices in an attempt to thwart Jerry's entry? Or would Tom maintain prices in a spirit of "live and let live"?

If Jerry Inc. entered the industry, they expected total profits of $50 million if Tom accommodated Jerry's decision to enter. On the other hand, if Tom tried to "punish" the entrant by driving down prices, Jerry anticipated losing a total of $100 million.

After some research into Tom's financial status, Jerry had made the following estimates. Currently (i.e., before Jerry's entry), Tom stood to make $500 million from its operations in the industry. This sum would be reduced to $400 million if Tom were to accommodate Jerry's decision to enter. Fighting the entrant would cost Tom $200 million.

Shortly before Jerry's CEO was to make a final decision on entry, she received a disturbing telephone call from her counterpart at Tom, leaving the distinct impression that Tom would drive down prices if Jerry were to enter. Jerry could ill afford the consequent loss of $100 million. Should Jerry enter the industry?

Harvard Business School case 9-189-092, revised October 25, 1991. This case was prepared by Professor Adam Brandenburger. Copyright © 1988 by the President and Fellows of Harvard College.

The Business School Endowment

A philanthropist wished to make a gift of $10 million, but was unsure which of two well-known business schools, Eastern Business School (EBS) or Western Business School (WBS), to endow. To resolve the dilemma, he summoned a representative from each institution and explained the procedure he planned to use. He would start by placing a check for $1 million on the table. The representative from EBS could then choose to take it or to leave it. If the check was left on the table, the philanthropist would replace it with a check for $2 million and give the WBS representative the option to take it or to leave it. If this second check was left on the table, it would be replaced with a check for $3 million and the EBS representative given the choice to take it or to leave it. The procedure would terminate as soon as a check was picked up. If the final check—for $10 million—was not picked up, the philanthropist would take the check back and dismiss the two representatives in disgust.

Should the EBS representative take the initial check for $1 million? Or should he leave it on the table in the hope that the WBS representative would likewise leave the check for $2 million? And what should he do then?

The Prisoner's Dilemma

Two suspects, 1 and 2, were taken into custody and placed in separate cells.[1] The district attorney was certain that they were guilty of a specific crime, but he did not have enough evidence to convict them at a trial. So, he visited each suspect in turn and pointed out that the prisoner had two alternatives: to confess to the crime the police department was sure he had committed, or not to confess. If neither suspect confessed to the crime, the district attorney threatened to book them for the crime. If both suspects confessed, they would be prosecuted but the district attorney would recommend less than the most severe sentence. If one confessed and the other did not, then the confessor would be allowed to go free for turning state's evidence, whereas the other would be prosecuted with the utmost vigor.

The above decision problem can be represented in the form of a "payoff matrix" (see Figure 8.1).

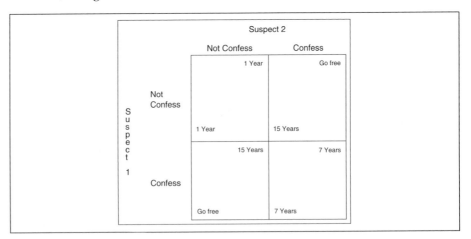

Figure 8.1

---

[1] The following description of this famous game is taken from R. Luce and H. Raiffa, *Games and Decisions*, New York: Wiley, 1957.

In Figure 8.1 the rows show the choices facing suspect 1 and the columns the choices facing suspect 2. Each cell in the matrix shows the payoff to suspect 1 in the lower left-hand corner and the payoff to suspect 2 in the upper right-hand corner. For example, the bottom left-hand cell shows that if suspect 1 confesses while suspect 2 does not, then 1 will go free while 2 will receive a 15-year sentence. What would you, as suspect 1, do?

Another version of the Prisoner's Dilemma (with payoffs in dollars instead of number of years in prison) is illustrated in Figure 8.2.

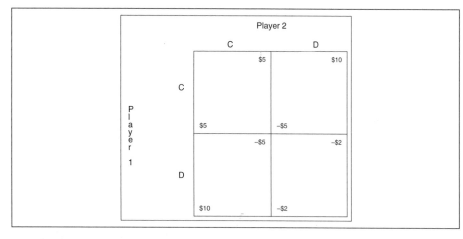

Figure 8.2

Again, each player has a choice of two strategies: C (for "Cooperate") and D (for "Defect"). The players must make their choices simultaneously—without knowing of the other's choice. If both choose C, then each gets a payoff of $5. If player 1 chooses C and player 2 D, then the payoffs are –$5 (i.e., a loss of $5) and $10, respectively. Similarly, if player 1 chooses D and player 2 C. If both choose D, then each receives a payoff of –$2.

Suppose this latter game is played not once but repeatedly. At each repetition (trial), the players make their choices simultaneously and then receive the payoffs resulting from that trial. How would you, as player 1, play if the game were repeated: (a) 10 times; (b) many times?

▼   ▼   ▼

CASE

CGE vs. Dowpont

The Lake Superior Mining District (LSMD) comprises the principal iron mining areas of Michigan, Minnesota, and Wisconsin. The LSMD produces a major fraction of all U.S. iron ore, largely through open-pit mining. The iron ore is found in a long stratum of taconite, a particularly hard rock that cannot be broken on a large scale by mechanical means. The normal method of mining is therefore to drill a grid of vertical holes (typically 40 ft. deep and 9"–12" in

Harvard Business School case 9-191-089, revised April 1, 1994. This case was based on an earlier case by Richard F. Meyer, Classic Greek Explosives Company (C), HBS #174-047. Copyright © 1990 by the President and Fellows of Harvard College.

diameter), fill them with explosives, and then blast a layer of rock. Since the holes often fill with water, the explosive has to be water-resistant; thus watergels are the principal explosive used at almost all mines.

The annual volume of watergels used in the LSMD is approximately 1 million cwt. This volume is supplied entirely by CGE and Dowpont, each of whom has a watergel plant in the LSMD and maintains a fleet of pump trucks to pump the gels into the holes. Both CGE and Dowpont have considerable overcapacity; in fact, either one could alone just about supply the entire needs of the District without having to add to their physical plant. Each had originally hoped to become the dominant producer in the District. This has created intense competition, most recently in the form of a vicious price war. Since explosives only account for approximately 1% of the cost of iron production, the watergel price war in the LSMD in no way stimulates demand for watergels: it merely reduces revenues for both CGE and Dowpont.

The recent price war was so severe that watergels are currently being sold at a small margin above variable cost. CGE's variable cost is $6.00/cwt and Dowpont's variable cost is $6.30/cwt. CGE had originally hoped that this cost advantage would permit them either to drive Dowpont out of the market altogether, or else to reduce Dowpont to the position of a second source of supply. In spite of CGE's aggressive price cutting, however, Dowpont has shown no signs of dropping out of the LSMD market. In fact, Dowpont has countered every price move of CGE promptly. Dowpont has not tried to underprice CGE, but has been intent on protecting its own contribution from the LSMD business as well as possible. At present, Dowpont's price is around $6.75/cwt, and CGE is trying to establish a new pricing strategy.

Although there are no significant objective differences in performance between the CGE and Dowpont watergels, it would be naive to think that the entire LSMD market will always swing to the lower-priced product. First of all, there are subjective differences in the perceptions of different mine operators: some prefer Dowpont, others swear by the CGE gels. Second, there are historical ties, personal friendships, and recollections of credit extended (or refused!) in difficult times. Also, Dowpont is in a position to purchase substantial quantities of products from some of the steel companies owning certain of the mines (i.e., Dowpont has the better trade relations). And finally, many mines want to split their business in order to be assured of a second source of supply in emergencies. It was estimated that at equal watergel prices Dowpont would take 55% of the market and that at a price differential of $1.00/cwt, 25% of the customers would be attracted to the lower-priced producer. In other words, if CGE were $1.00/cwt cheaper than Dowpont, CGE would take about 70% of the market. And vice-versa, if CGE were $1.00/cwt more expensive than Dowpont, CGE could expect about 20% of the market. To summarize, if Dowpont charges a price P_D and CGE charges a price P_C, sales of each would be:

Dowpont: $550{,}000 + 250{,}000\,(P_C - P_D)$ cwt

CGE: $450{,}000 - 250{,}000\,(P_C - P_D)$ cwt

Tables 8.1 and 8.2 are worksheets for "simulating" the success of possible pricing strategies. Tables 8.3 and 8.4 represent the period of payoffs to CGE and Dowpont, respectively, of various combinations of prices.

Table 8.1

	Dowpont Price	CGE Price	Dowpont Contribution	CGE Contribution
1.	6.75			
2.				
3.				
4.				
5.				
6.				
7.				
8.				
9.				
10.				

Table 8.2

	CGE Price	Dowpont Price	CGE Contribution	Dowpont Contribution
1.		6.75		
2.				
3.				
4.				
5.				
6.				
7.				
8.				
9.				
10.				

Table 8.3

Total Dollar Contribution for CGE ($000s)

CGE's Price	$6.75	7.00	7.25	7.50	7.75	8.00	8.25	8.50	8.75	9.00	9.25	9.50	9.75	10.00	10.25	10.50
Dowpont's Price																
$10.50	750	1000	1250	1500	1750	2000	2250	2375	2441	2475	2478	2450	2391	2300	2178	2025
10.25	750	1000	1250	1500	1750	2000	2138	2219	2269	2288	2275	2231	2156	2050	1913	1744
10.00	750	1000	1250	1500	1750	1900	1997	2063	2097	2100	2072	2013	1922	1800	1647	1463
9.75	750	1000	1250	1500	1663	1775	1856	1906	1925	1913	1869	1794	1688	1550	1381	1181
9.50	750	1000	1250	1425	1553	1650	1716	1750	1753	1725	1666	1575	1453	1300	116	900
9.25	750	1000	1188	1331	1444	1525	1575	1594	1581	1538	1463	1356	1219	1050	850	619
9.00	750	950	1109	1238	1334	1400	1434	1438	1409	1350	1259	1138	984	800	584	338
8.75	713	888	1031	1144	1225	1275	1294	1281	1238	1163	1056	919	750	550	319	56
8.50	666	825	953	1050	1116	1150	1153	1125	1066	975	853	700	516	300	53	0
8.25	619	763	875	956	1006	1025	1013	969	894	788	650	481	281	50	0	0
8.00	572	700	797	863	897	900	872	813	722	600	447	263	47	0	0	0
7.75	525	638	719	769	788	775	731	656	550	413	244	44	0	0	0	0
7.50	478	575	641	675	678	650	591	500	378	225	41	0	0	0	0	0
7.25	431	513	563	581	569	525	450	344	206	38	0	0	0	0	0	0
7.00	384	450	484	488	459	400	309	188	34	0	0	0	0	0	0	0
6.75	338	388	406	394	350	275	169	31	0	0	0	0	0	0	0	0

Table 8.4

Total Dollar Contribution for Dowpont ($000s)

CGE's Price	$6.75	7.00	7.25	7.50	7.75	8.00	8.25	8.50	8.75	9.00	9.25	9.50	9.75	10.00	10.25	10.50
Dowpont's Price																
$10.50	0	0	0	0	0	0	0	210	473	735	998	1260	1523	1785	2048	2310
10.25	0	0	0	0	0	0	198	444	691	938	1185	1432	1679	1926	2173	2419
10.00	0	0	0	0	0	185	416	648	879	1110	1341	1573	1804	2035	2266	2498
9.75	0	0	0	0	173	388	604	819	1035	1251	1466	1682	1898	2113	2329	2544
9.50	0	0	0	160	360	560	760	960	1160	1360	1560	1760	1960	2160	2360	2560
9.25	0	0	148	332	516	701	885	1069	1254	1438	1623	1807	1991	2176	2360	2544
9.00	0	135	304	473	641	810	979	1148	1316	1485	1654	1823	1991	2160	2329	2498
8.75	123	276	429	582	735	888	1041	1194	1348	1501	1654	1807	1960	2113	2266	2419
8.50	248	385	523	660	798	935	1073	1210	1348	1485	1623	1760	1898	2035	2173	2200
8.25	341	463	585	707	829	951	1073	1194	1316	1438	1560	1682	1804	1926	1950	1950
8.00	404	510	616	723	829	935	1041	1148	1254	1360	1466	1573	1679	1700	1700	1700
7.75	435	526	616	707	798	888	979	1069	1160	1251	1341	1432	1450	1450	1450	1450
7.50	435	510	585	660	735	810	885	960	1035	1110	1185	1200	1200	1200	1200	1200
7.25	404	463	523	582	641	701	760	819	879	938	950	950	950	950	950	950
7.00	341	385	429	473	516	569	604	648	691	700	700	700	700	700	700	700
6.75	248	276	304	332	360	388	416	444	450	450	450	450	450	450	450	450

JUDO AND THE ART OF ENTRY

This exercise[2] explores the strategic interaction between a dominant firm and a fringe competitor contemplating entry into the market. Crucial to the entry decision is the possible reaction of the entrenched incumbent firm. Entry is worthwhile only if the incumbent firm is "accommodating." When faced with such a situation, what are good entry strategies? To examine this question in more detail, let us specify the structure of the market in more detail.

Consumer Demand

Demand in the market has been estimated to be:

$$Sales = 12 - Price \ .$$

The relationship may be easily interpreted. There are twelve potential customers, and each would like to purchase exactly one unit of the product. However, each consumer has a different "willingness to pay." If the going price is, say, $4, then only 8 (= 12 − 4) customers wish to purchase the product.

The potential entrant, firm E, is able to supply exactly the same product as firm I, the incumbent; that is, there are no differences in product quality. The key to competition is the price that each firm charges for its product. Customers always wish to purchase from the firm with the lower price. Thus, if the incumbent's price is lower than the price charged by the entrant, the market remains with the incumbent. If the entrant's price is lower, customers flock to the entrant. There is, however, a certain amount of "brand loyalty." If both firms charge exactly the same price, consumers prefer to stay loyally with firm I.

Costs

The entrenched firm, firm I, has another advantage. Because of economies of scale and learning effects, its costs are lower than those of firm E. Suppose that firm I's unit costs are $2, while those of firm E would be $3.

The Current Situation

At present, firm I is the only one operating in the market and has established a market price of $7. Of course, if firm E were to enter the market and undercut this price, firm I could react competitively and match E's price. Because of brand loyalty, market demand would stay with the incumbent. Furthermore, firm I has a cost advantage and enough capacity (i.e., 12 units) to meet the whole market if necessary. Any price at which firm E can make money (above $3) can easily be matched by firm I. It would appear that from firm E's point of view, the prospects of profitable entry look pretty grim.

Questions

1. Suppose firm E decides to enter the market with a plant that has a capacity of 9 units (and unit cost of $3). How will the incumbent react? Is it worthwhile for firm E to enter?

Harvard Business School case 9-187-165, revised April 1, 1994. This case was prepared by Professor Vijay Krishna. Copyright © 1987 by the President and Fellows of Harvard College.

[2] This exercise is based on the paper by J. Gelman and S. Salop, "Judo Economics: Capacity Limitation and Coupon Competition," *Bell Journal of Economics*, 14 (1983): 315–325.

2. Next, consider the following "small is beautiful" strategy for the potential entrant. The entrant deliberately chooses a *small* plant with a capacity of only 1 unit and undercuts the incumbent by charging a price of $4 (recall that the incumbent's established price is $7). However, because firm E has only a limited capacity, not all customers willing to pay $4 for the product can be served, and the overflow will surely go to firm I. Let us look at this more closely. There are 8 (= 12 – 4) customers willing to pay $4 for the product, but firm E can only supply one "lucky" customer. Thus, the seven unsatisfied remaining customers have no recourse but to buy from firm I or not buy at all. Of course, only those unsatisfied customers whose willingness to pay exceeds $7 will actually purchase from firm I.

   Suppose that the lucky customer, able to purchase the product at the lower price of $4, is chosen at random from the 8 actually willing to buy at $4. This means that the probability that any one of the 8 is actually able to buy at $4 is 1/8. Thus, on average, the market remaining for firm I has shrunk to 7/8 of its original size. Putting this another way, the remaining market demand for firm I can be written as follows:

   $$Expected\ Sales\ of\ Firm\ I = 7/8 \times Original\ Demand$$

   $$= 7/8 \times (12 - Firm\ I's\ Price)$$

   For instance, if firm I lowers its price to $5 in response to E's entry, its expected sales are $(7/8) \times (12 - 5) = 6.125$.

   In response to the "small is beautiful" strategy, firm I has two options:

   (a) It can continue to charge a price of $7 and serve the demand overflow from firm E as outlined above. Call this the *accommodating* response.

   (b) It can match firm E by cutting its own price to $4, thereby protecting its turf. Call this the *aggressive* response.

   Which of these two responses should the entrant anticipate? Does the "small is beautiful" strategy really look beautiful?

3. How would your answer to question 2 change if the entrant randomly *gives away* a "transferable" coupon that entitles the holder to the right to buy one unit from the entrant at a price of $4?[3]
   (HINT: Since the coupon is transferable, and can be sold, what price will it fetch and how does this affect firm I's demand? As an example of this, you might want to think of transferable coupons issued by airlines.)

4. Would the entrant prefer to *sell* its coupon?

5. Would it be in the interests of the incumbent to honor the coupons sold by the entrant?

▼   ▼   ▼

FOURAKER MINING & METALS CORP.

Fouraker Mining & Metals, operator of a medium-scale molybdenum mine in the western U.S., was a technically sophisticated but marginally profitable producer of molybdenum ore concentrate. In its efforts to improve operating

Harvard Business School case 9-175-098, revised October 22, 1991. This case was prepared by Gerald Allan, Research Associate, under the direction of Professor John S. Hammond. Copyright © 1974 by the President and Fellows of Harvard College.

---

[3] A transferable coupon does not have the name of the customer on it. Thus, whoever presents it to firm E is entitled to buy a unit at a price of $4.

profits, Fouraker had just entered into an exclusive supply arrangement with Siegel & Company, Inc. to purchase a biochemically produced material called "Flozyme," which greatly increased molybdenum mineral recovery from each ton of ore mined. The arrangement required Fouraker to purchase the additive weekly, in small lots, at a price set each week by Siegel. Walter Lightdale, Fouraker's purchasing manager, was in the process of establishing a purchasing strategy under the new arrangement.

Fouraker Mining

Fouraker Mining was started in 1952 by a consulting geologist, Mr. L. Fouraker, and a research metallurgist, Dr. Henry Holmes. It was founded to develop a large, low-grade deposit of molybdenum ore on which Mr. Fouraker had long held mining claims, using chemical processes pioneered by Dr. Holmes. For the next six years, they struggled to finance both the rapidly expanding pilot plant operation and the exploration and development of the ore. By 1958 the process had been adequately tested and the mining operation had expanded to the point at which the company was almost breaking even.

In order to develop the ore fully and expand the plant to its most efficient size, Mr. Fouraker obtained an investment of $16 million from a large international mining company in return for a 45% interest in the firm. Holmes and Fouraker personally held 10% each of the equity, with the remaining interest widely dispersed among individuals who had helped finance Fouraker Mining's first ten years. The balance of the $60 million capitalization was provided by banks and various equipment suppliers. In subsequent years there was a marked increase in scale of operations but the company was only barely profitable ($1.2 million before-tax profit on $37.7 million sales in 1973).

Siegel & Company, Inc.

Siegel & Company was a small West Coast producer of proprietary carbohydrate derivatives used in the manufacture of certain prepared foods and drugs. It had been founded shortly after World War II by a young biochemist, Sydney Siegel, in order to commercialize a number of promising new biologically active substances on which he had obtained patents.

Despite the smallness and informality of its operation, Siegel & Company had become extremely profitable in recent years as significant markets began to develop for its highly specialized, costly products. Produced in carefully scheduled and interdependent batches, most products were sold exclusively to single users—a consequence of Siegel's past joint-venture method of funding the majority of its research programs. Typically, the joint-venture agreements allowed Siegel to retain patents and the rights to manufacture any resulting products, while the sponsor held exclusive rights to use and/or distribute the products.

Flozyme

Although the basic extractive process for molybdenum was well known and in widespread use, Fouraker Mining had succeeded in greatly enhancing its efficiency by special techniques, including the use of special additives to increase yields. Its continuing research had revealed that use of Flozyme substantially improved their recovery of molybdenum minerals when introduced into the process at rates equivalent to a few hundred pounds per week.

An extremely light and chemically unstable powder, Flozyme was a byproduct of a complex, biological-organic chemical process. Dr. Holmes had learned of Flozyme's surface-activating behavior from a brief description of the process in a professional journal. On the strength of a few laboratory-scale tests, Holmes recommended that Fouraker Mining undertake large-scale process testing of Flozyme so that its precise effect on molybdenum recovery and the economics associated with its use could be accurately established.

In return for exclusive rights to buy Siegel's entire output of Flozyme—should it prove successful in this application—Fouraker Mining agreed to fund a research program in which both the production and application of the Flozyme byproduct were to be investigated. After several years of sporadic activity on this program, Flozyme's effectiveness was proven to Fouraker's satisfaction.

Because Flozyme was a byproduct, the yield of the process's main product was greatly affected by the amount of Flozyme desired. Volume production of Flozyme was possible only through extensive and costly recycling of the main product. Fouraker had learned that Flozyme production added considerably to total process costs—the cost increment becoming larger as Flozyme output increased. Prior to the sale of Flozyme, any byproduct material had been disposed of as a waste product.

The Purchasing Arrangement

In the absence of a market for Flozyme outside Fouraker Mining, Siegel had decided to quote weekly an appropriate unit price for the reagent and let Fouraker place its order based on that price. Siegel hoped that prices and quantities would eventually stabilize at levels acceptable to both firms. With the above procedure established, Mr. Fouraker assigned the purchase responsibility to his purchasing manager, Mr. Lightdale. Mr. Lightdale was to base his weekly decisions solely on the profit-contribution information (Exhibit 1) developed by Fouraker's production superintendent, the chief process engineer, and himself during the final Flozyme tests.

An equivalent tabulation of incremental profits for Siegel & Co., shown in Exhibit 2, was also available from a project report exhibit prepared by Siegel chemists at the conclusion of the test program. It was regarded as very reliable and would undoubtedly be used by Siegel in its pricing decision. The same report contained the information shown in Exhibit 1.

Because of its great effect on the main process, Sydney Siegel had decided to handle the sale of Flozyme personally in order to keep close watch on the joint process and its combined economics. Weekly, Mr. Siegel would telex a price, in dollars per pound, to Fouraker, and Fouraker would in turn transmit an order quantity, in 20-lb. drums, for delivery two weeks hence. Fouraker had been advised that batches of up to 20 drums per week could be produced and that each batch had an active life of ten days at most. This meant that shipments would have to be used within ten days of manufacture, or discarded.

Exhibit 1

FOURAKER MINING & METALS CORP.
CONTRIBUTION AS A FUNCTION OF PRICE AND QUANTITY

Price	Quantity 1	2	3	4	5	6	7	8	9	10	11	12	13	14	15	16	17	18	19	20
1	160	570	960	1,330	1,680	2,010	2,320	2,610	2,880	3,130	3,360	3,570	3,760	3,930	4,080	4,210	4,320	4,410	4,480	4,530
2	140	530	900	1,250	1,580	1,890	2,180	2,450	2,700	2,930	3,140	3,330	3,500	3,650	3,780	3,890	3,980	4,050	4,100	4,130
3	120	490	840	1,170	1,480	1,770	2,040	2,290	2,520	2,730	2,920	3,090	3,240	3,370	3,480	3,570	3,640	3,690	3,720	3,730
4	100	450	780	1,090	1,380	1,650	1,900	2,130	2,340	2,530	2,700	2,850	2,980	3,090	3,180	3,250	3,300	3,330	3,340	3,330
5	80	410	720	1,010	1,280	1,530	1,760	1,970	2,160	2,330	2,480	2,610	2,720	2,810	2,880	2,930	2,960	2,970	2,960	2,930
6	60	370	660	930	1,180	1,410	1,620	1,810	1,980	2,130	2,260	2,370	2,460	2,530	2,580	2,610	2,620	2,610	2,580	2,530
7	40	330	600	850	1,080	1,290	1,480	1,650	1,800	1,930	2,040	2,130	2,200	2,250	2,280	2,290	2,280	2,250	2,200	2,130
8	20	290	540	770	980	1,170	1,340	1,490	1,620	1,730	1,820	1,890	1,940	1,970	1,980	1,970	1,940	1,890	1,820	1,730
9	0	250	480	690	880	1,050	1,200	1,330	1,440	1,530	1,600	1,650	1,680	1,690	1,680	1,650	1,600	1,530	1,440	1,330
10	-20	210	420	610	780	930	1,060	1,170	1,260	1,330	1,380	1,410	1,420	1,410	1,380	1,330	1,260	1,170	1,060	930
11	-40	170	360	530	680	810	920	1,010	1,080	1,130	1,160	1,170	1,160	1,130	1,080	1,010	920	810	680	530
12	-60	130	300	450	580	690	780	850	900	930	940	930	900	850	780	690	580	450	300	130
13	-80	90	240	370	480	570	640	690	720	730	720	690	640	570	480	370	240	90	-80	-270
14	-100	50	180	290	380	450	500	530	540	530	500	450	380	290	180	50	-100	-270	-460	-670
15	-120	10	120	210	280	330	360	370	360	330	280	210	120	10	-120	-270	-440	-630	-840	-1,070
16	-140	-30	60	130	180	210	220	210	180	130	60	-30	-140	-270	-420	-590	-780	-990	-1,220	-1,470
17	-160	-70	0	50	80	90	80	50	0	-70	-160	-270	-400	-550	-720	-910	-1,120	-1,350	-1,600	-1,870
18	-180	-110	-60	-30	-20	-30	-60	-110	-180	-270	-380	-510	-660	-830	-1,020	-1,230	-1,460	-1,710	-1,980	-2,270
19	-200	-150	-120	-110	-120	-150	-200	-270	-360	-470	-600	-750	-920	-1,110	-1,320	-1,550	-1,800	-2,070	-2,360	-2,670
20	-220	-190	-180	-190	-220	-270	-340	-430	-540	-670	-820	-990	-1,180	-1,390	-1,620	-1,870	-2,140	-2,430	-2,740	-3,070

Exhibit 2

SIEGEL & COMPANY
CONTRIBUTION AS A FUNCTION OF PRICE AND QUANTITY

Price \ Quantity	1	2	3	4	5	6	7	8	9	10	11	12	13	14	15	16	17	18	19	20
1	7.5	10	7.5	0	-12.5	-30	-52.5	-80	-112.5	-150	-192.5	-240	-292.5	-350	-412.5	-480	-552.5	-630	-712.5	-800
2	27.5	50	67.5	80	87.5	90	87.5	80	67.5	50	27.5	0	-32.5	-70	-112.5	-160	-212.5	-270	-332.5	-400
3	47.5	90	127.5	160	187.5	210	227.5	240	247.5	250	247.5	240	227.5	210	187.5	160	127.5	90	47.5	0
4	67.5	130	187.5	240	287.5	330	367.5	400	426.5	450	467.5	480	487.5	490	487.5	480	467.5	450	427.5	400
5	87.5	170	247.5	320	387.5	450	507.5	560	607.5	650	687.5	720	747.5	770	787.5	800	807.5	810	807.5	800
6	107.5	210	307.5	400	487.5	570	647.5	720	787.5	850	907.5	960	1,007.5	1,050	1,087.5	1,120	1,147.5	1,170	1,187.5	1,200
7	127.5	250	367.5	480	587.5	690	787.5	880	967.5	1,050	1,127.5	1,200	1,267.5	1,330	1,387.5	1,440	1,487.5	1,530	1,567.5	1,600
8	147.5	290	427.5	560	687.5	810	927.5	1,040	1,147.5	1,250	1,347.5	1,440	1,527.5	1,610	1,687.5	1,760	1,827.5	1,890	1,947.5	2,000
9	167.5	330	487.5	640	787.5	930	1,067.5	1,200	1,327.5	1,450	1,567.5	1,680	1,787.5	1,890	1,987.5	2,080	2,167.5	2,250	2,327.5	2,400
10	187.5	370	547.5	720	887.5	1,050	1,207.5	1,360	1,507.5	1,650	1,787.5	1,920	2,047.5	2,170	2,287.5	2,400	2,507.5	2,610	2,707.5	2,800
11	207.5	410	607.5	800	987.5	1,170	1,347.5	1,520	1,687.5	1,850	2,007.5	2,160	2,307.5	2,450	2,587.5	2,720	2,847.5	2,970	3,087.5	3,200
12	227.5	450	667.5	880	1,087.5	1,290	1,487.5	1,680	1,867.5	2,050	2,227.5	2,400	2,567.5	2,730	2,887.5	3,040	3,187.5	3,330	3,467.5	3,600
13	247.5	490	727.5	960	1,187.5	1,410	1,627.5	1,840	2,047.5	2,250	2,447.5	2,640	2,827.5	3,010	3,187.5	3,360	3,527.5	3,690	3,847.5	4,000
14	267.5	530	787.5	1,040	1,287.5	1,530	1,767.5	2,000	2,227.5	2,450	2,667.5	2,880	3,087.5	3,290	3,487.5	3,680	3,867.5	4,050	4,227.5	4,400
15	287.5	570	847.5	1,120	1,387.5	1,650	1,907.5	2,160	2,407.5	2,650	2,887.5	3,120	3,347.5	3,570	3,787.5	4,000	4,207.5	4,410	4,607.5	4,800
16	307.5	610	907.5	1,200	1,487.5	1,770	2,047.5	2,320	2,587.5	2,850	3,107.5	3,360	3,607.5	3,850	4,087.5	4,320	4,547.5	4,770	4,987.5	5,200
17	327.5	650	967.5	1,280	1,587.5	1,890	2,187.5	2,480	2,767.5	3,050	3,327.5	3,600	3,867.5	4,130	4,387.5	4,640	4,887.5	5,130	5,367.5	5,600
18	347.5	690	1,027.5	1,360	1,687.5	2,010	2,327.5	2,640	2,947.5	3,250	3,547.5	3,840	4,127.5	4,410	4,687.5	4,960	5,227.5	5,490	5,747.5	6,000
19	367.5	730	1,087.5	1,440	1,787.5	2,130	2,467.5	2,800	3,127.5	3,450	3,767.5	4,080	4,387.5	4,690	4,987.5	5,280	5,567.5	5,850	6,127.5	6,400
20	387.5	770	1,147.5	1,520	1,887.5	2,250	2,607.5	2,960	3,307.5	3,650	3,987.5	4,320	4,647.5	4,970	5,287.5	5,600	5,907.5	6,210	6,507.5	6,800

SIEGEL & COMPANY, INC.

Siegel & Co. had just entered into an unusual agreement with Fouraker Mining & Metals Corp. to supply Fouraker with a special process additive called "Flozyme." The additive had proven most effective in increasing Fouraker Mining's recovery of molybdenum minerals and was thought to offer a potentially significant contribution to the mining firm's overall profitability. However, production of the Flozyme product was complicated by its interference with a primary process of which it was a byproduct. Costly recycling was needed to obtain the required volumes of both products. Consequently, determination of an appropriate price for Flozyme was currently a problem of some importance for Siegel.

Siegel & Company

Siegel & Company was a small West Coast producer of proprietary carbohydrate derivatives used in the manufacture of certain prepared foods and drugs. It had been founded shortly after World War II by a young biochemist, Sydney Siegel, in order to commercialize a number of promising new biologically active substances on which he had obtained patents.

Despite the smallness and informality of its operation, Siegel & Company had become extremely profitable in recent years as significant markets began to develop for its highly specialized, costly products. In 1973, the company earned almost $1.5 million before taxes from the sale of seven major, and several dozen minor, products. (This profit represented nearly 60% of sales.) Produced in carefully scheduled and interdependent batches, most products were sold exclusively to single users—a consequence of Siegel's past jointventure method of funding the majority of its research programs. Typically, the joint-venture agreements allowed Siegel to retain patents and the rights to manufacture any resulting products, while the sponsor held exclusive rights to use and/or distribute the products. Mr. Siegel was highly satisfied with the exclusive distribution arrangements and low-volume production since this allowed him to concentrate on research and kept him free from time-consuming and uninteresting marketing duties.

Fouraker Mining & Metals Corp.

Fouraker Mining & Metals, operator of a medium-scale molybdenum mine in the western U.S., was a technically sophisticated but marginally profitable producer of molybdenum ore concentrate. In its efforts to improve operating profits, Fouraker had entered into the exclusive supply arrangement with Siegel & Co. to purchase Flozyme, a biochemically produced material that greatly increased molybdenum mineral recovery from each ton of ore mined. The arrangement required Fouraker to purchase the additive weekly, in small lots, at a price set each week by Siegel.

The company was started in 1952 by a consulting geologist, Mr. L. Fouraker, and a research metallurgist, Dr. Henry Holmes. It was founded to develop a large, low-grade deposit of molybdenum ore on which Mr. Fouraker had long held mining claims, using chemical processes pioneered by Dr. Holmes. For the next six years, they struggled to finance both the rapidly expanding pilot plant operation and the exploration and development of the ore itself. By 1958, the process had been adequately tested and the mining operation had expanded to the point at which the company was almost breaking even.

Harvard Business School case 9-175-099, revised October 22, 1991. This case was prepared by Gerald Allan, Research Associate, under the direction of Professor John S. Hammond. It was developed from the well-known Fouraker-Siegel bargaining experiments (L.E. Fouraker and S. Siegel, Bargaining Behavior, New York: McGraw-Hill, 1963). Copyright © 1975 by the President and Fellows of Harvard College.

In order to develop the ore fully and expand the plant to its most efficient size, Mr. Fouraker obtained a major financing commitment from a large international mining company in return for a substantial interest in the firm. Holmes and Fouraker, along with the many individuals who had helped finance Fouraker Mining's first ten years, retained a controlling interest.

Flozyme

Although the basic extractive process for molybdenum was well known and in widespread use, Fouraker Mining had succeeded in greatly enhancing its efficiency by special techniques, including the use of special additives to increase yields. Its continued research had revealed that use of Flozyme substantially improved their recovery of molybdenum minerals when introduced into the process at rates equivalent to a few hundred pounds per week.

An extremely light and chemically unstable powder, Flozyme was a byproduct of a complex, biological-organic chemical process. Fouraker had apparently learned of Flozyme's surface-activating behavior from an article appearing in a professional journal and had carried out some preliminary testing to ascertain the material's potential for recovery enhancement.

In return for exclusive rights to buy Siegel's entire output of Flozyme—should it prove successful in this application—Fouraker Mining agreed to fund a research program in which both the production and application of the Flozyme byproduct were to be investigated. After several years of sporadic activity on this program, Flozyme's effectiveness was proven to Fouraker's satisfaction.

Because Flozyme was a byproduct, the yield of the process's main product was greatly affected by the amount of Flozyme desired. Volume production of Flozyme was possible through extensive and costly recycling of the main product. Flozyme production added considerably to total production costs—the cost increment becoming larger as Flozyme output increased. Prior to the sale of Flozyme, any byproduct material had been disposed of as a waste product.

The Purchasing Arrangement

In the absence of a market for Flozyme outside Fouraker Mining, Siegel had decided to quote weekly an appropriate unit price for the reagent and let Fouraker place its order based on that price. Siegel hoped that prices and quantities would eventually stabilize at levels acceptable to both firms.

To guide his pricing decisions, Mr. Siegel had drawn up a table of profit contributions for Flozyme in various weekly production batch sizes (see Exhibit 1). Selling the product in weekly lots would allow Flozyme to be produced under the same schedule as the primary product. Weekly, he would telex his price, in dollars per pound, to Fouraker Mining's purchasing manager, Walter Lightdale, who would in turn transmit the quantity, in 20-lb. drums, that Fouraker wished to order for delivery two weeks hence. Fouraker had been informed that batches of up to 20 drums per week could be produced and that each batch had an active life of at most ten days. This meant that shipments would have to be used within ten days of manufacture, or discarded.

Mr. Siegel also possessed a profit contribution tabulation, similar to his own, that had been prepared by Fouraker Mining's engineering and purchasing groups (see Exhibit 2). This tabulation was part of the project report that summarized test program results and economics for Flozyme, a report that also contained the information in Exhibit 1.

Exhibit 1

SIEGEL & COMPANY
CONTRIBUTION AS A FUNCTION OF PRICE AND QUANTITY

Price \ Quantity	1	2	3	4	5	6	7	8	9	10	11	12	13	14	15	16	17	18	19	20
1	7.5	10	7.5	0	-12.5	-30	-52.5	-80	-112.5	-150	-192.5	-240	-292.5	-350	-412.5	-480	-552.5	-630	-712.5	-800
2	27.5	50	67.5	80	87.5	90	87.5	80	67.5	50	27.5	0	-32.5	-70	-112.5	-160	-212.5	-270	-332.5	-400
3	47.5	90	127.5	160	187.5	210	227.5	240	247.5	250	247.5	240	227.5	210	187.5	160	127.5	90	47.5	0
4	67.5	130	187.5	240	287.5	330	367.5	400	426.5	450	467.5	480	487.5	490	487.5	480	467.5	450	427.5	400
5	87.5	170	247.5	320	387.5	450	507.5	560	607.5	650	687.5	720	747.5	770	787.5	800	807.5	810	807.5	800
6	107.5	210	307.5	400	487.5	570	647.5	720	787.5	850	907.5	960	1,007.5	1,050	1,087.5	1,120	1,147.5	1,170	1,187.5	1,200
7	127.5	250	367.5	480	587.5	690	787.5	880	967.5	1,050	1,127.5	1,200	1,267.5	1,330	1,387.5	1,440	1,487.5	1,530	1,567.5	1,600
8	147.5	290	427.5	560	687.5	810	927.5	1,040	1,147.5	1,250	1,347.5	1,440	1,527.5	1,610	1,687.5	1,760	1,827.5	1,890	1,947.5	2,000
9	167.5	330	487.5	640	787.5	930	1,067.5	1,200	1,327.5	1,450	1,567.5	1,680	1,787.5	1,890	1,987.5	2,080	2,167.5	2,250	2,327.5	2,400
10	187.5	370	547.5	720	887.5	1,050	1,207.5	1,360	1,507.5	1,650	1,787.5	1,920	2,047.5	2,170	2,287.5	2,400	2,507.5	2,610	2,707.5	2,800
11	207.5	410	607.5	800	987.5	1,170	1,347.5	1,520	1,687.5	1,850	2,007.5	2,160	2,307.5	2,450	2,587.5	2,720	2,847.5	2,970	3,087.5	3,200
12	227.5	450	667.5	880	1,087.5	1,290	1,487.5	1,680	1,867.5	2,050	2,227.5	2,400	2,567.5	2,730	2,887.5	3,040	3,187.5	3,330	3,467.5	3,600
13	247.5	490	727.5	960	1,187.5	1,410	1,627.5	1,840	2,047.5	2,250	2,447.5	2,640	2,827.5	3,010	3,187.5	3,360	3,527.5	3,690	3,847.5	4,000
14	267.5	530	787.5	1,040	1,287.5	1,530	1,767.5	2,000	2,227.5	2,450	2,667.5	2,880	3,087.5	3,290	3,487.5	3,680	3,867.5	4,050	4,227.5	4,400
15	287.5	570	847.5	1,120	1,387.5	1,650	1,907.5	2,160	2,407.5	2,650	2,887.5	3,120	3,347.5	3,570	3,787.5	4,000	4,207.5	4,410	4,607.5	4,800
16	307.5	610	907.5	1,200	1,487.5	1,770	2,047.5	2,320	2,587.5	2,850	3,107.5	3,360	3,607.5	3,850	4,087.5	4,320	4,547.5	4,770	4,987.5	5,200
17	327.5	650	967.5	1,280	1,587.5	1,890	2,187.5	2,480	2,767.5	3,050	3,327.5	3,600	3,867.5	4,130	4,387.5	4,640	4,887.5	5,130	5,367.5	5,600
18	347.5	690	1,027.5	1,360	1,687.5	2,010	2,327.5	2,640	2,947.5	3,250	3,547.5	3,840	4,127.5	4,410	4,687.5	4,960	5,227.5	5,490	5,747.5	6,000
19	367.5	730	1,087.5	1,440	1,787.5	2,130	2,467.5	2,800	3,127.5	3,450	3,767.5	4,080	4,387.5	4,690	4,987.5	5,280	5,567.5	5,850	6,127.5	6,400
20	387.5	770	1,147.5	1,520	1,887.5	2,250	2,607.5	2,960	3,307.5	3,650	3,987.5	4,320	4,647.5	4,970	5,287.5	5,600	5,907.5	6,210	6,507.5	6,800

Exhibit 2

FOURAKER MINING & METALS CORP.
CONTRIBUTION AS A FUNCTION OF PRICE AND QUANTITY

Price \ Quantity	1	2	3	4	5	6	7	8	9	10	11	12	13	14	15	16	17	18	19	20
1	160	570	960	1,330	1,680	2,010	2,320	2,610	2,880	3,130	3,360	3,570	3,760	3,930	4,080	4,210	4,320	4,410	4,480	4,530
2	140	530	900	1,250	1,580	1,890	2,180	2,450	2,700	2,930	3,140	3,330	3,500	3,650	3,780	3,890	3,980	4,050	4,100	4,130
3	120	490	840	1,170	1,480	1,770	2,040	2,290	2,520	2,730	2,920	3,090	3,240	3,370	3,480	3,570	3,640	3,690	3,720	3,730
4	100	450	780	1,090	1,380	1,650	1,900	2,130	2,340	2,530	2,700	2,850	2,980	3,090	3,180	3,250	3,300	3,330	3,340	3,330
5	80	410	720	1,010	1,280	1,530	1,760	1,970	2,160	2,330	2,480	2,610	2,720	2,810	2,880	2,930	2,960	2,970	2,960	2,930
6	60	370	660	930	1,180	1,410	1,620	1,810	1,980	2,130	2,260	2,370	2,460	2,530	2,580	2,610	2,620	2,610	2,580	2,530
7	40	330	600	850	1,080	1,290	1,480	1,650	1,800	1,930	2,040	2,130	2,200	2,250	2,280	2,290	2,280	2,250	2,200	2,130
8	20	290	540	770	980	1,170	1,340	1,490	1,620	1,730	1,820	1,890	1,940	1,970	1,980	1,970	1,940	1,890	1,820	1,730
9	0	250	480	690	880	1,050	1,200	1,330	1,440	1,530	1,600	1,650	1,680	1,690	1,680	1,650	1,600	1,530	1,440	1,330
10	-20	210	420	610	780	930	1,060	1,170	1,260	1,330	1,380	1,410	1,420	1,410	1,380	1,330	1,260	1,170	1,060	930
11	-40	170	360	530	680	810	920	1,010	1,080	1,130	1,160	1,170	1,160	1,130	1,080	1,010	920	810	680	530
12	-60	130	300	450	580	690	780	850	900	930	940	930	900	850	780	690	580	450	300	130
13	-80	90	240	370	480	570	640	690	720	730	720	690	640	570	480	370	240	90	-80	-270
14	-100	50	180	290	380	450	500	530	540	530	500	450	380	290	180	50	-100	-270	-460	-670
15	-120	10	120	210	280	330	360	370	360	330	280	210	120	10	-120	-270	-440	-630	-840	-1,070
16	-140	-30	60	130	180	210	220	210	180	130	60	-30	-140	-270	-420	-590	-780	-990	-1,220	-1,470
17	-160	-70	0	50	80	90	80	50	0	-70	-160	-270	-400	-550	-720	-910	-1,120	-1,350	-1,600	-1,870
18	-180	-110	-60	-30	-20	-30	-60	-110	-180	-270	-380	-510	-660	-830	-1,020	-1,230	-1,460	-1,710	-1,980	-2,270
19	-200	-150	-120	-110	-120	-150	-200	-270	-360	-470	-600	-750	-920	-1,110	-1,320	-1,550	-1,800	-2,070	-2,360	-2,670
20	-220	-190	-180	-190	-220	-270	-340	-430	-540	-670	-820	-990	-1,180	-1,390	-1,620	-1,870	-2,140	-2,430	-2,740	-3,070

INDEX

C

yield-management problems, 43

Zeckendorf Company, case study,
98–102